Sumptuary Law in Italy 1200–1500

CATHERINE KOVESI KILLERBY

CLARENDON PRESS · OXFORD

This book has been printed digitally and produced in a standard specification in order to ensure its continuing availability

OXFORD
UNIVERSITY PRESS

Great Clarendon Street, Oxford OX2 6DP

Oxford University Press is a department of the University of Oxford.
It furthers the University's objective of excellence in research, scholarship,
and education by publishing worldwide in

Oxford New York

Auckland Cape Town Dar es Salaam Hong Kong Karachi
Kuala Lumpur Madrid Melbourne Mexico City Nairobi
New Delhi Shanghai Taipei Toronto
With offices in
Argentina Austria Brazil Chile Czech Republic France Greece
Guatemala Hungary Italy Japan South Korea Poland Portugal
Singapore Switzerland Thailand Turkey Ukraine Vietnam

Published in the United States
by Oxford University Press Inc., New York

Oxford is a registered trade mark of Oxford University Press
in the UK and in certain other countries

Published in the United States
by Oxford University Press Inc., New York

Reprinted 2005

ISBN 0-19-924793-5

IN MEMORY OF

JULIUS AND PAUL KOVESI

two much-loved Italophiles

ACKNOWLEDGEMENTS

In 1974, in a footnote to his economic history of Italy in *Storia d'Italia*, Philip Jones remarked that he had in preparation an article on the subject of sumptuary legislation. Unfortunately that article was not written but, as his last doctoral student, I had the wonderful opportunity to take advantage of the rich reference material accumulated by Philip and the stimulation of his ideas on the subject, often handed to me on his trade-mark scraps of paper. I owe him a great debt. Others have also been generous with their time and ideas. I wish to thank Bill Kent for initial encouragement to an academic in distress, as well as for his later comments. Lorenzo Polizzotto first got me hooked on Renaissance Italy and has been a valued friend and critic ever since. Trevor Dean and Bernadette Paton have been both good friends and great sources of ideas and information. Conversations with John Vickers, Patricia Crawford, Philippa Maddern, and Natalie Tomas were also helpful, and Joy Damousi's comments on the material in Chapter 6 led me to rethink much of it. Claude Eilers allowed me to consult his thesis on Roman Republican sumptuary legislation, thereby saving me from several errors in Chapter 1, and Brian Bosworth's close reading of the same chapter led to many changes. Mark Edwards, Neil O'Sullivan, and Andrew McGowan all offered invaluable assistance with the translation of Nicolosa Sanuti's treatise, used in Chapter 6, and my mother, Janet Kovesi Watt, translated several letters for me. John Kinder generously offered suggestions for my translations of Italian material, as did Ron Ridley for my Latin. Needless to say, I take full responsibility for any weaknesses.

I have also incurred many financial and institutional debts. The Gladys Krieble Delmas Foundation, the Mary Walters Memorial Bursary from the Australian Federation of University Women, the Christina Drake Fund for Italian Studies, the Arnold, Bryce and Read Funds, and Magdalen College, Oxford, all made possible a long visit to Italy to accumulate primary material. A Hackett Studentship from the University of Western Australia together with a British Commonwealth Overseas Research Studentship enabled me to spend three years at Oxford trawling the extraordinary holdings of the Bodleian Library, and the Seton-Watson Senior Scholarship gave me two memorable years at Oriel College, Oxford. This book would not have been finished, however, if it were not for a sabbatical from the University of Melbourne, and for that I wish to offer especial thanks to Peter McPhee.

I have dealt with some of the subject matter of this book in other publications. Cambridge University Press have kindly given me permission to reproduce material from 'Practical Problems in the Enforcement of Italian Sumptuary Law 1200–1500', from T. Dean and K. Lowe (eds.), *Crime, Society and the Law* (1994). Oxford University Press have kindly given permission for me to use material from '"Heralds of a Well Instructed Mind": Nicolosa Sanuti's Defence of Women and Their Clothes', in *Renaissance Studies*, 13/3 (1999), 255–82.

This book is also the product of ongoing discussion with my greatest friend and critic, Jeremy Killerby. Many of its key ideas stem from discussions with him, and he has been critically engaged with my work from our very first discussions. Lydia, Alex, Marcus, and Julius Killerby have all put up with their mother working at odd hours, and I would like to thank them for their tolerance.

Finally I wish to thank several people who have helped on the production side: my Oxford Historical Monographs editor, George Holmes, for his kindness and for his great patience in awaiting the arrival of my finished manuscript; the History editors Anne Gelling, Ruth Parr, and Dorothy McCarthy for overseeing the operation with such goodwill and patience; Rowena Anketell, my copy-editor, for her scrupulous attention to detail and helpful suggestions; and Elizabeth Wood-Ellem for the index.

Catherine Kovesi Killerby

University of Melbourne

CONTENTS

Abbreviations x

Note on Money x

Note on Measurements x

Introduction 1

1. Ancient and Early Medieval Precedents 9

2. The Origins and Characteristics of Italian Sumptuary Law 23

3. Money and People 41

4. Ambition and Social Order 61

5. The Church and Sumptuary Law 92

6. Women and Sumptuary Law 111

7. Problems of Enforcement and the Failure of Sumptuary Law 133

Bibliography 165

Index 181

ABBREVIATIONS

ACF	Archivio comunale, Ferrara
ASB	Archivio di Stato, Bologna
ASF	Archivio di Stato, Florence
ASP	Archivio di Stato, Perugia
ASS	Archivio di Stato, Siena
ASV	Archivio di Stato, Venice
BNF	Biblioteca Nazionale, Florence

A NOTE ON MONEY

Because this study spans three centuries and examines over forty towns, the question of money is difficult. Monetary systems varied from one Italian city or state to the other, and, of course the relative worth of these currencies varied tremendously over the three-century time span of this study as cities' fortunes waxed or waned. I have not, therefore, attempted to translate any of the currencies, but have left them in the original.

A NOTE ON MEASUREMENTS

The main unit of measurement for cloth was the *braccio*, or, the arm's length. However, the length of an Italian arm seemed to have varied from city to city. In Florence, for example, a *braccio* was 58 cm, whilst in Piacenza it was 66 cm. A *braccio* could be further subdivided into measurements of a *palmo* (palm), or, smaller still, a *dito* (finger). Yet again, however, there seems to have been no standard length for Italian palms and fingers. The situation is further complicated by the fact that fabric widths varied also, although generally speaking, a width of silk was narrower than a width of woollen cloth.

Introduction

There was rude simplicity of old . . .

Ovid

The commercial revolution which Italy underwent from the twelfth century onwards brought wealth to many and created an economic momentum which continued into the following centuries. It also brought an enormous variety of new luxury goods onto the Italian markets, goods that were not only redistributed for profit abroad but were enthusiastically consumed, and soon produced, in Italy itself. So marked was this luxury consumption, both in comparison to what had gone before and to levels elsewhere in Europe at the time, that it has been suggested that 'modern consumer society, with its insatiable consumption setting the pace for the production of more objects and changes in style, had its first stirrings, if not its birth, in the habits of spending that possessed the Italians in the Renaissance'.[1] Paradoxically, however, in the literature of these centuries of prosperity there is a persistent refrain that is suffused with nostalgia for a lost golden age of simple virtue, the 'buon tempo antico', and which condemns the new luxury and the effete habits of modern times.[2] Thus Riccobaldo da Ferrara describes in favourable terms an Italy under the Emperor Frederick as having 'coarse and rustic customs and usages' while 'now many dissolute habits have stifled these early customs, many indeed which lead to the destruction of the soul. Parsimony has been changed into extravagance.'[3] Similarly, Dante's forefather Cacciaguida condemns the excesses of Dante's city and describes the Florence of his own day as 'sober and modest'.[4] A few decades later, Franco Sacchetti deplored the rapidity with which the fashions throughout Italy altered, again contrasting it with the stability of previous years.[5] Such idealizations of the past are common to many societies undergoing rapid

[1] R. Goldthwaite, 'The Economy of Renaissance Italy: The Preconditions for Luxury Consumption', *I Tatti Studies: Essays in the Renaissance*, 2 (1987), 16.

[2] For a more detailed discussion of this issue see C. T. Davis, 'Il buon tempo antico', in N. Rubinstein (ed.), *Florentine Studies: Politics and Society in Renaissance Florence* (London, 1968), 45–69, and P. J. Jones, 'La storia economica dalla caduta dell'impero romano al secolo XIV', in *Storia d'Italia*, 2* (Turin, 1974), 1777–84.

[3] A. Masséra, 'Dante e Riccobaldo', *Bollettino della società dantesca italiana*, NS 22 (1915), 168–200.

[4] *Paradiso*, XV. 97–129.

[5] *Il trecentonovelle*, ed. A. Lanza (Florence, 1984), *novella* 178, pp. 402–3.

economic, social, and political change. It was not just chroniclers, poets, and satirists, however, who were critical of the new wealth in Italy and who longed for simplicity and virtue. Churchmen and city statesmen were also concerned with increasing sumptuousness and, by the end of the fifteenth century, jurists and humanists were expressing their opinions on the matter. Perhaps the most voluminous evidence of this preoccupation in the late Middle Ages and Renaissance is the large body of laws enacted designed to restrict and regulate all aspects of luxury consumption and excess. Between 1200 and 1500 governments in over forty Italian cities enacted more than 300 of these so-called sumptuary laws, and they continued to do so well into the eighteenth century. It is the aim of this study to examine the nature of these laws up to 1500 and thereby relate them to the circumstances, the framework of ideas, and the habit of mind which gave rise to them.

The category 'sumptuary laws' can be a diffuse and vague one. Among the ancient Romans, the early *leges sumptuariae* tended to concentrate upon the regulation of dining habits.[6] Their main legal text, however, the *Digest*, concentrated on the regulation of funerals. Moreover, modern historians of ancient sumptuary law include in this category not only laws which regulated dining habits and funerals, but also clothing. This is justified etymologically on the grounds that all these laws regulated expense (*sumptus*), and not just expenditure per se, but, more specifically, expenditure on luxury goods. Whilst such a definition is adequate to describe what is meant by ancient sumptuary laws, it does not fully encompass the range of the later Italian sumptuary legislation. The majority of rubrics in these Italian laws are, it is true, concerned with consumption of luxury goods and excessive expenditure, but Italian lawmakers also grouped other concerns under the heading of *leggi suntuarie* which were not strictly concerned with luxury consumption at all. Loud wailing and weeping at funerals, for instance, or disorderly conduct at wedding festivities and banquets, could hardly be termed luxurious or even expensive, yet these activities were forbidden repeatedly in sumptuary laws. What can be said of all the many subjects dealt with in Italian sumptuary legislation is that they were all concerned with various manifestations of excess and, in particular, with excess in the consumption of luxury goods. To ensure that at all times we are discussing what the Italians of this period regarded as a sumptuary law, rather than with the ancient etymology of the term or later definitions of it, all the concerns specified in Italian sumptuary laws will be discussed in what follows, no matter how diverse.

[6] Gellius, *Noctes Atticae*, 2. 24.

In order to deal adequately with the development and nature of sumptuary law in Italy the time span of this study is necessarily large. It begins with the first provisions against consumption in the thirteenth century (with one isolated provision in the mid-twelfth century) and follows their rapid spread throughout the Italian peninsula to cities under every type of political regime. The year 1500 was chosen as the cut-off point, not because legislative activity started to decline then—on the contrary it continued unabated—but because by this date legislation had become so frequent that its interest for the specific purposes of the study diminishes. Moreover, with the beginning of the Italian wars, the political dynamic of Italian cities complexified in a way that makes analysis increasingly complicated. Because of the large time span of this study, and the number of laws and towns studied, this book has not been organized in strict chronological fashion but follows a thematic scheme.

The frequency and fervour of sumptuary legislation in late medieval and Renaissance Italy has meant that historians have not failed to notice it, and there are numerous references in a variety of historical works to these laws. Perhaps surprisingly, however, there has been no comprehensive study of sumptuary legislation in Italy. Previous work on sumptuary laws may be loosely divided into three categories. Into the first falls the transcription, usually in the nineteenth and early twentieth centuries, of one or more of the sumptuary laws of an individual city to which a brief introduction on sumptuary legislation or luxury in the relevant city was often attached.[7] This approach is essentially one of making available primary material in a local context. The second approach examines the laws not primarily to explain them, but as source material for details of the private lives and customs of Italians in the period. Antonio Bonardi is representative of this approach when he says: 'For the Middle Ages and for several centuries of the modern era no other historical source, in my opinion, gives a better understanding of the private life of the various social classes than sumptuary laws.'[8] Historians like Bonardi have used the minutely detailed prescriptions of the laws to provide information about clothing and fashion, interior furnishings, funeral, baptismal and marriage customs,

[7] See e.g. A. Fabretti, 'Statuti e ordinamenti suntuari intorno al vestire degli uomini e delle donne in Perugia dall'anno 1206 al 1536 (raccolti ed annotati)', *Memorie della reale accademia di scienze di Torino*, ser. 2b, 38 (1888), 137–232; G. Del Giudice, 'Una legge suntuaria inedita del 1290: Commento storico-critico', *Atti dell'accademia pontaniana*, 16/2 (1886), 1–319; and, more recently, R. E. Rainey, 'Sumptuary Legislation in Renaissance Florence', Ph.D. thesis (Columbia Univ., 1985).

[8] 'Il lusso di altri tempi in Padova: Studio storico con documenti inediti', *Miscellanea di storia veneta*, 3rd ser., 2 (1910), p. ix.

and childbirth rituals. These appear in the many *vita privata* studies of individual Italian towns[9] as well as in histories of Italian costume,[10] and studies such as that of Sharon Strocchia on death and its rituals in Florence, and Peter Thornton's on the Renaissance Italian interior.[11] In addition, the laws, and in particular their preambles, have furnished material for those studying the social, economic, and political aspects of the rising level of luxury in Italy during the period.[12]

Finally, there have been a few general studies of Italian sumptuary law. One of the earliest is that of Denholm-Young and Kantorowicz who, in their edited transcription of a fifteenth-century jurist's tract questioning the legality of episcopal sumptuary laws, included a brief introduction to the subject which focused on three Italian towns (Milan, Florence, and Venice).[13] Over thirty years later, the historian of costume Rosita Levi Pisetzky, in her five-volume *Storia del costume in Italia*, included brief summaries of the characteristics of northern Italian sumptuary laws for each century of her study and added a bibliography of many laws. Widely known and more recent is the work of Diane Owen Hughes who has written several articles on the subject.[14] Owen Hughes's early article 'Sumptuary Law and Social Relations' provides a stimulating view of the broad spectrum of governments' sumptuary concerns, although her main interest is in laws restricting women's clothing, and deals with a selection of laws passed in the north of Italy. After a later fascinating article on earrings, Owen Hughes re-

[9] See e.g. L. Frati, *La vita privata in Bologna dal secolo XIII al XVII* (2nd edn., Bologna, 1928); L. T. Belgrano, 'Della vita privata dei genovesi', *Atti della società ligure di storia patria*, 4 (1886), 79–273; E. Pandiani, 'Vita privata genovese nel rinascimento', *Atti della società ligure di storia patria*, 47 (1915), 119–201; G. Biagi, *The Private Life of the Renaissance Florentines* (London, 1896).

[10] See e.g. R. Levi Pisetzky, *Storia del costume in Italia*, 5 vols. (Milan, 1964–9); J. Herald, *Renaissance Dress in Italy, 1400–1500* (London, 1981); F. Gabotto, 'Per la storia del costume nel medio evo subalpino', *Bollettino storico bibliografico subalpino*, 13 (1909), 1–28.

[11] Strocchia, *Death and Ritual in Renaissance Florence* (Baltimore, 1992) and Thornton, *The Italian Renaissance Interior 1400–1600* (London, 1991).

[12] For the best use of sumptuary laws for this purpose and for a useful introduction to the subject of sumptuary legislation itself see Jones, 'Storia economica', 1469–1810, esp. 1777 ff.

[13] Denholm-Young and Kantorowicz, 'De Ornatu Mulierum: A Consilium of Antonius de Rosellis with an Introduction on Fifteenth Century Sumptuary Legislation', *Bibliofilia*, 35 (1933), 315–35 and 440–56.

[14] 'Sumptuary Law and Social Relations in Renaissance Italy', in J. Bossy (ed.), *Disputes and Settlements: Law and Human Relations in the West* (Cambridge, 1983), 69–99; 'Distinguishing Signs: Ear-Rings, Jews and Franciscan Rhetoric in the Italian Renaissance City', *Past and Present*, 112 (Aug. 1986), 3–59; 'Regulating Women's Fashion', in C. Klapisch-Zuber (ed.), *Silences of the Middle Ages: A History of Women in the West*, ii (Cambridge, Mass., and London, 1992), 136–58.

visited women and sumptuary law in 1992, placing the issue more closely within the context of women's history. J. A. Brundage, too, focuses on restrictions against women, in particular against prostitutes, in a study centred on fifteen towns, all in the north of the peninsula.[15]

Geographical and chronological overselectiveness has, however, distorted our understanding of the phenomenon of sumptuary legislation as a whole, for it has led to attempts to explain the legislative impulse in terms of the type of government studied. However, hundreds of legislative bodies in Italy, in every variety of political regime, whether despotic, republican, monarchical, or foreign, enacted sumptuary provisions. This would seem to suggest that the overconsumption of luxury goods posed problems to all these societies regardless of political and ideological particulars. Whilst it cannot be claimed that this study is exhaustive, as archival work remains to be done, it examines all known sumptuary laws in Italy (some 300) enacted over a three-century period in over forty towns across the peninsula. I realize, of course, that such wide coverage lays me open to many potential inaccuracies and hope that those whose specific expertise is much greater than mine will be able to correct these. What I hope to provide, however, is a comparative and structural framework within which and against which more specific studies may be made.

A further problem in most studies of sumptuary law is that, while the laws themselves have been examined, enforcement records have not. From the fact that sumptuary legislation failed to contain luxury consumption and that the lawmakers were aware of this and yet continued to enact new laws, many have concluded that the impulse to legislate was irrational, or that the lawmakers had no real desire to see their laws succeed, and that we can therefore impute to them motives other than those which they themselves have professed. Thus Bistort said that 'sumptuary laws, in every time and place, . . . led to nothing; they did nothing but forbid in order then to tolerate, to threaten in order then to pardon; they were abused and ridiculed; they were in sum, as Boccardo said, erroneous, absurd, unjust, immoral'.[16] The view is a common one, even if more subtly expressed by others. According to Zanelli the legislators were forced 'uselessly to multiply the laws, often to correct them and acknowledge that too narrow restraints had been not only useless but harmful'.[17] And similarly Pierro:

15 'Sumptuary Laws and Prostitution in Late Medieval Italy', *Journal of Medieval History*, 13 (1987), 343–55.

16 'Il magistrato alle pompe nella repubblica di Venezia: Studio storico', *Miscellanea di storia veneta*, 3rd ser., 5 (1912), 9 citing Boccardo, *Economia politica* (Turin, 1869), i. 303.

17 'Di alcune leggi suntuarie pistoiesi dal XIV al XVI secolo', *Archivio storico italiano*, 5th ser., 16 (1895), 206.

'What were the results of sumptuary legislation, as much opposed by contemporaries as ridiculed by posterity? None or almost none.'[18] The view is often one of early modern man as a species rationally distinct from modern man: 'in those times so different from our taste and from the modern way of doing things, the magistracy did not believe it inopportune to concern itself with women's fashion and, with laws, to oppose excessive luxury in clothing and jewels'.[19]

The failure to consider enforcement records and to give due weight to the real problems which excess luxury created in these societies has led some of the most recent historians of sumptuary law to conclude that the actual process of legislating was mostly a cathartic exercise for legislators beset with problems that they could not fully identify or deal with. As J. M. Vincent describes it, the constant revising and renewal of the ordinances, 'whatever other motives they may have had, saved the face of the lawmakers, who felt obliged to make some public declaration on the subject' although 'centuries of experience seemed to teach these city councils little or nothing as to the actual nature of sumptuary law'.[20] And Diane Owen Hughes says:

> We must distinguish between *enforcement* which failed, and *legislating*, which achieved objects of its own . . . Renaissance legislators tried to create order at those points in social organization where structure was ambivalent, particularly where social ideology was in conflict with many social practices . . . These structural inconsistencies, for which there was no real cure, created social tensions which the legislation sought to remedy and which the *process* of legislating may have eased.[21]

So, the dominant view of the lawmakers is that they were not committed to the ideals they professed in legislation of a pure and austere society, the 'buon tempo antico'. Rather, legislation was mostly talk, a way for the lawmakers to pretend to themselves and to others that they were true to these ideals. However, neither the preambles and contents of the laws nor the enforcement records allow for such a readily dismissive conclusion. Though not wanting to deny that other impulses, irrational, unexpressed, or otherwise, may indeed have been present while legislators drew up their laws, this study takes as its primary point of departure the words of the lawmakers themselves as explanatory statements. The aim of this study, in

[18] 'Le leggi suntuarie e il problema demografico nel medioevo', *Politica sociale*, 2 (1930), 21.

[19] Pandiani, 'Vita privata genovese', 154.

[20] 'Sumptuary Legislation', in *Encyclopaedia of the Social Sciences*, xiv (New York, 1930–4), 133.

[21] 'Sumptuary Law and Social Relations', 96 and 99.

other words, is to examine sumptuary legislative activity as, first and foremost, a rational activity, before looking elsewhere for explanations. It will be seen that the profound economic and social transformation that Italy underwent as a result of the opening of new trade routes, and the concomitant availability of luxury commodities and increased wealth, gave rise to a multitude of social, economic, moral, and political problems. It was to these that the laws were most often addressed. Ineffective instruments though they were, they were yet one of statesmen's few tools.

Further, it will be argued that the failure of the laws was not usually due to a lack of desire to implement them, but to a combination of other factors. The first and unavoidable problem lay in the inappropriateness of legislation as a tool with which to control luxury consumption. The forms luxury can take are virtually endless, but enforceable sumptuary legislation is necessarily specific. This means that sumptuary laws are, by their very nature, self-defeating: to curb luxury by the outlawing of one form that luxury happens to be taking itself generates new forms as the way to avoid prosecution. Secondly, the legislative problem was aggravated by a lack of desire to condemn luxury consumption outright. It should be emphasized that no government in this period regarded luxury as an evil in itself. It was the context of its use, by whom and for what purpose, that determined the approval or censure of luxury. In the economic sphere the demand for luxury goods was seen to stimulate production and so was to be encouraged. At the same time, luxury consumption also led to the dissipation of reliable sources of capital, also necessary for a strong economy, and so was to be condemned. In politics, luxury could be used to mark the divinity of a king or the power of the ruling body and, on a national level, it could help to demonstrate the power of a state in comparison with its neighbours. But, for these same reasons, luxury was also a useful tool for the politically ambitious and so in these circumstances was to be deplored. On a social level, the display of luxury could help to maintain accepted views of the social order: it could underline the exclusive status of the nobility, or the professional status of doctors, lawyers, and the educated elite.[22] But equally, luxury could be used to erode class distinctions, and could encourage public disorder. The positive economic, political, and social functions of luxury combined with its religious use as a means to worship, meant that morally, too, luxury was acceptable and was to be encouraged. But luxury could also foster weakness, moral inanition, and

[22] See N. McKendrick, J. Brewer, and J. H. Plumb, *The Birth of a Consumer Society: The Commercialization of Eighteenth-Century England* (London, 1982), 2.

focus attention on the fleshly concerns of the world and so again demand condemnation.

The unavoidable clash between the positive and negative functions of luxury and the seeming contradiction of disallowing luxury on certain occasions and to certain people whilst permitting or positively promoting its use in others, created the impression to those subject to the law, and to later writers on sumptuary law, that there was a lack of clear legislative policy. The practical and conceptual difficulties of legislation meant that the lawmakers found themselves beset by a dilemma that ensured for them many centuries of conflict, compromise, and ultimate failure.

1

Ancient and Early Medieval Precedents

> because our beginnings go back a very long way, the recounting in brief of other ancient histories seems to me necessary to our undertaking.
>
> Giovanni Villani

The concern with luxury consumption in late medieval and Renaissance Italy was not an isolated historical phenomenon. Nor, as may be thought, was it a peculiarly Christian one. Attempts to explain Italian sumptuary legislation by linking it to any particular type of government, set of religious beliefs, geographical location, or to a paternalistic form of government, soon encounter difficulties. Indeed expressions of concern at the level of consumption of luxury goods, whether in laws, treatises, or popular literature, can be found in societies spanning two and a half thousand years with governments as diverse in form as they were geographically dispersed. A survey of legislative precedents to medieval Italian laws reveals not only that the Italians were employing long-established means to combat perennial problems, but also the powerful heritage of classical ideals, as well as Christian morality from which, to a large extent, the Italians' views of excess and their condemnation of it were drawn.

I

Sparta seems to have been the earliest Western society to enact sumptuary legislation, but little is known of it. Traditionally sumptuary legislation has been attributed to Lycurgus[1] and has been seen in the context of Spartan rigour and discipline, attributes which have, more recently, been the focus of some scrutiny.[2] Other later, and unfortunately undatable, laws forbade women to wear jewellery, cosmetics, perfume, or dyed clothing.[3]

[1] See R. Garner, *Law and Society in Classical Athens* (London, 1987), 140 for the problems associated with the correct attribution of Lycurgan laws and also A. Andrewes, 'Eunomia', *Classical Quarterly*, 32 (1938), 100–2.

[2] See A. J. Holliday, 'Spartan Austerity', *Classical Quarterly*, 17 (1977), 111–26.

[3] S. Pomeroy, *Goddesses, Whores, Wives and Slaves: Women in Classical Antiquity* (New York, 1975), 36.

These limited expressions of luxury consumption in the Archaic period gradually became more pronounced, and for this later writers were to blame Spartan women. Certainly by the fourth century BC, through dowries and other inheritances, women controlled two-fifths of Spartan land, and some apparently forsook their traditional role as childbearers, devoting their money and time instead to racehorses and clothing.[4] In the mid-third century BC, King Agis enacted a series of reforms designed to redistribute the land[5] but, in Plutarch's arguably biased and moralistic view, these failed because of women's refusal to abandon their new-found ease and luxury.[6] Spartan women were also criticized by Aristotle who blamed their behaviour for certain aspects of Sparta's decline.[7] This linking of political weakness with the moral degeneracy of women and, conversely, of a strong state with the virtue of women, was to be echoed later by both the Romans and the Italians.

There are also restrictions on luxury in the earliest Athenian laws of whose content we have any clear knowledge.[8] In the sixth century BC Solon formulated legislation to regulate many aspects of the Athenians' public life including feasting, mourning, and women's clothing. Women were the main focus of Solon's sumptuary laws. He restricted their trousseaus to three garments and banned the use of personal ornaments.[9] In addition he used clothing as a means to signify women of virtuous character. Respectable women were to wear wool or linen while prostitutes were to wear filmy, saffron-coloured material.[10] Women were further restricted in Solon's funerary legislation. He reduced the numbers of women allowed to enter the deceased's room or participate in the funeral procession to those over 60 and to family members,[11] required women to follow the men in the procession, and forbade excessive lamentation. Furthermore, the lying-in-state of the

[4] Pomeroy, *Goddesses, Whores, Wives and Slaves*, 36 and 38.

[5] Plutarch, *Lives, Agis*, in *Plutarch on Sparta*, trans. R. J. A. Talbert (Harmondsworth, 1988), 57–9.

[6] Ibid. On the background to this see P. Cartledge and A. Spawforth, *Hellenistic and Roman Sparta* (London and New York, 1989), 42–6.

[7] Aristotle, *Politics*, 2. 6. 5–11 (1269^b–1270^a).

[8] The first written laws in Athens were those of Drakon in 621/20 BC. All that is known of these is that they were severe and that homicide was dealt with. The dating of early Athenian legislation is complicated by the fact that, from the 6th cent. BC, Solon's name became synonymous with the law regardless of whether a particular law was actually a later addition or amendment to Solon's original legislation. For more on this see D. M. MacDowell, *The Law in Classical Athens* (London, 1978), 42–3.

[9] W. K. Lacey, *The Family in Classical Greece* (London, 1968), 87; Plutarch, *Solon*, 20. 4.

[10] Pomeroy, *Goddesses, Whores, Wives and Slaves*, 83. Prostitutes also had to be registered and were subject to a special tax, see ibid. 89.

[11] 'Family' was defined as those within the degree of children of cousins.

body (*prothesis*) now had to be indoors where formerly it had been in the courtyard; the sacrifice of an ox was forbidden; and there were limits to the amount of clothing, food, and drink which might be buried with the body.[12]

There is also evidence of funerary legislation elsewhere in Greece during the fifth century. At Iulis on Keos in about 420 BC legislation restricted the cost of garments for the corpse to 100 drachmas, specified that the bier be simple, that only traditional victims be sacrificed, and that the mourners maintain silence on the way to the tomb. At Delphi, around 400 BC, funeral costs were also limited and, during the funerary procession, there were to be no long pauses, silence was to be kept, and no one was to lament the former dead.[13]

Athenian sumptuary legislation in the Hellenistic period further restricted the position of women. During the government of Demetrius of Phalerum (317–307 BC) a board of 'regulators of women' was established (*gynaikonomoi*) (although this not only censored women's conduct but sought to limit excess at dinner parties). Some have argued that there is evidence of Aristotelian elements in this legislation.[14] Whilst this has been contested by others,[15] Aristotle's beliefs themselves are important as they, more than any ancient Greek legislation, had a profound impact upon medieval and Renaissance theories regarding luxury and women. Aristotle's beliefs that, as the deliberative part of woman's soul was impotent, she needed supervision, and that virtue consisted in a mean between two opposing excesses, provided a powerful ethical framework with which to support moderation and with which to regulate women in particular. A neo-Pythagorean treatise concerning women's clothing is typical of those promoting moderation as the supreme virtue. This advocated that the body

> be provided with a proper measure of clothing, bathing, anointing, hair-setting, and all those items of gold and precious stones that are used for adornment . . . to wear dresses that are excessively styled and elaborately dyed with purple or some other colour is a foolish extravagance. For the body desires merely not to be cold or, for the

[12] See Plutarch, *Solon*, 21; MacDowell, *Law in Classical Athens*, 109; Pomeroy, *Goddesses, Whores, Wives and Slaves*, 80; D. C. Kurtz and J. Boardman, *Greek Burial Customs* (London, 1971), 142–6. For some interpretations of this legislation see M. Gagarin, *Early Greek Law* (Los Angeles, 1986), 18 and Pomeroy, *Goddesses, Whores, Wives and Slaves*, 57.

[13] Lacey, *Family in Classical Greece*, 232 citing W. Dittenberger, *Sylloge Inscriptionum Graecarum* (3rd edn.), 1218, 438, 132 ff. See also H. J. Gehrke, 'Politik und Philosophie bei Demetrios von Pahleron', *Chiron*, 8 (1978), 168–9 nn. 200–2 for sumptuary initiatives in places other than Athens.

[14] See Pomeroy, *Goddesses, Whores, Wives and Slaves*, 131, and also 134–5.

[15] See Gehrke, 'Politik', 149–93.

sake of appearance, naked; but it needs nothing else . . . if a woman is well off, she has nothing to complain about; if not, it doesn't do to yearn.[16]

To the extent that they regulated the consumption or display of luxury goods of one form or another, it is appropriate to describe the Greek laws outlined above as sumptuary. However, it was the Romans who first applied the term 'sumptuary' to a law, using the term for their dining laws. In addition, the Romans enacted other laws regulating *sumptus* in funerals and clothing, although they themselves never defined these laws as sumptuary. Overall, the Romans seem to have been far more interested than the Greeks in controlling extravagance; certainly they had more extravagance to control. Wealthy Roman citizens spent large amounts of money not only on clothing but also on food for their tables, importing (amongst other things) anchovies from Pontus and wine from Greece. In 264 BC gladiatorial games were introduced and by 186 BC lions and panthers were being brought great distances at considerable cost to pander to the Romans' passion for spectacle. This luxurious lifestyle reached its peak under the Empire. Indeed Augustus claimed to have erected 408 marble pillars and to have provided 8,000 gladiators and 3,000 wild beasts for the arena. The excesses of Caligula and Nero too are infamous and were apparently emulated by many citizens according to their means.[17] Perhaps it is not too surprising, then, that from the Twelve Tables in the fifth century BC[18] to the fourth century AD, the Romans passed many regulations restricting consumption. Of these, by far the greatest number were concerned with excesses of the table, true *leges sumptuariae*, but women's extravagance, men's clothing, gladiatorial display, luxury in general, funerals, furniture, and the exchange of gifts were also dealt with.[19]

The very earliest Roman sumptuary law, contained in the Twelve Tables, concerned excessive expenditure on funeral ceremonies. According to Cicero, these regulations were drawn from the laws of Solon, and are in the tenth table.[20] This law forbade the use of worked wood in fu-

[16] See Pomeroy, *Goddesses, Whores, Wives and Slaves*, 134–5, citing H. Thelseff, *The Pythagorean Texts of the Hellenistic Period*, trans. F. R. Levin (Abo, 1965), 142–5.

[17] J. Hastings (ed.), *Encyclopaedia of Religion and Ethics*, viii (Edinburgh, 1915), 204.

[18] Traditionally 481–450 BC.

[19] For general information and chronologies of Roman sumptuary law see B. Kübler, 'Sumptus', in A. Pauly, G. Wissowa, W. Kroll, and K. Witte (eds.), *Real-Encyclopädie der klassischen Altertumswissenschaft*, 4a (Stuttgart and Munich, 1894–), 901–8; A. Berger, *Encyclopedic Dictionary of Roman Law: Transactions of the American Philological Society*, NS 43/2 (Philadelphia, 1953); C. Eilers, 'Roman Republican Sumptuary Legislation', MA thesis (McMaster Univ., Ontario, 1989), *passim*, and esp. 28.

[20] Cicero, *De Legibus*, 2.59.

neral pyres, a dowry of more than three robes or of purple tunics, and the participation of more than ten flute players in the ceremony.[21] The number of flute players was also limited to ten in a later aedile's edict which also forbade a dowry of garlands (if these had not been earned in the games or as a reward for bravery), gold clamps which were used to attach false teeth, the anointing of the corpse by slaves, drinking bouts, wine spiced with myrrh, frankincense, and the use of professional female mourners.[22] The only other attempt to regulate funeral practices was by the dictator Sulla with his *lex Cornelia* of AD 81.

The few laws restricting women's extravagance can, to some extent, be seen to relate to the Roman conception of the ideal citizen. Contemporary literature abounds with examples of a nostalgia for a bygone age of simple virtue.[23] According to this, it was a tough people who had founded the city in whose success the Romans now basked, and there was a constant clash between this ideal and the present reality. As described by Ovid, the

> Sabine dames of old under king Tatius would perchance have wished to cultivate their paternal acres rather than themselves when the matron, sitting rubicund in her high seat, span assiduously with hardened thumb, and herself penned up the lambs her daughter had pastured, herself set the twigs and cleft logs upon the hearth. But your mothers have borne delicate girls. You wish your bodies to be covered with gold-embroidered gowns, you wish to vary the dressing of your perfumed locks, you wish to have hands that shine with gems; you adorn your necks with stones sought from the East, and so large that the ear finds two a burden to bear.[24]

While Ovid may have exaggerated the simple purity of his Roman ancestors, his depiction of contemporary Roman women does seem to have some basis. The Punic wars had increased the wealth of many women through inheritances from relatives who had died in battle and so the rich Roman matron, unlike her more secluded counterparts in classical Athens, had more opulent dress, costly vehicles, and many more slaves who gave her the leisure to accompany her husband to dinner parties, to visit friends, attend festivals, and so on.[25] With the disastrous defeat of the Romans at the battle of Cannae in 216 BC, the display of such wealth must have seemed to

[21] See Kübler, 'Sumptus', 901–80.

[22] Ibid.

[23] See e.g. Ovid, *The Art of Love, and Other Poems*, trans. J. H. Mozley, ed. G. P. Gould (Cambridge, Mass., 1979), 127: 'There was rude simplicity of old, but now golden Rome possesses the vast wealth of the conquered world. See what the Capitol is now, and what it was: you would say they belonged to different Jupiters'; Seneca, *De Tranquillitate Animi* in which he yearns for 'the moderation of past ages'; and Juvenal, *Satire*, I. 34.

[24] 'Face Cosmetics', in *Art of Love*, 3.

[25] Pomeroy, *Goddesses, Whores, Wives and Slaves*, 170.

epitomize the abandonment of the old ideals that Roman men considered to have led to military defeat. The following year, in an effort to restore women's conduct and costume to a level more appropriate to a military situation, the *lex Oppia* was passed. This restricted the gold jewellery a woman could wear to half an ounce, prohibited dresses of varicoloured fabrics, and forbade women to ride in certain types of carriages within a mile of Rome or in the Roman towns except on occasions of religious festivals.[26] Still more restrictions were enforced the following year, 214 BC, when all the funds of wards, single women, and widows were deposited with the state.[27]

Despite the defeat of Hannibal in 201 BC, the Oppian law remained in effect. In 195 BC, however, its repeal was proposed and, in a rare display of public disaffection, Roman women demonstrated in the streets. Whether these women were protesting on their own behalf, or whether they had been encouraged by men eager to display wealth once more through their women, was and is a matter of debate.[28] Whatever the motive, the appeal was successful and the Oppian law was abolished.

The next law concerning women was the *lex Voconia* of 169 BC. This was a succession law in which no woman could inherit an estate worth more than a certain amount[29] and, of female agnates, only the deceased's sister was entitled to intestate succession. After the *lex Voconia*, there was no more legislation concerning women for over a century until the *lex Julia* of 46 BC which contained general prohibitions for men and women against luxury including the use of pearl jewellery, the wearing of purple and other costly clothing, and the use of litters.[30] With another *lex Julia*, this time under Augustus in 18 BC, women's clothes and adornment again came under attack. The laws are then silent on the subject until the reign of

[26] On the *lex Oppia* see P. Culham, 'The Lex Oppia', *Latomus*, 41 (1982), 786–93, who shows that the law prohibited wearing not owning as is maintained by Berger, *Encyclopedic Dictionary*, 557 and Pomeroy, *Goddesses, Whores, Wives and Slaves*, 178. There may have been an earlier clothing law, the *lex Metilia de fullonibus* of 217 BC, but its date and purpose are unclear: see Eilers, 'Roman Republican Sumptuary Legislation', 6–7.

[27] Pomeroy, 'Goddesses, Whores, Wives and Slaves', 178.

[28] This debate is reported in Livy, 34. It is the only source for the law as all other ancient references to the *lex Oppia* are obviously derived from Livy.

[29] The historical sources do not agree on the amount, see Berger, *Encyclopedic Dictionary*, 561.

[30] The only information about Caesar's rules on clothing is at Suetonius, *The Twelve Caesars*, trans. R. Graves (Harmondsworth, 1989), Julius Caesar 43, p. 33: 'He denied the use of litters and the wearing of purple robes or pearls to all except to those of a designated position and age, and on set days' ('Lecticarum usum, item conchyliatae vestis et margaritarum nisi certis personis et aetatibus perque certos dies ademit'). *Personis* is sexually ambiguous, perhaps intentionally so.

Elagabalus in AD 218–22 during which the dress and etiquette of women was regulated according to rank.[31]

The concept of the ideal citizen is most apparent in the Roman legislation concerning the behaviour of men. The word chosen by both Juvenal and Cicero to describe a true noble Roman is *gravitas*.[32] The precepts of *gravitas* required a Roman to be a good soldier and a good statesman, a man with no time for, or concern with, frivolity. Hence he should have short hair, be clean-shaven, and wear a simple knee-length tunic, or a long gown if he was an elder or official.[33] Later the toga, the distinguishing dress of the Roman citizen, came to be seen as a symbol of all that was dignified, sober, and upright in the Roman male. But Roman men, like their women, were attracted by the new luxury goods being brought into the city and, in an effort to control consumption, in 46 BC the *lex Julia* restricted the wearing of purple and other luxurious clothes, while in the reign of Tiberius the use of silk by men was forbidden.[34] The latter restrictions, as reported by Tacitus, led to some debate. Whilst Quintus Haterius and Octavius Fronto not only denounced the extravagance of male clothing but also argued for further restrictions on silver plate, furniture, and slaves, Gaius Asinius Gallus argued for the merits of such items as compensation for responsibilities of state, and pointed out that, in any case, moderation is a relative concept:

> The extension of the empire has meant the growth of private fortunes. This is nothing new; indeed it is in keeping with the most ancient history. Wealth meant one thing to the Fabricii, another to the Scipios. It must be judged in relation to the country. When the nation was poor, people's houses were small. In its present grandeur individuals, too, expand. In slaves, plate, or any other article for use, the only criterion of moderation or excess is the owner's means. Senators and knights have special property qualifications, not because they are intrinsically different, but because their precedence in station, rank, and honours warrants special provision for their mental and physical well-being. Otherwise leading men would have all the worries and dangers, and none of their compensations.[35]

Nero also placed prohibitions on the use of the expensive amethystine and Tyrian purple dyes in clothing (although his motives were for personal gain rather than the common good).[36] The only other Roman legislation con-

[31] Pomeroy, *Goddesses, Whores, Wives and Slaves*, 182.

[32] A. Ribeiro, *Dress and Morality* (London, 1986), 22.

[33] Ibid.

[34] Tacitus, *The Annals of Imperial Rome*, trans. M. Grant (Harmondsworth, 1989), 2. 33, p. 92 and Dio Cassius, 57. 15. 1.

[35] Tacitus, *Annals*, 2. 33, pp. 92–3.

[36] Suetonius, *Twelve Caesars*, trans. Graves, Nero 32. 37, p. 230.

cerning men's clothes is that of Honorious between AD 397 and 416 in which trousers, a barbarian influence, were outlawed.[37]

It was the areas of food and gladiatorial display, however, which attracted most vigilance from the state. In all, eleven laws were passed limiting excess of the table, more than double the number against any other subject, and three were passed concerning gladiatorial display. Whilst excess at the table and in the arena did not conform to the principles of *gravitas*, historians have argued that this alone cannot account for the number of laws in these areas.

David Daube has highlighted the Roman concern with *ambitus*.[38] This was the effort of the politically ambitious to win votes by whatever means were available but, in particular, by the banqueting of friends, the hosting of public games, the distribution of gifts, and the display of expensive attire. As Daube explains it, such behaviour was reprehensible on several counts. First, a man behaving in this way was 'doing business, he was buying, and buying, moreover, a commodity which ought not be for sale'. Secondly, *ambitus* 'often involved an unworthy degree of self-ingratiation with the public', and, finally, 'recourse to *ambitus* showed that the man could not succeed by virtue of his and his family's reputation and real qualities'.[39] If Daube is correct, then this desire to check the politically ambitious certainly explains the sub-clause of the *lex Antia* of 71 BC in which magistrates and magisterial candidates (with some exceptions) were prohibited from accepting invitations to banquets.[40] It also helps to explain restrictions on expenses involved in gladiatorial displays, pompous funerals, and the one law forbidding the exchange of gifts, except on New Year's Day, passed during the reign of Tiberius.[41]

Daube's general explanation of Roman laws regulating expenditure is his theory of the 'non-tipper'.[42] This is based on contemporary evidence that Roman senators were worried about having to live up to the precedents of extravagance set by other senators, and yet were ashamed of being thought miserly. To avoid such an accusation they could, of course, simply have spent lavishly. But if they had neither the desire nor money to do so, and yet did not wish to be compared unfavourably with their prodigal contemporaries, then what better solution than to outlaw prodigality and render their

[37] See S. Dill, *Roman Society in the Last Century of the Western Empire* (London, 1905), 297.

[38] *Roman Law: Linguistic, Social and Philosophical Aspects* (Edinburgh, 1969), 126.

[39] Ibid.

[40] Kübler, 'Sumptus'; Berger, *Encyclopedic Dictionary*, 547.

[41] Kübler, 'Sumptus'.

[42] Daube, *Roman Law*, 124 ff.

own disposition undetectable? Chaim Wirszubski's explanation is similar and is based upon Livy's account of the protest over the *lex Oppia*.[43] Wirszubski suggests that the advocates of sumptuary legislation desired to strengthen the unity of the senatorial class by preventing, or at least arresting, differentiation in standards of living. In other words, they sought to maintain uniformity within the one social body of senators.

Whatever the motives for Roman sumptuary law, there was increasing debate in Rome as to whether moderation was properly a matter for the individual or the state and, given the problems of enforcement, whether passing laws was, in fact, detrimental to the public good. As reported by Tacitus, the Emperor Tiberius argued against new sumptuary measures, not because he agreed with increasing luxury but because he 'knew how undignified it would be to start something which he could not maintain, or could only maintain by humiliating and disgracing eminent men'. As the emperor concluded: 'the remedy lies with the individual. If we are decent, we shall behave well—the rich when they are surfeited, the poor because they have to.'[44]

II

The advent of Christianity brought more force to traditional condemnations of luxury consumption. Now indulgence in luxury could be seen not just as irrational, immoderate, and potentially threatening to society, but as a sin. In the New Testament itself, however, there is remarkably little on the subject of luxury. Whilst it is implicitly condemned by Jesus ('How hard it is for those who have riches to enter the kingdom of God!', Mark 10: 23–4), it was only St Paul who dealt with it overtly and only in relation to women. In his first letter to Timothy, Paul directs the women in the assembly 'to wear suitable clothes and to be dressed quietly and modestly, without braided hair or gold and jewellery or expensive clothes; their adornment is to do the sort of good works that are proper for women who profess to be religious'.[45] Similarly in his first letter to Peter, Paul instructs married women: 'Do not dress up for show: doing up your hair, wearing gold bracelets and fine clothes; all this should be inside, in a person's heart, imperishable: the ornament of a sweet and gentle disposition—this is what is precious in the sight of God.'[46]

[43] Livy, 34. 1 ff., and Wirszubski, *Libertas as a Political Idea at Rome during the Late Republic and Early Principate* (Cambridge, 1968), 27–8.

[44] Tacitus, *Annals*, 3. 52–5, pp. 143–5.

[45] 1 Tim. 2: 9–11.

[46] 1 Pet. 3: 3–5.

These words of advice from Paul were taken one step further by early Christian moralists who were adamant in their damnation of luxury as a vice. The earliest and most influential of the Christian tracts on the subject was that of Tertullian. Drawing from the controversial *Book of Henoch*,[47] Tertullian condemns all finery and the arts that produce it on the grounds that these owe their existence to the fallen angels and hence also, by implication, to the devil. He then condemns false hair because 'you may be putting on a holy and Christian head the cast-offs of hair of some stranger who was perhaps unclean, perhaps guilty and destined for hell';[48] coloured garments because 'what legitimate honour can garments derive from adulteration with illegitimate colours? God is not pleased by what he Himself did not produce. We cannot suppose that God was unable to produce sheep with purple or sky-blue fleeces. If He was able, then He chose not to do it, and what God refused to do certainly cannot be lawful for man to make.'[49]

This same notion of perverting God's creation is apparent in Tertullian's attitude to make-up:

For, surely, those women sin against God who anoint their faces with creams, stain their cheeks with rouge, or lengthen their eye-brows with antimony. Obviously, they are not satisfied with the creative skill of God; in their own person, without doubt, they censure and criticize the Maker of all things! Surely they are finding fault when they try to perfect and add to His work, taking these their additions, of course, from a rival artist. This rival artist is the Devil.[50]

Tertullian is also quite clear in his assignation of love of finery to love of, and absorption in, the world.[51] It is modesty that he stresses and his final admonition to Christians is to 'Dress yourselves in the silk of probity, the fine linen of holiness, and the purple of chastity. Decked out in this manner, you will have God Himself for your lover.'[52]

While Tertullian professes to be addressing both sexes, he devotes only one chapter (book 2, chapter 8) out of a total of twenty-two to men's indulgence in finery, and this imbalance, found in the New Testament as well, was to be carried on by later Christian theologians.[53] Moreover, while the implications of the biblical attitude towards luxury are quite clear, the lack of direct condemnation of finery in the Bible meant that Tertullian was

[47] 'The Apparel of Women' (*De cultu feminarum*), trans. E. A. Quain, in *Tertullian: Disciplinary, Moral and Ascetical Works* (R. J. Deferrari (gen. ed.), *The Fathers of the Church*, 40; New York, 1959), 1. 3, pp. 121–2.

[48] Ibid. 2. 7, p. 139.

[49] Ibid. 1. 8, p. 126.

[50] Ibid. pp. 135–6.

[51] Ibid. pp. 133–4.

[52] Ibid. 2. 13, p. 149.

[53] Cf. Cyprian and also Thomas Aquinas in Ch. 5, below.

largely on his own in formulating an exact and appropriate Christian response. His influence on subsequent theologians in the matter was immense and it is his attitude and arguments, though often moderated, which are found repeatedly in later treatises. Cyprian, for instance, virtually paraphrased Tertullian's views in his treatise *The Dress of Virgins*. Cyprian's main contribution to the theological formulation of attitudes to private conspicuous consumption of luxury goods lay in his superior rhetorical style which rendered Tertullian's arguments more palatable to other theologians. Both Augustine and Saint Jerome refer to Cyprian rather than to Tertullian as an authority in this matter, Jerome recommending Cyprian's treatise as a manual of instruction for virgins in his own pastoral care.[54]

For the first few centuries of its existence, however, the Christian condemnation of excess had no means of enforcement. But, when in 337 Christianity became institutionalized as the main religion of the Empire, the legal framework of the Romans could be wedded to the peculiarly Christian view of excess. There are indications, however, that there was some theological debate in this period as to whether the Church should regulate the dress of its lay members. In a letter of Augustine written to Possidius appears the following: 'I should not like you to make any impulsive regulation forbidding the use of jewelry or fine clothing, except that those who are neither married nor desirous of being married ought to be thinking about how to please God. But worldly people think of worldly things: if husbands, how to please their wives; if wives, how to please their husbands.'[55]

Augustine does conclude, however, that the 'true and unique adornment of Christian men and women is a good character, not lying paint, or even gold or the ostentation of fine apparel'. That Augustine's appreciation of the difficulties involved in the Church legislating for the laity in this matter was more widespread is perhaps indicated by the fact that the only ecclesiastical sumptuary laws of this period are directed to the Church's own representatives, the

[54] See Augustine, *De doctrina christiana*, 21. 47–9 ed. H. J. Vogels (*Florilegium patristicum*, 24; 1930), 56, and A. E. Keenan's introd. to Cyprian, 'The Dress of Virgins', in *Saint Cyprian Treatises*, trans. R. J. Deferrari, in *Saint Cyprian Treatises* (Deferrari (gen. ed.), *The Fathers of the Church*, 36; New York, 1958), 28. Cf. *Saint Augustine's Commentary on the Lord's Sermon on the Mount*, trans. D. J. Kavanagh, in *Writings of Saint Augustine*, 3 (Deferrari (gen. ed.), *The Fathers of the Church*, 11; Washington, 1963), 149: 'When a man dazzles by immoderate adornment of the body and its raiment or by the splendor or whatever else he may possess, by that very fact he is easily shown to be desirous of worldly display; he deceives nobody by a crafty semblance of holiness.'

[55] *Saint Augustine Letters*, vol. v trans. W. Parsons, *Writings of Saint Augustine*, 13 (R. J. Deferrari (gen. ed.), *The Fathers of the Church*, 32; New York, 1956), letter 245, p. 229.

clergy. In these ecclesiastical statutes the combination of Roman law and Christian morals can clearly be seen and it is here that the next substantial body of sumptuary legislation can be found.

In the second Council of Nicaea (787), a canon was entitled 'Clerics shall wear modest and unostentatious clothing and not array themselves in gay and showy apparel embroidered with silk'.[56] The reasons put forward are ones of appropriateness ('All luxury and gaudy apparel are foreign to the sacerdotal state') and tradition ('From early times every cleric wore modest and unostentatious garments'). In the fourth Council of Constantinople (869–70), bishops were the sole focus of a sumptuary canon which cautioned them 'not to wear the pallium to satisfy a spirit of self-love' and that if they had been monks before being raised to the office of bishop then they 'must retain the monastic habit'.[57]

Ecclesiastical sumptuary pronouncements continued to be fairly general in nature until the thirteenth century. In 1096 at a synod in Rouen and in 1102 at a synod in London, the clergy were urged simply to adhere more strictly to their clerical dress and to have their heads tonsured.[58] Similarly, a canon of the second Lateran Council in 1139 commanded that both bishops and clerics should 'not by superfluity, dissensions, or the color of their clothes, nor in their tonsure, offend the sight of those whose model and example they ought to be'.[59] In 1191 the Council of Toulouse decreed that any cleric with long hair should be excommunicated until he cut it;[60] and at the Council of Montpellier in 1195 slashings of the hems of clerical robes were forbidden.[61] By the thirteenth century, however, more detailed prohibitions appear. For instance, a canon of the fourth Lateran Council in 1215 decreed that in the matter of dress clerics must have

> a becoming crown and tonsure . . . Their garments must be worn clasped at the top and neither too short nor too long. They are not to use red or green garments or curiously sewed together gloves, or beak-shaped shoes or gilded bridles, saddles, pectoral ornaments [for horses], spurs, or anything else indicative of superfluity. . . . Buckles may under no condition be worn, nor sashes having ornaments of gold or silver, nor rings, unless it be in keeping with the dignity of their office.[62]

The details in this passage suggest that luxurious commodities were by

[56] Canon 16 in H. J. Schroeder, *Disciplinary Decrees of the General Councils* (St Louis, Mo., 1937), 151.

[57] Canon 27, ibid. 176.

[58] Ribeiro, *Dress and Morality*, 35.

[59] Schroeder, *Disciplinary Decrees*, 199–200.

[60] J. Evans, *Dress in Medieval France* (Oxford, 1952), 76.

[61] Owen Hughes, 'Sumptuary Law and Social Relations', 73.

[62] Schroeder, *Disciplinary Decrees*, 257.

then more widely available, that indulgence in them was increasing, and that tailoring techniques had improved, allowing for greater variety in fashion—all factors requiring a more concerted attempt by the Church authorities to keep their officers in line.

Similar ecclesiastical prohibitions against excess were issued at fairly regular, if large, intervals for the rest of the medieval period.[63] The common factor in all these enactments was their exclusively moral character and clerical focus. Conspicuously absent in the early ecclesiastical sumptuary decrees, indeed, is any statement concerning the luxurious habits of the Church's lay members. Apart from questions concerning the jurisdiction of the Church in passing secular sumptuary laws, which will be dealt with in Chapter 5, one reason for a lack of such laws in this early period is the level and distribution of luxury goods. Before the twelfth century, luxurious commodities were hard to come by and the general level of wealth in the population does not seem to have been very high. What wealth there was tended to be concentrated in large institutions such as royal families and the Church. Whether or not Church authorities had any desire to pass laws directed to the laity in this early period, the Church's lack of such decrees coupled with regular decrees against clerical excess can partly be explained in terms of the increasing availability of luxury goods to the Religious.

III

For the early medieval period, the only secular governing body concerned to restrict consumption of luxury goods by its subjects was that of Charlemagne and his successor, Louis le Débonnaire. In his sumptuary ordinance of 808, Charlemagne forbade all his subjects from buying or selling a *sayon double* tunic for more than 20 sou and the more basic *sayon simple* for more than 10 sou. The fur-lined *rochet* that was worn over the tunic was restricted to the price of 30 sou if lined with marten, sable, or otter, and to 10 sou if lined with cat fur.[64] According to Baudrillart, by these preventive measures Charlemagne hoped to arrest what he saw as a disorder contrary to custom and opposed to society, religion, and the good of the state.

[63] See e.g. the Council of Montpellier, 1216, canons 1, 2, and 3 cited in Bistort, *Magistrato alle pompe*, 245; the Council of Vienne, 1311–13, in Schroeder, *Disciplinary Decrees*, 387 ff.; the Council of Paris, 1323, in G. D. Mansi (ed.) (continued and supplemented under the editorship of L. Petit and J. B. Martin), *Sacrorum conciliorum nova et amplissimo collectio*, 53 vols. (Florence, 1759–1962), 25. 730; the Council of Constance, 1414–18, in Schroeder, *Disciplinary Decrees*, 455.

[64] H. J. Baudrillart, *Histoire du luxe privé et public depuis l'antiquité jusqu'à nos jours*, 4 vols. (Paris, 1878–80), i. 66–7.

Charlemagne's successor, Louis le Débonnaire, forbade the wearing of silk and ornaments of silver and gold.[65] The imbalance in wealth of the general population as opposed to the Church, however, is once more indicated by the fact that Louis was especially severe with ecclesiastics in his kingdom. He disallowed them rings, belts, knives, and shoes ornamented with precious stones and the use of golden reins when riding mules, horses, or palfreys.[66]

Overall, then, there was little legislative activity designed to control luxury in the early medieval period. The Church provides the most examples, and even these are not very plentiful when compared with ancient precedents and with those of the later Middle Ages and the Renaissance. However, it is important to note that, whenever luxury was of a level sufficient to merit concern, there was no hesitation on the part of the appropriate ruling bodies, whether sacred or secular, to pass legislation. The efforts of Tertullian, Cyprian, Augustine, Jerome, and other theologians to formulate and promulgate the Christian response to luxury, together with the Church's legislative efforts, ensured that a powerful legacy of moral condemnation could be handed down to, and drawn upon by, later secular governments to bolster their own sumptuary enactments.

[65] Baudrillart, *Histoire du luxe privé et public*, 67. [66] Ibid. 69.

2

The Origins and Characteristics of Italian Sumptuary Law

The chief enjoyment of riches consists in the parade of riches.

Adam Smith

From the end of the Carolingian Empire until the mid-twelfth century, no European government, with the exception of the Church, passed sumptuary laws. The Church's interest in restricting luxury continued throughout the early medieval period but was focused exclusively on the clergy. Then, from the mid-twelfth century onwards, secular laws restricting various aspects of luxury consumption made a gradual reappearance until by the early fourteenth century they were being issued with increasing frequency all across Europe from London to Sicily. Sumptuary legislation was not adopted with equal fervour by all countries. Governments in Germany, Switzerland, and England, for example, did not begin to legislate until the fourteenth century.[1] Late medieval sumptuary legislation, indeed, seems to originate in Italy, France, and Spain and, of the three countries, it is Italy, particularly northern Italy, which is most rewarding to study. Not only does Italy have the earliest recorded sumptuary law in the period, but its legislation is more frequent, wide ranging, and detailed than that of any other region in Europe. This chapter is not, however, concerned with determining why Italy should have led the way in sumptuary legislation, or why laws were passed there at all. Such questions will form the basis of subsequent chapters. Here instead we are concerned simply to establish the chronology, distribution, and general characteristics of Italian sumptuary legislation for it is only from the basis of these facts that we can begin to tackle the question 'why?'.

[1] German governments began legislating in 1350, see L. C. Eisenbart, *Kleiderordnungen der deutschen Städte zwischen 1350 und 1700: Ein Beitrag zur Kulturgeschichte des deutschen Burgertums* (Gottingen, 1962), 5–6, and G. Hampel-Kallbrunner, *Beiträge zur Geschichte der Kleiderordnungen, mit besonderer Berücksichtigung Österreichs* (Vienna, 1962); the Swiss began in 1304, see J. M. Vincent, *Costume and Conduct in the Laws of Basel, Bern, and Zurich, 1370–1800* (Baltimore, 1935), 1; and the English began in 1316, see N. B. Harte, 'State Control of Dress and Social Change in Pre-Industrial England', in D. C. Coleman and A. H. John (eds.), *Trade, Government and Economy in Pre-Industrial England: Essays presented to F. J. Fisher* (London, 1976), 132–65.

I

The earliest sumptuary enactment of the late Middle Ages stands somewhat apart. It is contained in Genoa's first law code, the *Breve della campagna* of 1157, a full seventy-two years earlier than any other European sumptuary law.[2] Although it only banned the use of sable furs over the value of 40 *soldi* to trim hems, and although this ban was then omitted from the code's reissue in 1161, it is nonetheless significant. First it shows that Genoa's government felt, if only for a short period, that luxury consumption could be a problem and one which came within the proper jurisdiction of the law. Further, it expressed two of the various conflicting attitudes towards luxury that were to be a constant problem in devising and enforcing an effective sumptuary law. For, whilst restraining private luxury, and thereby condemning individual displays of finery, this law provided for the display of public wealth. As representatives of their city, legates to other states and visitors to the papal, royal, or imperial courts could apply for a licence to wear the furs that were otherwise banned, thereby implicitly holding up the display of wealth as something honourable and worthy of admiration.

After this isolated Genoese provision, sumptuary legislation does not reappear until the early thirteenth century when France and Spain as well as Italy became preoccupied with the problem of excess. The French and Spanish laws take the form of royal decrees and seem primarily concerned with maintaining the accepted order of society by restraining the ambitions of nobles and of the lower orders. In 1229 King Louis VIII of France issued a decree limiting the excess of his nobles' wardrobes.[3] In 1234 King James of Aragon approved a sumptuary law which restricted his subjects' consumption of meat to two meals a day, one in the morning and one in the evening, and forbade them from wearing many items of clothing and jewellery, all of which were luxury goods principally made and worn by Arabs.[4] In 1258 a law of Alfonso X of Castile gave precise details as to the dress permitted to the various ranks of the upper orders of society, with unrestrained indulgence reserved only for the king: 'The King may wear as many suits of clothing as he wishes . . . no one except the King may wear a scarlet rain cloak . . . no one may wear sendal or silk except the King or a noble knight.'[5]

[2] F. Niccolai, *Contributo allo studio dei più antichi brevi della campagna genovese* (Milan, 1939), 125–6.

[3] P. Kraemer, *Le Luxe et les lois somptuaires au moyen âge* (Paris, 1920), 33–4.

[4] Del Giudice, 'Legge del 1290', 84–6.

[5] 'A Thirteenth-Century Castilian Sumptuary Law', *Business History Review*, 37/1–2 (1963), 98–100.

In 1279 King Philippe le Hardi of France limited the consumption of food by his subjects and restricted the cost and amount of clothing and riding accoutrements that could be worn on a graded scale according to the value of land owned by an individual.[6] A few years later, in 1283, King Philippe directed his legislative attention to the middle ranks, a group not mentioned in his law of 1279, forbidding their women from wearing the distinctively aristocratic adornment of crowns.[7] The middle ranks, together with nobles, also featured in Philippe le Bel's restrictions of 1294.[8] The perceived need for Philippe's law was underlined by his wife, Jeanne of Navarre, who, while on a visit to Ghent, declared: 'I believed myself to be the only queen and here I am seen with hundreds!'[9] The wealth of the clergy also featured in these royal decrees. Both the law of Alfonso X and that of Philippe le Hardi in 1279 placed detailed restrictions on the dress of the clergy. It would seem that wealthy clerics were to be feared no less than the wealthy laity.

Thirteenth-century royal decrees can also be found in the south of Italy. In 1272 Charles I of Anjou sanctioned a law for Messina.[10] Similarly, the vice-regents of the Kingdoms of Sicily and Puglia approved a sumptuary law in 1290. The existence of these and later southern Italian laws should be stressed. Denholm-Young and Kantorowicz, echoing Burckhardt, claimed that sumptuary legislation in Italy was restricted to the north of the peninsula while 'in Naples there was liberty of dress for all, as far as the state was concerned'.[11] Modern historians of sumptuary law have also focused their studies on the north of Italy and seem unaware of the southern Italian laws.[12] Certainly, after the fourteenth century, sumptuary legislation in the south of Italy is not as frequent as in the north, but its existence from as early as 1272 should be noted lest we be tempted to assume that Italian sumptuary legislation was a northern, essentially republican, phenomenon. It is true, however, that it was the governments of city states in northern Italy who

[6] H. Duplès-Agier, 'Ordonnance somptuaire inédite de Philippe le Hardi', *Bibliothèque de l'École des Chartres*, 3/5 (1854), 176–81.

[7] Del Giudice, 'Legge del 1290', 136 and 162–5; Baudrillart, *Histoire du luxe*, iii 252.

[8] J. Favier, *Philippe le Bel* (Paris, 1979), 126–7; Fabretti, 'Statuti suntuari', 153: 'accennavano a moderare lo sfarzo della borghesia o dal ceto medio, che, prestamente arricchite, talvolta sorpassava nei godimenti del banchettare e nella ricchezza delle vesti il fasto della nobilità'.

[9] M. Lériget, *Des lois et impôts somptuaires* (Montpellier, 1919), 76: 'Je croiyais être seule reine, et j'en vois ici par centaines!'

[10] Del Giudice, 'Legge del 1290', 120–2. This law was revoked the following year.

[11] Denholm-Young and Kantorowicz, 'De Ornatu Mulierum', 330 and J. Burckhardt, *The Civilization of the Renaissance in Italy* (1860: Oxford, 1945), 220 and 245.

[12] See Owen Hughes, 'Sumptuary Law and Social Relations', and Brundage, 'Sumptuary Laws and Prostitution', *passim*.

were most prolific in the passage of sumptuary laws and who developed the early, isolated provisions into sophisticated legal documents with a character and purpose different in many respects from those of royal governments in the south of Italy and elsewhere in Europe.

II

After the Genoese law of 1157, the earliest hint of legislative activity in northern Italy comes from Bologna. Fra Giovanni da Vicenza, leader of the so-called 'Allelujah movement', came to Bologna in 1233. Among his many exhortations for repentance was a condemnation of women's ornate head-dresses. He urged women to veil themselves modestly instead. So inspired and impressed were the Bolognese that they gave him their statute books to alter as he saw fit.[13] Unfortunately we have no indication of the details of Fra Giovanni's law nor of the extent to which it was enforced or observed after the initial religious enthusiasm had waned, and there is no record of any further sumptuary legislation in Bologna for another twenty years.

Brescia legislated against certain funeral practices sometime between 1200 and 1276.[14] In 1242 Reggio also legislated against excess at funerals.[15] In 1249 Siena restricted the length of the trains of women's dresses.[16] Two years later, in 1251, a similar ban was issued by San Gimignano,[17] and Parma followed suit in the provisions added to its statutes between 1258 and 1266.[18] Bassano restricted wedding and funeral practices in a statute compiled between 1259 and 1265.[19] Perugia attacked wedding celebrations in 1266;[20] Padua restricted baptismal and wedding celebrations in 1277.[21]

[13] A. Sorbelli (ed.), *Corpus chronicorum bononiensum*, 2/1, 'Cronaca A' (L. A. Muratori (gen. ed.), *Rerum italicarum scriptores*, 18; new edn., Città di Castello, 1905), 102.

[14] A. Cassa, *Funerali, pompe, conviti* (Brescia, 1887), 35. There is a great disorder in the early statutes and provisions of Brescia so Cassa cannot be more precise.

[15] A. Cerlini (ed.), *Consuetudini e statuti reggiani del secolo XIII* (*Corpus statutorum italicorum*, 16; Milan, 1933), 36.

[16] Denholm-Young and Kantorowicz, 'De Ornatu Mulierum', 331; Owen Hughes, 'Sumptuary Law and Social Relations', 73; Jones, 'Storia economica', 1784.

[17] R. Davidsohn, 'Jagd, Spiel, Luxus', in *Forschungen zur Alteren Geschichte von Florenz*, ii (Berlin, 1900), 324. Levi Pisetzky thought the war against trains only began in 1275 with Gregory X's supposed ban. She corrects Fabretti who claimed it began in 1278, see *Storia del costume*, i. 259.

[18] A. Ronchini (ed.), 'Adjectiones ab anno MCCLXVI', in *Statuta communis parmae digesta anno* MCCLV (Parma, 1856), 406.

[19] G. Fasoli (ed.), 'Statuti del comune di Bassano dell'anno 1259 e dell'anno 1295', *Reale deputazione di storia patria per le Venezie: Monumenti storici*, NS 2 (1940), 41 and 134.

[20] Bonardi, 'Lusso di altri tempi', 5.

[21] Ibid. 9–10.

In 1281 funeral practices were under discussion in Florence.[22] Sumptuary laws were also passed in Prato (1283), Pisa (1286), Ferrara (1287), Verona (1295), Cremona (1297), Fabriano (1299), Venice (1299), Mantua (1302), and so on, all across the peninsula. And, while new laws were being devised, old laws were being revised, so that legislative activity directed towards luxury became a characteristic feature of northern Italian life in this period.

The chronology, distribution, and frequency of Italian sumptuary laws from their origins until 1500 are indicated in Table 2.1. This table is the result of an examination of the published primary and secondary material with additions from archival documents. Some qualifications, however, should be entered. In a study of such wide scope as the present one, it is not feasible to examine the unpublished primary sources exhaustively, and therefore I have had to depend, to a great extent, upon the work and preoccupations of other historians. For instance, the table suggests that Florence and Venice passed many more sumptuary laws than other cities. While this may indeed be the case, as will be argued, it might, on the face of it, simply be a reflection of the current preoccupation with the history of these two cities. Their archives have been more thoroughly trawled than those of other cities, so one should not be surprised that more of their laws have been discovered and published. Again, looking at the published laws of Genoa, it looks as though there were no laws in the fourteenth century and that there was then a sudden cluster of them in the fifteenth century. But it could also be that records of Genoese sumptuary laws for the fourteenth century have been mislaid, or destroyed, or simply insufficiently examined. And for some cities, like Milan and Naples, archival material has, of course, been completely destroyed. Furthermore, historians examining sumptuary legislation have, on the whole, been far more interested in laws restricting women's clothing than with those against men's clothing, funeral, wedding, baptismal, and post-partum practices. This has led, not only to certain emphases in their studies, but to fewer published sources for these other areas of sumptuary concern.

To redress some potential imbalances in the table, a variety of other sources was also examined. Wherever gaps appeared, either chronologically or geographically, contemporary chronicles and histories of the city in question were consulted. Reassuringly, these sources seemed to confirm the general outlines of the table. Cities such as Florence, Venice,

[22] Rainey, 'Legislation in Florence', 44–5, citing the *Consulte e Pratiche*; no provision survives so one cannot be certain when the Florentines began sumptuary legislation.

TABLE 2.1. Distribution and chronology of Italian sumptuary laws

Town	Dates of sumptuary laws	Total
Agrigento	1426	1
Ancona	*c.*1500	1
Aquila	*c.*1375	1
Arezzo	1327	1
Aspra Sabina	1417	1
Bassano	1259, 1295	2
Bergamo	1331, 1343, 1352, 1374, 1391, 1482, 1491	7
Bologna	1233, 1250, 1260, 1276, 1289, 1294,1299, 1301, 1309, 1310, 1313, 1335, 1352, 1357, 1376, 1394, 1398, 1401, 1453, 1474, 1476	21
Brescia	1200–76, 1277, 1442, 1466, 1473, 1477, 1481, 1492, 1495, 1497, 1499	11
Castel Fiorentino	1305	1
Como	1335	1
Cremona	1297, 1300, 1387	3
Fabriano	1299, 1415	2
Faenza	1410	1
Ferrara	1287, 1420, 1434, 1447, 1453, 1456, 1460, 1467, 1476	9
Florence	1281, 1290, 1299, 1301, 1307, 1318, 1322–5, 1330, 1334, 1338, 1339, 1341, 1345, 1348, 1349 (× 2), 1351, 1352, 1354, 1355, 1356, 1357, 1359, 1363, 1364, 1365, 1373, 1376, 1377, 1379, 1384, 1388 (× 2), 1392, 1393, 1396, 1402, 1406, 1412, 1415 (× 2), 1419, 1420, 1427, 1433, 1439, 1449, 1456, 1459 (× 2), 1463, 1464, 1467, 1472 (× 3), 1473 (× 2), 1475, 1483, 1497	61
Forlì	1359	1
Genoa	1157, 1402, 1403, 1413, 1440, 1443, 1445, 1449, 1450, 1452, 1453, 1474, 1484, 1487 (× 2), 1488 (× 2), 1489, 1494	19
Gubbio	1371, 1469, 1484	3
Imola	1334	1
Lucca	1308, 1331, 1337, 1342, 1346, 1350, 1362, 1372, 1380, 1382, 1383, 1440, 1458, 1473, 1482, 1484, 1489, 1498	18
Mantua	1302	1
Milan	*c.*1343, 1351, 1396, 1421, 1498	5
Modena	1327–36	1
Montalboddo	1366	1

Town	Dates of sumptuary laws	Total
Orvieto	1398	1
Padua	1277, 1287, 1398, 1440, 1460	5
Parma	1258–66, 1316–25, 1421, 1422, 1424	5
Perugia	1266, 1279, 1318, 1322, 1342, 1366, 1400, 1402, 1416, 1445, 1460, 1469, 1472, 1475, 1485	15
Pescia	*c.*1262, 1339	2
Pisa	1286, 1302, 1305, 1350, 1386, 1463	6
Pistoia	1332, 1333, 1360, 1439	4
Prato	1283	1
Ravenna	1331	1
Reggio	1242, 1277, 1313	3
Rome	1429, 1469, 1473, 1487	4
Saccomurro	1311	1
San Gimignano	1251, 1267	2
Sarzana	1330	1
Savona	1325, 1430, 1452	3
Sicily	1272, 1290 (& Puglia), 1309 (& Puglia), 1330, 1340, 1383, 1421 (×4), 1423, 1426, 1437, 1451	14
Siena	1249, 1277, 1284, 1292, 1306, 1324, 1330, 1339, 1343, 1348, 1349, 1374, 1411, 1412, 1424, 1426, 1433, 1460, 1471, 1472, 1473	21
Tivoli	1305, 1308	2
Treviso	1432	1
Vellano	1367	1
Venice	1299, 1306, 1334, 1336, 1339, 1348, 1356, 1360, 1365, 1400, 1403, 1420, 1421, 1425, 1430, 1433, 1437, 1441, 1443 (×2), 1445, 1450, 1453, 1454, 1456, 1459, 1460, 1463, 1465, 1466, 1472 (×2), 1475, 1476, 1480, 1483, 1488, 1489, 1494, 1495, 1497, 1499	42
Verona	1295, 1328, 1332, 1441, 1446, 1450, 1460, 1490, 1499	9
Viterbo	1237, 1251, 1444, 1449, 1469, 1472, 1485, 1488	8

Siena, and Bologna, which all enacted numerous sumptuary laws, have chronicles and other histories which also refer regularly to sumptuary laws, either in passing, or at some length. Cities such as Mantua, Parma, and Milan, on the other hand, with few extant sumptuary laws, have only rare references in contemporary sources to sumptuary legislative activity.[23] Whilst the table is certainly not definitive and whilst more archival research is clearly called for, the general distribution and frequency of laws which it indicates is, one feels, largely correct.

One point immediately to be noted is that sumptuary legislation in Italy was primarily an urban phenomenon. Toubert, in his study of the fourteenth-century rural statutes of Lombardy, has found a few examples of rural sumptuary laws, particularly in Riperia d'Orta, Orzinuovi, Isola d'Orta, and Bellano, but they are not as detailed as urban laws, and are concerned solely with the splendour of weddings and funerals.[24] Likewise, the hill village of Camporotondo in the March of Ancona passed brief sumptuary provisions between 1322 and 1366 dealing with funerals, weddings, and gifts on the birth of a child.[25] However, the published statutes of most other rural areas in northern Italy do not contain any sumptuary provisions. There are none in the statutes of Sambuca (1291), Frignano (1337–8),[26] Averrara and Val Taleggio (1313 and 1368), Valsassina (1388), Dervio and Corenno (1389),[27] Cittadella (1366–88),[28] nor in the statute of Gabiano (1421).[29] Not only does this lack of sumptuary provisions provide us with further information, by default, of the geography of the laws, but it is also revealing as to the way in which sumptuary legislation spread across the peninsula and the influence of one city upon another.

The statute of Frignano of 1337–8, for instance, a region in the Apennines near Modena, seems to a great extent to imitate the Modenese statute of 1327.[30] However, while the latter contains a sumptuary provision, none appears in Frignano's statute. Similarly, despite the creation of Cittadella by the Paduans in 1220 and the close involvement of the Paduans with its statute of 1366–88, no sumptuary provision was included. Again,

[23] This situation is confirmed also by historians who have worked in these archives. In particular I wish to thank David Chambers and Daniel Bueno de Mesquita for sharing their knowledge of the Mantuan and Sforza archives respectively.

[24] 'Les Statuts communaux et l'histoire des campagnes lombardes au XIVe siècle', *Mélanges d'archéologie et d'histoire*, 72 (1960), 503 n. 3.

[25] D. Cecchi (ed.), *Statuta castri campirotundi* (Milan, 1966). Because of their brevity and sporadic nature, these rural sumptuary laws have not been included in the table.

[26] Q. Santoli, A. Sorbelli, and F. Jacoli (eds.), *Statuti dell'Apennino Tosco-Modenese (Sambuca Pistoiese, Frignano), secoli XIII–XIV* (*Corpus statutorum italicorum*, 2; Rome, 1913).

[27] E. Anderloni (ed.), *Statuti dei laghi di Como e di Lugano del sec. XIV*, i: 'Statuti di Averrara e val Taleggio degli anni MCCCXIII e MCCLXVIII'; 'Statuto di Dervio e Corenno dell'anno MCCCLXXXIX'; 'Statuti della Valsassina dell' anno MCCCLXXXVIII' (*Corpus statutorum italicorum*, 3; Rome, 1913).

[28] G. Ortalli, G. Parolin, and M. Pozza (eds.), *Statuti di Cittadella del secolo XIV* (Rome, 1984).

[29] M. Brusasca (ed.), *Statuti di Gabiano* (Milan, 1955).

[30] Santoli et al. (eds.), *Statuti dell'Apennino Tosco-Modenese*.

despite the fact that Padua itself passed under Venetian control in 1405, and despite the fact that Venice enacted several sumptuary laws in this period, it was not until 1440 that the Paduan *Consiglio*, on its own initiative, voted for another law against excess. Only then were the provisions of this law put before the Venetian Senate for approval.[31] In 1463, despite their position as overlords of Pisa, it was not the Florentines who imposed a law upon the city, but rather the Pisans themselves who petitioned for a law to be approved for them by the Florentines.[32]

More persistence was required by the Lucchese when under the rule of the Della Scala. In 1336 they thought that their sumptuary law of 1331 required revision. However, Guglielmo Scannabecchi, the captain-general, refused to approve their revisions. His reason was that such prohibitions in other cities governed by the Scaligeri were not observed by the populace. The *Anziani* of Lucca, determined to get their revisions approved, wrote personally to Alberto and Mastino della Scala requesting them to order Scannabecchi to enact their proposed new law. In this petition, as justification for their law, the Lucchese drew attention to the fact that other cities in Tuscany dealt with abuses of luxury by means of similar legislation: 'Our Lords. To keep our women to honest customs and to restrain the lavish expenses made by the citizens of Lucca in the ornaments and weddings of their women, in banquets, feasts and also in obsequies for the dead, there were for a longer time in the city of Lucca, in similar manner to the customs of other Tuscan cities, ordinances and chapters composed and confirmed.'[33] The Lucchese must finally have received a positive response from the Della Scala as their desired law was put into effect the following year. What is interesting in this case is that all the parties concerned in the dispute seemed well aware of the sumptuary laws of other cities. Scannabecchi felt legislation was not an effective means to combat the problem of luxury because of its failure in other towns, whereas the *Anziani* argued for the use of legislation as a practical means to combat what they felt were problems in the city precisely because other towns also used such legislation.

The reasoning of the *Anziani* was employed by their own citizens in

[31] Bonardi, 'Lusso di altri tempi', 12.

[32] Rainey, 'Legislation in Florence', 466–7.

[33] S. Bongi (ed.), *Bandi lucchesi del secolo decimoquarto: Tratti dai registri del R. Archivio di stato in Lucca* (Bologna, 1863), 309: 'Domini nostri. Ad reprimendum in honestos mores mulierum, et prodigas expensas que fiebant per cives lucanos in ornamentis et nuptiis dominarum suarum, conviviis et commestionibus, ad etiam in exequiis defunctorum, fuerunt in civitate lucana, iuxta ritum aliarum civitatum Tuscie, quedam ordinamenta et capitula diutius composita et firmata'.

1380. In this year some of the principal citizens of Lucca felt that the city's laws were having little effect. Again, rather than questioning the principle of legislating in the first place, they felt that more sumptuary provisions were called for and that in this matter 'we can take example from our neighbours, who have all most wisely provided for this'.[34] These petitions would seem to confirm the opinion of Giovanni Villani who claimed that the Florentine sumptuary ordinances of 1330 'were highly commended, because they were useful and honest; and almost all the cities of Tuscany and many others in Italy sent off to Florence for an example of the said ordinances and ratified them in their own cities'.[35]

It would appear, then, that while cities were fully aware of the sumptuary laws of other towns, it was only when they perceived the level of luxury consumption by their citizens as a problem that they turned to their neighbours for example or requested laws from the dominant power. In fact sumptuary legislation was never imposed on a city by another, and there is only one instance of a town adopting a law verbatim from another when Bergamo in 1343, under the Visconti, adopted the Milanese funeral law.[36] Even when cities were consciously imitating the laws of another, as in the case of Messina with Aragon in 1290,[37] or Pistoia with Florence in 1330,[38] there is always some regional variation in measurements, fashion terminology, exemptions or lack of them, gradations of fines, methods of enforcement, uses to which fines were to be put, and so on. Indeed it is because of their great individual detail that sumptuary laws have proved such rich sources for social historians and historians of costume. All the towns which enacted sumptuary laws were facing similar problems and, not surprisingly, they turned to one another for example in methods to deal with them. Nonetheless, whilst the sumptuary laws of Renaissance Italy rapidly became formulaic, and whilst there is a great similarity in many of them, sumptuary legislation always remained highly tailored to individual needs.

With sumptuary legislation spread over such a wide area, to what extent can it be linked to a particular form of government? Certainly several his-

34 S. Bongi (ed.), *Bandi lucchesi*, 311: 'Et di questo possiamo prendere exemplo dalli nostri vicini, che tutti saviamente ci hanno proveduto.'

35 *Cronica*, 10. 153: 'e molto furono commendati i detti ordini, perocché furono utili e onesti; e quasi tutte le città di Toscana e molte altre d' Italia mandarono a Firenze per esempio di detti ordini, e confermargli nelle loro città'.

36 See A. Pinetti, 'La limitazione del lusso e dei consumi nelle leggi suntuarie bergamesche (sec. XIV–XVI)', *Atti dell'Ateneo di scienze lettere ed arti in Bergamo*, 24 (1915–17), 47: 'quaedam capitula facta in Mediolano pro funeribus et sepulturis'.

37 Del Giudice, 'Legge del 1290', 86.

38 Zanelli, 'Leggi suntuarie pistoiesi', 207.

torians have tried to trace its origins, not to the prima facie problems posed by luxury consumption to governments, but rather to the nature of the governments themselves. It is in this context that the limitations of a restricted geographical and chronological study of sumptuary legislation are most apparent. For, although the proliferation of sumptuary legislation in northern Italy makes this region worthy of study, the nature of the legislation cannot be understood in isolation from the context of the royal laws passed in the south of Italy and elsewhere in Europe. Thus Brundage says that 'kings and parliaments paid little heed to regulating women's dress',[39] and Owen Hughes, too, links the rise of sumptuary legislation with the development of republican governments. Legislation first appears, she says, in the middle of the thirteenth century, 'in communes which had admitted the "popolo" in at least a partial way into the government'.[40] She cites Siena in 1249, Bologna in 1260, and Florence in 1281 as evidence. Nonetheless King Louis VIII passed a law in 1229 (which Owen Hughes herself cites in her next paragraph). Possibly her claim was meant to apply to Italy alone. Even so it still does not account for the southern Italian royal decrees. Indeed the Sicilian and Puglian law of 1290 was approved in a *parlamento* by the prelates and nobles of the realm in which the popular element of the *Sindaci della Università* was absent. Here, then, were nobles agreeing to restrict their own lifestyle.

Even without these examples of royal legislation, a thesis based on the new assertiveness of the *popolo* encounters difficulties which will be dealt with at a later point. For the moment suffice to say that it seems to be a mistake to try to link the origins of medieval sumptuary legislation to a particular form of government for that is to misunderstand its essential purpose. The laws appear in late medieval Europe across the board in monarchical, despotic, and republican states. As Bonardi expresses it: 'One is not to believe that sumptuary legislation derived from one particular form of government, because in Italy for example the democratic republic of Florence and the aristocratic one of Venice, the monarchies of Piedmont and of Naples and so also the duchy of Milan when it was a province of Spain, had, albeit in different measure, their provisions against luxury.'[41]

Although all these forms of government experimented with sumptuary legislation, certain governments, it is true, became more absorbed in it than others. After their early legislative attempts, monarchical regimes enacted laws rather sporadically. Likewise most despotic regimes within Italy

39 'Sumptuary Laws and Prostitution', 346.
40 'Sumptuary Law and Social Relations', 72 ff.
41 'Lusso di altri tempi', 4.

passed fewer laws than their republican counterparts. It was republican governments, particularly those of Florence and Venice, which seemed to have taken to the idea of sumptuary legislation with most enthusiasm. Within three centuries, indeed, Florence enacted an astonishing sixty-one sumptuary prohibitions that we know of, and Venice passed at least forty-three. So far as is known, no other city approached this number. The next in line is Bologna (with 21), followed by Siena (21), Genoa (19), Lucca (18), Perugia (15), Brescia (11), and Verona (9). The average, however, is closer to five.

What then of the general format of these laws, and what subjects fell into the spotlight of sumptuary concern? The earliest sumptuary laws are not very long and do not have a wide range of concerns. They usually have no introduction but simply and briefly state what is to be banned. For instance, the Genoese law of 1157 states (rather curiously in the first and third persons):

> In no manner will I, within the jurisdiction of this city, buy or sell to anyone of this same jurisdiction a single sable worth more than 40 *soldi* . . . and nor shall my wife, children nor any of my family in the future be allowed to wear borders of sable above the aforesaid value, except he who already owns such an item or who should in the future set out on a legation anywhere. Furthermore if for other reasons any people desire to go to the papal court or that of the king or emperor, they may wear fur borders of more than the aforesaid value with a licence from the Consuls.[42]

In a similar curt style, the sumptuary law of Reggio in 1242 says:

> Concerning obsequies for the dead of the kind we have determined to be observed, namely that no more than twelve candles are to be offered or carried for the obsequies of anyone: nor is any oblation to be made with double candlesticks or candles . . . and whoever contravenes the law is to be fined 100 *soldi* and the *podestà* is to conduct inquiries diligently concerning these contraventions.[43]

Despite their brevity, what is noteworthy in early laws such as these is their detail. The Genoese law specifies exemptions, the Reggian law specifies the penalty for contravention with a warning to the enforcement officer, and both laws specify the exact limits of sumptuary expense. Both these laws, though, were limited in their focus; they were each designed to restrict one aspect of luxury consumption only. As the thirteenth century progressed and the private wealth of a large section of the population increased, together with the availability of luxury goods, there was wider scope for elaborate clothing and

[42] Niccolai, 'Antichi brevi', in *Contributo*, 125–6.
[43] Cerlini (ed.), *Consuetudini reggiani*, 36.

ceremonial. Legislators concerned to limit luxury consumption now had to deal with many more areas and with many more aspects of the same area. Accordingly, sumptuary laws of the late thirteenth century are usually much longer than earlier examples and contain several rubrics. For instance, the 1277 funeral law of Reggio has, not just a single paragraph as in 1242, but ten separate rubrics each with its own heading, including:

- Concerning customs for the dead.
- About not having a wake (*cridamentum*).
- About not wailing and weeping for any deceased.
- Concerning the coffin after the deceased has been etc.
- That the wife, mother, and daughter etc.[44]

Often the list of sumptuary rubrics includes several different subjects, not just different aspects of the same subject. The Bolognese sumptuary law of 1289, for instance, contains the following rubrics:

- About the penalty for those bringing gifts to any bride.
- About the penalty for those wailing at obsequies for the dead.
- About the penalty for sending gifts to any cleric or religious.
- About the penalty for wearing dresses, trains, crowns of pearls, etc.
- That no more than twenty men can accompany anyone to a ring ceremony.
- That no one can go to a ring ceremony unless invited.
- About confetti and excessive noise at a ring ceremony.[45]

Likewise, the 1299 Venetian sumptuary law has rubrics concerned with wedding gifts, wedding ceremonial and feasting, clothing for men and women, and ornaments of pearls.

With so many different subjects dealt with in a single law, legislators obviously felt the need to unify the rubrics and make it clear that they all dealt with one concern, namely ostentation and luxury. From the mid-thirteenth century many laws are preceded by a preamble which frequently provides justification for the law. These preambles are a rich source for understanding the motives of the legislators and will be drawn upon extensively in the following pages. For the moment a few examples will suffice. One of the earliest preambles is that prefacing the Sicilian and Puglian law of 1290. This long preamble describes the benefits to be derived from moderation and temperance and stresses the evils arising from the useless superfluity of

[44] C. Campori, 'Del governo a comune in Modena secondo gli statuti ed altri documenti sincroni', in *Statuta civitatis mutine* (*Monumenti di storia patria delle provincie modenesi, Serie degli statuti*, 1; Parma, 1864), p. clxxiv.

[45] Frati, *Vita privata*, 267–74.

expenses. Temperance, it claims, consists of the enjoyment of things according to their true condition, with sufficiency not prodigality. It urges its targets to remember the sacred tradition concerning temperance which places it higher than all other virtues. After similar generalities, this preamble then considers the particular needs of the time. It recalls the horrors of the war between the factions of the Houses of Anjou and Aragon and pleads that, if moderation and frugality are virtues that are always of use, they were never more in need than now in the present conditions of the realm.[46]

The sumptuary law of Imola of 1334 states more simply that the law was enacted 'To revoke the grave and onerous expenses which have uselessly been made by all the men of the city and district of Imola from their wages for clothing and other various ornaments for men and women.'[47] The 1342 law from Perugia begins: 'To avoid the useless expenses which are continually made by the citizens and peasants of Perugia'.[48] The law of Verona from 1333 declares: 'In order to curb the vain ambition of women and to stop the useless and costly ornaments of their clothing, we decree with this most holy law that . . .'.[49] Still others, such as that of Siena of 1343, use the preamble as a more formal introduction and state only what the law will deal with and who was responsible for devising it:

In the name of God Amen. These are the ordinances made and composed by certain, wise men, one indeed from each *terziere* of the city of Siena, elected by the officers of the Nine Governors and Defenders of the Commune, revising and correcting the verbose ordinances concerning gifts given at the investiture of knights and concerning clothes and obsequies for the dead and ornaments for men and women; and also concerning weddings and feasts and other matters concerning these and similar occasions, written by me, Mino Fei, notary for the said elected *Sapientes*, in the year of our Lord 1343.[50]

46 Del Giudice, 'Legge del 1290', 2–3.

47 S. Gaddoni (ed.), *Statuti di Imola del secolo XIV, i. Statuti della città (1334)* (Milan, 1931), 223 ff.: 'Ad revocandas graves et honerosas expensas quas universi homines civitatis Imole et districtus non sine ipsorum reali stipendio circa vestes et alia varia ornamenta tam virorum quam mulierum, inutiliter faciebant'.

48 Fabretti, 'Statuti suntuari', 165: 'A skifare le spese inutele, le quale continuamente se faceano per glie citadine e contadine peruscine'.

49 L. Simeoni (ed.), 'Statuto suntuario a Verona nel XIV secolo', *Studi storici veronesi*, 2 (1949–50), 235: 'Perchè sia frenata la vana ambizione delle donne e cessi l'inutile e costoso ornamento delle loro vesti, decretiamo con questa santissima legge che'.

50 E. Casanova, *La donna senese del quattrocento nella vita privata* (Siena, 1901), (separately published extract from *Bollettino senese di storia patria*, 8) 54.

Once the basic structure of these laws was established in the thirteenth century, the only real change over the following two centuries was one of length and detail. In the fourteenth century not only did the preambles tend to become lengthier and more explanatory, but the number of rubrics could often be very large. The Sienese law of 1343, for instance, has sixty detailed rubrics, the Pisan law of 1350 has forty-seven, and the Florentine law of 1356 has forty-three. This pattern remained more or less the same in the fifteenth century although, if anything, the total number of rubrics in any one law tended to decline. The Bolognese law of 1474 has about fifteen separate chapters, and the 1491 law of Bergamo has twenty-nine. This slight overall decline in the number of rubrics in the fifteenth century could be explained by the increase in the total number of laws in the period. With new laws being enacted so frequently perhaps there was no need for the very lengthy but less frequent laws of the fourteenth century. By the sixteenth century, however, the length of laws once more increased and they became quite unwieldy documents. For example, the Bergamese law of 1540 has a preamble that is two pages long and which is followed by eighty-two chapters.

What then of the subjects covered by the laws? Figure 2.1 shows the range and number of Italian sumptuary concerns over three centuries. It should be emphasized that the graph does not show the number of rubrics passed on a particular subject within the same law for this could be quite misleading. For example, laws restricting certain fashions, by their very nature, require more rubrics to account for every possible permutation of fashion and interpretation of the law than those restricting ceremonies such as weddings and funerals. Hence one sumptuary law might contain thirteen rubrics restricting clothing and only three restricting funeral practices, yet this would not necessarily indicate a greater preoccupation with clothing. For the purposes of the graph, such a law has been quantified as one measure of concern with clothing and one with funerals. Further, several laws contain rubrics which cross the boundaries of more than one subject. One rubric, for example, might deal with gifts at weddings and gifts at christenings. In the graph such a rubric has been interpreted as a concern with wedding practices and christenings, rather than with the giving of gifts per se. The only rubrics that have been placed under the heading of gifts are those of a more general nature where it is stated that no gifts are to be given to any cleric or other Religious, nor to any knight at his investiture, and so on. Similarly, while funeral and wedding rubrics often deal with feasts, the category of feasts on the graph only includes rubrics which deal with feasts held on non-specific occasions. It should also be said that the categories of servants and minors refer to both sexes. Finally, the category

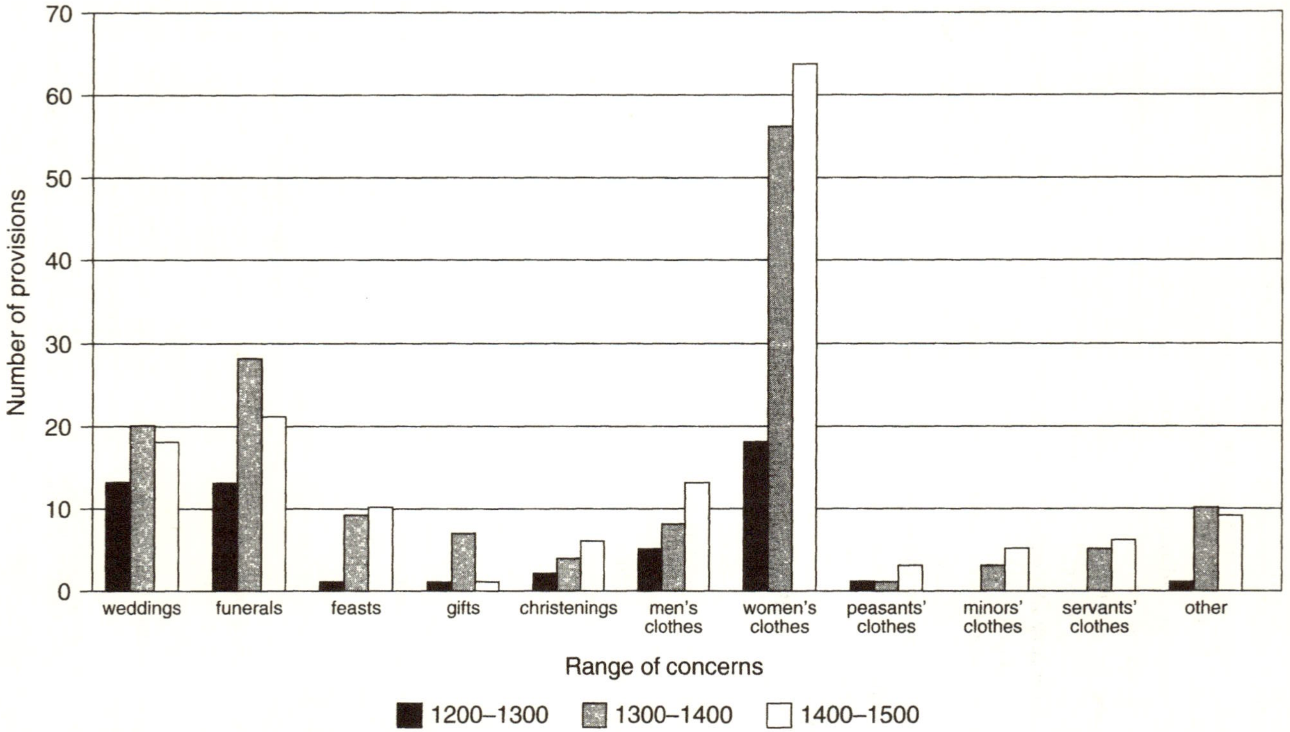

FIG. 2.1. The range and number of Italian sumptuary concerns

of 'other concerns' has been placed on the graph to cover subjects which were not dealt with frequently enough to warrant a place in their own right. Such subjects were riding accoutrements, coats of arms, inheritances, women riding in carriages or unaccompanied on horseback, public order on feast days, the clothing of foreigners visiting the city, and interior furnishings.

What is immediately apparent from the graph is that women's clothing, followed by funerals, and then weddings, were the subjects dealt with most frequently by legislators and that, of the three, it was women's clothing which received the most attention. This preponderance of legislation restricting what women could wear is the justification for Chapter 6, which is devoted solely to women's clothing.

Moreover, what is also notable from the graph is that, although the range of concerns expanded from the thirteenth century into the fourteenth, during the fifteenth century the main change was only one of degree of concern. Over the three centuries covered by this study, legislators concerned themselves with just about every area that fell into the sphere of ostentation and excessive luxury consumption, but with one notable exception. Apart from five examples, interior furnishings were not dealt with by legislators, despite the fact that interior furnishings throughout this period were often very costly. In the 1373 list of *gabelle* in Florence there was one specifying that, before anyone made, sold, or bought any piece of newly made furniture which cost more than 25 florins, both the seller and buyer had to pay a *gabella* of 15 florins.[51] A Bergamese law forbade the use of ultramarine, gold, and silver in any picture or interior ornament.[52] In a funeral law of Brescia, the draping of black cloth on the walls and tables in the deceased's house was forbidden.[53] In the Venetian law of 1476 no one was to have bed coverings or wall hangings of cloth of gold, cloth of silver, brocade, or of the silken materials velvet, satin, or *tabi*,[54] and in the Milanese law of 1498 at the time of a child's birth no one was to put on the bed any covers of plain silk or covers of silk which had been embroidered or worked in gold or silver or silk. In addition there were to be no cushions covered in silk or with gold and silver buttons or pearls or gems;

[51] Rainey, 'Legislation in Florence', 203–4.

[52] Pinetti, 'Limitazione del lusso', 65–6. Ornaments intended for a church were specifically exempted from this article: 'Salvis tamen picturis et ornamentis, quae fiunt in Ecclesia, aut aliis Ecclesiasticis vel piis locis: quae poenae applicentur ut supra et exequentur ut supra.'

[53] Cassa, *Funerali*, 80.

[54] Bistort, *Magistrato alle pompe*, 356–8. They could, however, use *taffeta* (plain woven silk), *zendado* (a very light silk textile), *catasamito*, and *ormesin* (a stronger, patterned fabric) for wall hangings.

no bed curtains or hangings made of silk or embroidered in any way; and no cradles worked in gold, silver, blue, or ultramarine.[55] A possible explanation for this lack of regulation of interiors is that the wearing of costly clothing, the hosting of elaborate weddings, funerals, christenings, feasts, or the giving of gifts were all opportunities for the public display of one's wealth. Furnishings, however ornate and costly, could only ever be guaranteed a limited audience of immediate friends and relatives. Of course there would on occasion be larger gatherings in the home but it is significant that the Brescian law cited above dealt only with furnishings at the time of a death, and the Milanese law with furnishings at the time of a birth, both occasions when just such a larger gathering of people might be expected into one's house. That legislators should concentrate on external adornment and the public display of wealth is further confirmation that they were not concerned necessarily with the restraint of luxury itself, but with the uses to which such luxury might be put.

Luxury consumption and the luxury trades were to transform Italy. Though the new wealth was obviously to be welcomed, governments were confronted by a host of concomitant social, economic, and political problems. What needs to be explored in detail is the ways in which governments connected these problems with the new luxury and sought to combat them through legislative activity. This will form the subject of subsequent chapters.

[55] E. Verga, 'Le leggi suntuarie milanesi: Gli statuti del 1396 e del 1498', *Archivio storico lombardo*, 25 (1898), 56.

3

Money and People

money . . . lies dead, converted into vanities

Venice, sumptuary law

Sumptuary laws presuppose the existence of two things: consumables and consumers. To explain the absence of sumptuary laws before the thirteenth century, one need only look to the absence of any large group of consumers in this period. That a sumptuary policy assumes an economy healthy enough to allow for the consumption of luxury goods has led many to overlook considerations of economic and demographic health as motivating factors in governments' actions, or at least to relegate them to a minor position. Thus we hear that sumptuary legislation cannot be 'linked in a simple or satisfying way to contemporary economic opinion or conditions. Born in a climate of expansion, it was several centuries old before Italian decline had set in'.[1] It may come as a surprise, then, that of explanatory motives cited in preambles, it is the dissipation of capital and the decline of marriages and births which appear most frequently. The importance for late medieval and Renaissance Italian governments of preserving and encouraging these two resources of money and people by means of sumptuary law forms the basis of this chapter.

I

The preamble to the Sienese sumptuary statute of 1412 is typical of many which stress economic considerations. This argued that 'It is necessary to make provisions to restrain superfluous expenditure from our citizens' purses, both rich and poor, for their own preservation and for the utility and honour of the commune.'[2] More explicitly, a statute from Bergamo claimed that it was necessary to legislate, 'owing to the bad nature of the times, [the city] being reduced to great poverty, and the luxury of the dress of women,

[1] Owen Hughes, 'Sumptuary Law and Social Relations', 72.

[2] C. Mazzi, 'Alcune leggi suntuarie senesi del secolo XIII', *Archivio storico italiano*, 4th ser., 5 (1880), 143.

of the food, of the ornaments of rooms and funeral obsequies being more than abundant, all of which is of manifest ruin to the citizens and also provokes the Divine Majesty to anger against us'.[3] Many Italian cities, it is true, were experiencing unprecedented economic expansion from the thirteenth century onwards, but these and similar preambles would seem to indicate that governments were not complacent about the stability of the economy. As Miller has pointed out, we should not assume that there were no such things as government economic policies in the late Middle Ages. 'It must be remembered', he says, 'that every medieval government had to grapple with one basic economic problem; that of its own maintenance. Fiscal policies, however elementary and hand-to-mouth, play a continuous part in the history of government.'[4]

One of the major economic concerns expressed by the laws was that capital should not be withdrawn from productive activity and that citizens should not be allowed to ruin themselves. Expenditure itself was not discouraged for it was recognized that the circulation of money was vital to the maintenance and improvement of trade and industry, but what was considered useless expenditure was universally condemned. This distinction was spelt out by the Venetians in 1466:

> Just as everyone has learnt through experience and each day there is greater and greater increase in the excessive and inordinate expenses made for women's dowries, clothes, ornaments as in many other things which, as much for the honour of God as for the honour of our ruler and for the public advantage of our citizens and our subjects, and that their material resources not be uselessly dissipated but rather be completely transformed into more useful and praiseworthy things for the citizens and subjects of our worthy state, it is to be provided that . . .[5]

This theme was a common one in sumptuary laws. In Perugia in 1342 a law was passed 'to avoid useless expenditures, which are continually made by women in the city of Perugia and its *contado*'.[6] In Imola in 1334 legislators

[3] Pinetti, 'Limitazione del lusso', 26. This led to a law in 1540 with 82 articles, see ibid. 66.

[4] See his introd. to C. M. Cipolla, 'The Italian and Iberian Peninsulas', in M. M. Postan, E. E. Rich, and E. Miller (eds.), *The Cambridge Economic History of Europe*, iii (Cambridge, 1963), 282.

[5] ASV, Compilazioni leggi, Busta 305, Pompe-Magistrato, Filza T, c. 235: 'Sicut per experientiam omnes intelligunt et quotidie magis ac magis crescunt excessive et inordinate expense tam in dotibus mulierum quam circa earum vestitum et ornamentum et in plurimus aliis rebus quibus tam pro honore Dei quam pro honore nostri dominii ad publico commodo civium et subditorum nostrorum et eorum facultates tam inutiliter non dissipentur sed in rebus utilioribus et laudabilioribus pro civibus et subditis nostris ac totius nostri Reipublice convertantur omnino providendum est'.

[6] Fabretti, 'Statuti suntuari', 165.

desired 'to revoke serious and onerous expenses which universally the men of the city of Imola and district uselessly make from their incomes for clothes and other various ornaments both for men and women'.[7] In Siena in 1348 a law referred to the 'useless and harmful expenses' incurred for costly mourning clothes,[8] as did funeral laws from Brescia in 1277 and 1473[9] and a funeral law of Verona from 1450 which declared it intended 'to avoid useless expenses made on the occasion of funerals'.[10]

An apparent flaw in these governments' economic thought here is their failure to consider that expenditure by the wealthy, though possibly foolish, provided income for artisans. That is, supposed impoverishment of one class, in this case the consumers, permitted the survival and enrichment of some members of another class, the artisans, thereby stimulating rather than stultifying the economy. Here, however, Cipolla explains the failure of governments to be moved by this kind of consideration by emphasizing their need to safeguard great private fortunes at a time when capital formation was dangerously scarce. As he says: 'if you consider the fundamental scarcity of capital in medieval society, the insufficiency of saving, the high rates of interest, it is hard to find substantial fault with the argument of the medieval authorities'.[11] Indeed, during this period, because of the scarcity of capital and the imperfections of the credit system, interest rates tended to stay at high levels. In general they fluctuated between 10 per cent and 50 per cent, and sometimes even higher. At the same time, the constancy of demand for necessary goods, such as grain, coupled with the insecurity of the supply of these goods, meant that their prices went through drastic fluctuations which often led to poverty, hunger, and even death for large sections of the population.[12]

In addition to this general picture, each city had its own particular circumstances which added further economic burdens. In Bologna, for instance, expenditure was in excess of income throughout the Bentivoglio supremacy (a situation common to many larger city states from the thirteenth century onwards), and government was only carried on by means of loans from members of the *Sedici* and other leading citizens.[13] The city's

7 Gaddoni (ed.), *Statuti di Imola*, 223.

8 Mazzi, 'Leggi senesi', 142 n. 1.

9 Cassa, *Funerali*, 36, addition of 1277 to an earlier law: 'per evitare le inutili spese che in addietro solevansi fare nei funebri accompagnamenti'. See also F. Odorici, *Storie bresciane*, 11 vols. (Brescia, 1853–65), vii. 127 (item 22, carte 46), and Cassa, *Funerali*, 38 (the law of 1473): 'Ad evitandas damnosas expensas et inutiles consuetudines'.

10 A. Magnano, 'Documenti per una storia delle leggi suntuarie veronesi', *Atti e memorie della accademia di agricoltura scienze e lettere di Verona*, 6th ser., 22 (1970–1), 266.

11 'Italian and Iberian Peninsulas', 421.

12 Ibid. 404.

13 C. M. Ady, *The Bentivoglio of Bologna: A Study in Despotism* (Oxford, 1969), 90.

position as a papal vicariate meant that salaries had to be paid to the papal legate and the papal treasurers, as well as to the officers of the commune. It meant also that there was a double set of authorities for the granting of gifts of salt, and other privileges, and for receiving exemptions from certain taxes. To this were added further burdens from the increasing activity and reputation of the government under the Bentivoglio; increasing numbers of envoys had to be housed at public cost; there was greater expenditure on display; and property and privileges passed from the commune to the Bentivoglio.[14]

In Florence, too, the city's costly expansionist policy, together with chronic warfare, bouts of plague, and famine, and banking failures such as that of the 1340s, meant that the city's governments were reduced to deficit-financing, and required increasing sums of money. In 1303 the commune's public debt stood at about 50,000 florins. By 1343 it had risen to about 600,000 florins, by 1364 to about 1,500,000 florins, and by 1400 it stood at about 3,000,000 florins.[15] And, while the production of luxury goods could bring a considerable income into a city (such as Parma, which in the mid-fifteenth century earned 60,000 ducats each year from its cloth trade with Venice alone), nonetheless the daily requirements of the citizens, and their expenditure on the luxury products of other cities, could lead easily to an overall deficit. In this same period the Parmese sent 2,000 ducats each week back to Venice to buy daily necessities or luxury items, amounting to an annual sum of 104,000 ducats, producing an overall deficit of 44,000 ducats.[16] Nor were such financial crises confined to the city states of northern Italy. In the mid-fifteenth century the Kingdom of Naples under King Alfonso, like other contemporary governments, was constantly faced with a chronic shortage of ready cash. It has been estimated that when in a state of war the ordinary revenues of the kingdom would fall short of needs by between 200,000 and 300,000 ducats a year, a sum which had to be raised both in Italy and in Spain by every means available. In 1446 King Alfonso admitted to the governor of Mallorca that he stood 'in great and extreme necessity'[17] and in November 1448 he returned to Naples to find all his treasure in pawn to merchants as security for their loans.[18]

[14] Ady, *The Bentivoglio of Bologna*, 177.

[15] B. Barbadoro, *Le finanze delle repubblica fiorentina* (Florence, 1929), 507 and 616; C. M. Cipolla, *The Monetary Policy of Fourteenth-Century Florence* (Berkeley and Los Angeles, 1982), 3 ff.

[16] A. Pezzana, *Storia della città di Parma*, 5 vols. ii (Parma, 1842), 211.

[17] A. Ryder, *The Kingdom of Naples under Alfonso the Magnanimous: The Making of a Modern State* (Oxford, 1976), 174 citing ACA Reg. 2699. 40^r, 30 Apr. 1446.

[18] Ibid., citing ACA Reg. 2940. 59^r, 27 Nov. 1448.

The necessity of channelling money into productive commercial activity was most acute for cities which had few natural resources and which depended on trading for their main livelihood. Venice, with its lack of terra firma (at least before the early fifteenth century); Genoa, with its low production of crops and manufactured goods; and Messina all recognized that their wealth and long-term financial stability depended upon the trading advantages to be had from their superior maritime positions. Thus, in a sumptuary statute of Venice from 1360 we read that 'Our state has become less strong because money that should navigate and multiply . . . lies dead, converted into vanities'.[19] And in the Messinese supplication to the king to approve their 1383 sumptuary law we hear that 'these *capitula*, by mature deliberation of our Council, have been discovered to be most evidently pertinent to the profit of the State and our citizens, especially since those citizens have been accustomed mostly to augment their livelihoods by trading at sea from which, little by little, they are being turned away'.[20] Similarly a Genoese law of 1449 begins: 'a great quantity of money which is kept dead and wrapped up in clothing and jewels, if converted into trade might bring great return and profits'.[21] For these cities the major resource was money. Money was conceived, indeed, not just as the simple source of riches and well-being, but as the main instrument with which to guarantee their continued survival. It made sense, then, to devise laws that would ensure that money remained in economic circulation rather than being used to satisfy desires that did not produce wealth.

This preoccupation with the conservation of capital and diversion of resources into trade also helps to explain the constant and strict regulation in most sumptuary laws of precious metals (gold and silver), and jewels (particularly pearls), regardless of the shifting prices or availability of such commodities.[22] The availability of gold and silver fluctuated through the period as new mines were alternatively discovered or depleted, but they were, overall, in short supply relative to demand. The shortage of silver especially reached famine proportions in the late fourteenth century and on into the fifteenth. And, while there had been shortages in previous

[19] M. M. Newett, 'The Sumptuary Laws of Venice in the Fourteenth and Fifteenth Centuries', in T. F. Tout and J. Tait (eds.), *Historical Essays by Members of the Owens College, Manchester* (London, 1907), 269.

[20] R. Gregorio, 'Leges somptuariae', in *Bibliotheca scriptorum qui res in Sicilia gestas sub Aragonum imperio retulere*, 2 vols., ii (Palermo, 1792), 530–1.

[21] F. Martignone, 'L'importanza del danaro nella mentalità dei Genovesi alla fine del Medio Evo', *Studi genuensi*, 9 (1972), 76.

[22] Owen Hughes sees this instead as evidence for a lack of developed economic interest in bullion. See her 'Sumptuary Law and Social Relations', 78.

centuries, especially in the seventh century, the silver famine of this later period was felt more acutely as it occurred in a more complex economy in which people were more reliant on the use of money than their ancestors had been. Gold, too, while more widely available, especially from the mines in Hungary, was also subject to shortages. There seems to have been a lack of gold from the late 1390s until the second decade of the fifteenth century, and then a further shortage developed into the 1440s. The bullion famine reached its worst point in the mid-1460s, and by then the economy of Europe had been under severe strain for three decades for the lack of means of payment, and silver had not been plentiful for over a century. The development of a system of credit was usually not sufficient to balance the resulting deflationary pressure. Both in the long and the short term, early modern Italy, and Europe as a whole, stayed under the threat of dangerous shortages of money.[23]

If sumptuary laws were used to conserve revenue, they were also used to raise it. Every sumptuary law imposed some kind of penalty upon offenders, and most commonly this was a fine of money. Although many cases of prosecutions successfully pressed have come to light,[24] not enough have been discovered (if indeed are still extant) to enable a reliable assessment of the amount of money a city was likely to raise from the collection of fines. Though it is unlikely that a great sum was earned in this way, it is worth emphasizing that money was collected, and that the documents indicate that most people prosecuted for violating the sumptuary laws confessed to the charges and agreed to pay the fine imposed.[25]

An alternative to fines, and one with a more overt motive of revenue raising, was the imposition by at least four cities of a straightforward luxury tax. In the sumptuary law of Viterbo of 1444 those wanting to wear prohibited items could do so by paying an annual tax renewable yearly.[26] However, in the sumptuary law issued in 1449 this option was no longer available.[27] Both Bologna and Florence tried to institute a luxury tax in 1299, but in both instances the experiment was short-lived. In the case of Bologna, the *Consiglio del popolo* allowed women to wear crowns or garlands of pearls, or to have gold and silver woven through their plaits provided they paid a

[23] P. Spufford, 'Coinage and Currency', in Postan and Miller (eds.), *Cambridge Economic History*, ii (2nd edn., Cambridge, 1987), 851–60. See also Cipolla, 'Italian and Iberian Peninsulas', 407.

[24] See Ch. 7, below.

[25] See ibid.

[26] G. Lombardi, *Galiane in rivolta: Una polemica umanistica degli ornamenti femminili nella Viterbo del Quattrocento*, 2 vols. (Rome, 1998), vol. i, p. lvii.

[27] Ibid., pp. cclxxv–cclxxviii.

yearly sum of 100 *soldi di bolognini* to the commune. On 8 July 1301, however, a new law decreed that it was now absolutely forbidden for any woman, no matter what her status, to wear crowns ornamented with pearls or circlets of beaten gold or silver.[28] The early Florentine effort was similarly brief, but from the 1360s onwards, faced with a succession of financial crises, the Florentines imposed a series of indirect taxes, or *gabelle*, upon luxurious items of clothing. The first list of *gabelle* was in December 1364, in the wake of the plague of 1363 and the war against Pisa (1363–4). This allowed for the payment of an annual tax of 100 gold florins by women (or by the men responsible for them) who wished to wear certain ornaments worth more than a specified value.[29] More explicit in motive was the provision of December 1373 which gave the officials of the mint the task of devising new ways of bringing money into the commune's coffers, and which resulted in a collection of *gabelle* for women who wished to wear items that were otherwise forbidden. According to Ammirato, this extra money was needed to send several citizens to Pistoia to reform the government there, and *gabelle* as an addition to a sumptuary law were decided upon because officials were reluctant to impose new taxes.[30] In August 1376 the officials of the mint supplemented the list of *gabelle* as yet more money was required to finance the commune's war with the papacy, the so-called War of the Eight Saints. The preamble to this list gave a threefold purpose for the new measures: to increase the income of the commune; to decrease the expenses of citizens; and to eliminate the unnecessary ceremonies and the 'excesses' indulged in by women.[31] If women decided to pay the tax in order to continue to wear extravagant items, then at least the commune could take advantage of this weakness, and if the high cost of the tax acted as a deterrent, then the commune could be reassured that money was not being dissipated on luxuries in this time of crisis. Either way, they believed, the system of *gabelle* would work to their monetary advantage. Exemptions from Florentine funeral sumptuary provisions could also be bought. Between 1384 and 1392, indeed, the commune sold at least 233 sumptuary exemptions for funerals.[32]

A *gabella* on the use of pearls in clothes and ornaments was also introduced in Genoa in 1402. A codex listing all *gabelle* collected from 1408 to 1445 in the Archivio di San Giorgio reveals that the annual proceeds from

[28] Frati, *Vita privata*, 30.
[29] Rainey, 'Legislation in Florence', 195.
[30] Ibid. 200 citing Ammirato, 2/1, p. 698, anno 1373.
[31] Ibid. 206–7.
[32] For an analysis of these exemptions see Strocchia, *Death and Ritual*, 67–73.

this tax on pearls were never less than 500 lire and in 1414 a total of 1,310 lire was collected.[33] Such taxes on luxury items would seem a particularly good way to raise revenue; not only because demand for luxury goods is relatively inelastic in that these goods do not respond so directly to price changes as most goods, but also because the rich consume proportionately more than the poor and therefore money would be provided by those most able to pay. However, the fact that only two cities employed the system of *gabelle*, and then only for a very limited period, favouring instead the system of a straightforward ban on luxury items, suggests that the raising of revenue was not the prime economic reason for a sumptuary policy.

More common seems to have been the desire to protect industry and promote a balance of trade through sumptuary and related measures. From the end of the thirteenth century in Italy, many areas which had been comparatively underdeveloped entered a period of rapid expansion. In most cases there was a conscious effort to industrialize and encourage new industries, which meant that many governments passed measures to protect fledgling industries. This led to much fiercer competition and the closing of markets for the older manufacturing centres which in turn encouraged further protective measures. At the beginning of the fourteenth century, for example, the wool industry in Pisa experienced a crisis due to the development of a wool industry in Florence. This Florentine industry itself underwent a crisis from the mid-fourteenth to the mid-fifteenth century. In Lucca, too, the thriving silk industry suffered in the fourteenth century because of the new silk industries at Bologna, Genoa, Venice, and later at Milan.

A frequent protectionist measure used by the Italians was the application of duties, but very often this was not considered sufficient. Many city authorities took the further precaution of imposing absolute prohibitions on the importation or selling of foreign manufactures on the home market. While such measures were very rare in the twelfth and thirteenth centuries when the interests of the mercantile class were dominant, they became increasingly frequent in the fourteenth and fifteenth centuries when the interests of the manufacturing classes predominated and, more especially, when competition was increasing, leading to further protective measures and still more competition. In 1305 the Pisans prohibited the importation of semi-finished woollen goods, a regulation which they reinforced in 1310. In 1336 this ban was extended to finished products as well, that is to foreign woollen cloth. In Florence, in 1317, 1319, and again in 1397, the importation of 'foreign cloths made and manufactured outside the city and district of

33 Belgrano, 'Vita privata dei genovesi', 217–18.

Florence' was prohibited. In 1458 the Florentines not only banned the import of cloth from elsewhere in Italy and from the south of France, but they provided for stricter control of the transit trade. In 1415 cloth from Turin and Perlasca was forbidden from entering the city of Milan. In 1420 shops in the city, district, or duchy of Milan were forbidden to sell or stock any woollen cloth which had not been made in territories subject to the duke. Only certain types of cloth which did not compete with local industries were allowed. Similar prohibitions were passed in 1454, 1460, 1471, 1474, 1476, and on into the sixteenth century. In July 1452, the Milanese imposed an embargo on foreign silk cloths and cloth of gold and silver, an embargo repeated several times in the course of the century. In Genoa, during the fifteenth century, it was forbidden to import for resale any silk manufactured abroad with the exception of taffeta and satin and any silk products produced by the Genoese colonies. Similarly in Venice, in the second half of the fifteenth century, regulations were passed ordering all public officials to wear only clothes of Venetian manufacture.[34]

These measures were designed to protect home industries, boost trade surpluses, and cut deficits. Other cities sought to accentuate these benefits by discouraging not just imported luxuries but also the consumption of home-produced luxury goods so that domestic producers might sell more abroad, thereby earning foreign exchange. This tactic was most attractive to economies that depended more upon trade than upon manufacture such as Genoa and Venice. For instance, both these cities restricted the use of sugar in confections, sauces, roasts, *confetti*, and similar items from the middle of the fifteenth century.[35] The timing of these restrictions coincided with the dominance of sugar in the battle for commercial predominance between these two cities. Here it is clear that the legislators wanted to ensure that most of the supplies of sugar reaching their ports should go to sea again to be sold elsewhere for maximum profit.[36]

This proto-mercantilist policy was reinforced by some cities, from the early thirteenth century, by measures designed to attract both foreign skilled artisans and foreign merchants, while seeking to prevent the movement of the factors of production and skilled workers out of the territory. Parma as early as 1211 sought to bolster its newly fledged cotton industry

[34] All from Cipolla, 'Italian and Iberian Peninsulas', 415–16. These protectionist laws are not included in Table 2.1.

[35] Genoa: 1484 (Belgrano, 'Vita privata dei genovesi' (1866), 171–2); 1494 (Pandiani, 'Vita privata genovese', 199–201); Venice: 1459 (Newett, 'Laws of Venice', 273 and ASV, Senato, Terra, Reg. IV, fo. 133); 1465 (ASV, Senato, Terra, Reg. V, fo. 149); 1472 (ASV, Senato, Terra, Reg. VI, fo. 193).

[36] See Martignone, 'Importanza del danaro', 74.

by attracting foreign artisans with favourable working privileges. The same methods were used in Bologna, over a period of some forty years (1230–70), to encourage artisans from Verona, Milan, Mantua, Lucca, Florence, and Prato. Padua, too, adopted this method in 1265 for its wool and cotton industries.[37] The same incentives were still being offered in the fifteenth century. The commune of Vicenza, for instance, in 1431 reduced the residence requirement of wool workers to five years, and allowed up to fifteen grants of citizenship for them per year.[38] In Pistoia, also, skilled artisans from Verona and from Lombard towns who might help in the development of the wool industry, were welcomed with attractive privileges.[39] And foreign merchants coming to Pistoia to buy cloth were exempt from all tariffs and from any threat of reprisals against them for debts owed by their countrymen.[40] At the same time the export of raw materials was discouraged,[41] whilst all rural inhabitants were required to take a solemn oath not to leave the territory of Pistoia with the intention of residing elsewhere unless they had first secured the permission of the *podestà*.[42]

The general economic policy pursued by Italian governments throughout this period was one in which reserves of capital were to be protected and channelled into productive activity and which allowed for the free flow of the factors of production (including artisans) into the district with no flow in the opposite direction. Exports were thus limited to manufactured articles which could command high prices in foreign markets.[43]

II

Even more precious as a resource than capital was a rising population. From the laws examined in this study it appears that the most pressing concern by

[37] Jones, 'Storia economica', 1724–5.

[38] See J. S. Grubb, *Firstborn of Venice: Vicenza in the Early Renaissance State* (Baltimore, 1988), 77.

[39] D. Herlihy, *Medieval and Renaissance Pistoia: The Social History of an Italian Town, 1200–1430* (New Haven, 1967), 157, citing L. Zdekauer (ed.), *Statutum potestatis comunis Pistorii anni MCCLXXXXVI* (Milan, 1888), 239.

[40] Ibid., citing Zdekauer (ed.), *Statutum comunis Pistorii*, 219.

[41] See e.g. Zdekauer (ed.), *Statutum comunis Pistorii*, 125, 36, 185.

[42] Ibid. 210.

[43] The flaw in this policy was that the majority of the Italian cities were pursuing the same goals and employing the same means to achieve them. If most cities banned the import and use of foreign manufactures then most were deprived of both home and foreign consumers of their lucrative luxury goods. But industries did in fact have markets, and this is because the situation was in reality more complex than this paradox suggests. Not all towns had sumptuary laws, particularly in the rest of Europe, and not all at the same time, and they were not always and everywhere enforced effectively or with a will.

far of legislators by the mid-fifteenth century was the effect, as they saw it, of indulgence in luxury goods on the marriage rate and hence on population levels. One of the earliest and clearest expressions of this concern is in a plea for a sumptuary law by the principal citizens of Lucca to the General Council in 1380:

it must please you to make provision on the immoderate and immodest ornaments of women because of which, and the excessive expenditure involved, great inconvenience and harm have occurred and still occur in our city and community: because there are a great number of young women to be married and similarly a great number of young men ready to take a wife who are unable to marry. And this because those who are ready to take a wife cannot withstand the large and excessive expenses incurred, and those women who are to be married cannot provide a dowry of great enough sufficiency to cover said expenses and their trousseaus. The inordinate multitude of furs, ornaments, pearls, garlands, belts, and other expenses that are required by custom for this are manifest to everyone. And for these reasons young women do not marry, and young men do not take wives, and so our city decreases: so that the old pass away and few young children are born.[44]

The Lucchese were not alone in expressing these fears. In 1463 the citizens of the subject city of Pisa begged the Florentine *Signoria* to pass a sumptuary law because, they claimed, their city was very poor and, apart from their other difficulties, 'there are about 900 nubile girls, more than 300 of whom are twenty four years of age and older, and many youths and men who might take these girls as wives instead remain without wives, as much as they wish to marry, on account of the great expenses that they would be required to make for the apparel and ornaments of married women, and especially because the dowries of these girls are so small, none of them having a dowry of more than 200 florins'.[45] The Pisans felt that if a restraint were imposed on the expenses for women's ornaments, many marriages which had not been possible might take place, resulting in the honour of God, the honour of these girls, and relief for the whole commune.[46] In Venice in 1430 the authorities prohibited the platform shoes favoured by the city's women not just because they required longer and hence more extravagant garments to cover them, but because it was feared that pregnant women

[44] Bongi (ed.), *Bandi lucchesi*, 311.

[45] Rainey, 'Legislation in Florence', 466–7.

[46] The Florentines responded with a sumptuary law on 7 Feb. 1462/3, cited in Rainey, 'Legislation in Florence', 505–6 nn. 89–90: 'et quod ipsi putant quod si quod frenem apponeretur huiusmodi expensis ita ut moderatis fierent, multa connubia fierent per die in illa civitate que non fiunt, ex quare honor Dei et ipsarum puellarum ad totius illius civitatis placitum in solamine sequeritur'.

would topple in them and induce miscarriages.[47] In Padua in 1504, in a particularly vitriolic preamble, we hear that

The nature and condition of the female sex, full of vanity through sloth, cause of many ills, and the lack of prudence of those who badly weigh their affairs and the harmful expenses made for new fashions and superfluous ornaments, lead this poor city of Padua to great misery, scandalize the minds of the good, who desire to live well, and, what is worse, disturb many marriages, which would have been made, if it were not for these lascivious and excessive luxuries, which are displeasing to God and to the world and are of bad example. And this occurs because no one wants to appear inferior to his companion, and many are constrained to spend more than their condition can support; and in this way the city is filled with poverty.[48]

In Milan in 1396 and 1498;[49] in Genoa in 1449 and in 1488;[50] in Venice in 1425, 1430, and 1460;[51] in Brescia in 1477;[52] in Ferrara in 1447 and 1453;[53] in Siena in 1424;[54] in Florence in 1433 and 1511,[55] and indeed throughout the fifteenth century and into the sixteenth, and all across the peninsula, city states passed sumptuary laws whose preambles and contents attest to similar concerns.

Although what is important here is that city rulers perceived there to be a decrease both in the number of marriages contracted and in the number of births, the evidence suggests that there was real cause for such fears. Over the fourteenth and fifteenth centuries there was a large-scale demographic decline in Italy. Between 1350 and 1450 no northern Italian city had increases in population that approached the records set in the period from about 1140 to 1280. What is uncertain, however, is whether this fall was due to a decrease in the birth rate coupled with a rise in the death rate, or solely

47 ASV, Compilazioni leggi, Busta 305, Filza T, 2 Mar. 1430.

48 Bonardi, 'Lusso di altri tempi', 13: 'La natura et condition del sexo femineo, pien de vanità per l'ocio, cason de molti mali, et la poca prudentia de chi mal misura i fati soi e le dannose spese in nove foge et superflui ornati, conduse questa povera cità de Padova a gran miseria, scandeleza la mente dei boni, che desidera ben viver, et che pezo e disturba molti matrimoni, che se faria, sel non fusse queste lascivie et excessive pompe, le qual dispiace a Dio e al mondo e sono de cativo esempio. E questo intervien che niun vuol apparer inferiore del compagno, e molti sono costretti a far più de quelo porta la sua condictione; e a tal partito la cità se impie de povertà.' These sentiments were repeated in the Paduan law of 1506 which was passed to restrain 'disonesti appetiti, dannose pompe e . . . le spese delle donne, che disturbano i matrimoni'.

49 E. Verga, 'Leggi suntuarie milanesi', 9.

50 Pandiani, 'Vita privata genovese', 193–4.

51 Newett, 'Laws of Venice', 272 and 276.

52 Cassa, *Funerali*, 78–9.

53 A. Frizzi, *Memorie per la storia di Ferrara*, 5 vols. (Ferrara, 1847–50), iii. 502; ix. 24–5.

54 Casanova, *Donna senese*, 81–2.

55 Rainey, 'Legislation in Florence', 505–6.

due to a rise in the death rate. Genicot argues that the fall in population was probably triggered off by a fall in the birth rate but that this alone would not have been too critical if it had not been accompanied by factors which led to an exceptional number of deaths.[56] Famine, pestilence, and war were constant features of the fourteenth and fifteenth centuries and they dealt a decisive blow to population levels that were already precarious. It has been estimated that the Black Death of 1348 and succeeding epidemics carried off from 35 per cent to 65 per cent of the rural and urban populations. By 1500 all the major cities were still struggling to regain their early fourteenth-century population levels (many not achieving this until the eighteenth or even nineteenth centuries).[57]

In Prato, for example, at the end of the thirteenth century and until about 1310, there were nearly 4,000 households, but by 1325 there were only about 3,400, and by 1339 2,760. The Black Death affected Prato badly and then the so-called 'children's plague' affected the rate of renewal of the next generation. The new attacks of plague between 1373 and 1394 reduced the population still further and, after the plague of 1400–1, Prato counted no more than 1,178 households. After 1410 the population finally stabilized at a mere 950 households, a figure which did not change until about 1470–80. Within the space of a century the population in terms of households had dropped by 72 per cent.[58] Similarly, in Florence, the recurrence of plague decreased the population from more than 90,000 in the early fourteenth century to less than 40,000 by the mid-fifteenth century.[59] In Pisa, it has been estimated, the late fourteenth-century population of about 15,000 was reduced to 10,000 by 1427–9.[60] In Venice in about 1300, estimates based on military enrolments put the population at 160,000.[61] But, within eighteen months of the plague first arriving in Venice in 1347, approximately three-fifths of the inhabitants of Venice were dead.[62]

The reduction in the population was accompanied by a change in the marriage pattern, although the nature of this pattern seems to have varied

56 'Crisis: From the Middle Ages to Modern Times', in Postan and Habakkuk (eds.), *Cambridge Economic History*, i. (2nd edn., Cambridge, 1966), 667–77. For further discussion of this issue and its effect upon the medieval economy and bibliographical references see Jones, 'Storia economica', 1486–93.

57 L. Martines, *Power and Imagination: City-States in Renaissance Italy* (Harmondsworth, 1979), see 229–30 for chart with approximate comparisons of the populations of fifteen towns.

58 C. Klapisch-Zuber, *Women, Family and Ritual in Renaissance Italy* (Chicago, 1985), 26.

59 See amongst others G. A. Brucker, *Renaissance Florence* (1969; Los Angeles, 1983), 55 ff.

60 B. Casini, *Aspetti della vita economica e sociale di Pisa dal catasto del 1428–1429* (Pisa, 1965), 9–11.

61 See F. C. Lane, *Venice: A Maritime Republic* (Baltimore, 1973), 18.

62 Ibid. 19.

considerably from one area to another. In Florence, for instance, by the first half of the fifteenth century men were marrying later in life than they had during the second half of the fourteenth century. The age for first marriage shifted from an average of 23.9 to 30.9.[63] At the same time women were marrying younger. The average age in Florence between 1351 and 1400 was 18 while between 1401 and 1450 it had dropped to 16.6.[64] Late first marriage for men and early first marriage for women increased the age differences between husbands and wives, resulting in marriages of shorter duration which led to a fall in the average number of offspring per family. This marriage pattern also meant, as David Herlihy has pointed out, that fathers felt constrained to 'engage in competitive bidding to attract reluctant grooms'.[65] The main financial burden of marriage shifted to the bride's family, the reverse dowry declined, and the true dowry became the main transfer of property involved in matrimony. This pattern may have been quite widespread as Aeneas Silvius Piccolomini also noticed an increased difference in ages of spouses in Vienna in 1440.[66] Other chroniclers, however, have noted that the immediate effect of the plague on its survivors was one of encouraging earlier marriages for both sexes and that women became astonishingly fecund, often giving birth to triplets.[67] If this was indeed the case, one would have expected the population rates to recover, but since the plague of 1348 and its successive outbreaks affected the least resistant members of the population most acutely, that is children and the elderly, a generation after the plague there was another falling-off of births. So, even if the outbreaks of plague encouraged earlier marriages in Italy, contrary to the Tuscan evidence, the vulnerability of children meant that such marriages did little to ease population problems. Further, even if the population levels were more critically affected by the death rate than by the birth rate, and even if governments were aware that this was so, factors such as famine, plague, and war were not ones that a government could easily control. Encouraging marriages and births, however, was something constructive and tangible and was, moreover, always going to be of benefit to a society facing a demographic crisis.

The connection of all this with indulgence in luxury goods may not be immediately clear. However, the dowry consisted of cash minus the value of

63 D. Herlihy, 'The Medieval Marriage Market', *Medieval and Renaissance Studies*, 6 (1976), 19.

64 Id. and C. Klapisch-Zuber, *Les Toscans et leurs familles* (Paris, 1978), p. 205, table 23.

65 Id., 'Medieval Marriage Market', 19.

66 Cited in Genicot, 'Crisis', 672.

67 Ibid. 675.

the trousseau and any other wedding gifts that a woman's family chose to bestow upon her.[68] So, while late first marriage encouraged larger dowries, increased sumptuousness in dress meant that the cost of trousseaus soared, decreasing the cash component of the dowry considerably.[69] Moreover, a tax had to be paid on all contracts which was calculated as a percentage of the value of the dowry, including the trousseau.[70] The effect of this situation on the dowry received by a man can be seen in the case of the Minerbetti family. When Andrea Minerbetti married Francesca Talenti in 1320, he received a dowry of 360 gold florins, 325 florins of which were cash with only 35 florins in gifts. But when Andrea di messer Tommaso Minerbetti married Maria di Piero Bini over a century later in 1493, he received a dowry of 800 florins, 240 florins of which was her *donora*, that is, nearly one-third of her dowry.[71] Again, when Francesco di Marco Datini gave his daughter Ginevra in marriage in 1406, her dowry consisted of 1,000 gold florins, but her trousseau was so lavish that her husband was left with a mere 161 florins in cash.[72] A further problem for grooms was that there was no way of calculating the value of the trousseau precisely. As Gregorio Dati commented after his marriage to his second wife Isibetta: 'I received the trousseau which my wife's cousins valued at 106 florins, in the light of which they deducted six florins from another account, leaving me with the equivalent of 100 gold florins. But from what I heard from her, and what I saw myself, they had overestimated it by thirty florins or more. However, from politeness, I said nothing about this.'[73]

Nor did the financial deductions cease once the trousseau arrived. Though it was not a legal requirement, it had become customary for grooms to provide a kind of counter-trousseau for their wives during the days or months before the marriage and within the year following. Recent work on Renaissance Italian marriage practices, drawing principally upon Tuscan material, indicates that very often the money spent on this customary adornment of the new bride and on furnishing the bridal chamber exceeded the value of the trousseau that she had brought with her. Marco Parenti, an extreme example, spent 700 *fiorini* on jewels and clothes for his bride, while her dowry, including the trousseau, came to less than 1,000

68 See R. Davidsohn, *Storia di Firenze*, 8 vols. (Florence, 1956–68), vii. 683–4, and Rainey, 'Legislation in Florence', 506 n. 94.

69 Rainey, 'Legislation in Florence', 469.

70 Ibid. 473–4.

71 Ibid. 507 nn. 100–1.

72 I. Origo, *The Merchant of Prato* (1957; London, 1984), 189.

73 Rainey, 'Legislation in Florence', 508, citing G. A. Brucker (ed.), *Two Memoirs of Renaissance Florence*: *The Diaries of Buonaccorso Pitti and Gregorio Dati*, trans. J. Martines (New York, 1967), 114.

fiorini. Other entries in Tuscan *ricordanze* specify sums that, if less than that paid by Marco Parenti, still amounted to a large share of the dowry and trousseau.[74] In the words of Giuliano di Michele Fusacchi of San Gimignano: 'When my son gets the dowry he will have to spend this amount or even more to clothe his wife.'[75] That too much emphasis should not be placed upon the financial burdens of the counter-trousseau, however, is suggested by the work of Christiane Klapisch-Zuber. She feels that the main role of these gifts from the husband was more symbolic than economic. Often, indeed, the husband would borrow gifts for his bride from friends, relatives, jewellers, or professional lenders for the nuptial period, returning them within a year.[76] Marco Parenti himself, although he bought rather than borrowed the gifts for his bride, lived to regret his extravagance. Three years after his marriage ceremonies he had picked apart all the gifts, selling off every pearl and gem.[77] Other husbands who bought rather than borrowed the gifts could turn them to profit, once the first year of marriage was past, by allowing professional lenders to lend them to other husbands.[78]

Overall, however, the obligations in money, clothing, and other gifts from both parties concerned in a marriage often resulted in a deadlock; because the father of the bride could not afford the amount promised for the dowry and expected of him for a trousseau and wedding festivities, he could not send his daughter to her husband even if she had been legally betrothed. Likewise, because the groom could often not produce his expected portion of gifts and clothing until he received at least a portion of the dowry, the bride could not be sent.

The most obvious and frequently employed way of dealing with this problem was simply to restrict women's clothing across the board. But often the dowry and clothing problems were attacked together. One of the earliest laws to do this was that of Messina in 1272. As the preamble to this law states:

As all the men of this city, who so far have women ornamented to excess and also who give immoderate dowries to each other, exceeding more than their means, were greatly burdened and completely impoverished, so that unless they were aided by appropriate remedy they were subject to the dangers of poverty and indigence, the

[74] See e.g. the examples given by Klapisch-Zuber, 'Women, Family and Ritual', 220–1 nn. 21–9.

[75] Ibid. 222 citing ASF, *Catasto*, 266, fo. 334.

[76] Ibid. 227.

[77] Ibid. n. 53, citing the *Ricordanze* of Marco Parenti, ASF, *Strozz.*, 2nd ser., 17 bis, fos. 3^v–23.

[78] Ibid. 228 n. 54.

statutes written below concerning moderation of ornaments, and the giving of said dowries and other of their circumstances were introduced. We consider it proper to confirm those statutes by royal beneficence.[79]

This law then proceeded to limit dowries to no more than a cash component of 3,000 *tarena* of gold and a trousseau of 1,000 *tarena*; restricted the number of guests invited to ten for each couple and the groom's companions to four; limited the weight and value of gold in a wide range of bridal garments; restricted the use of fabric with stripes; forbade the wearing of silk mantles; and specified that any gifts given by the groom to his spouse must be carried to her house 'honestly', concealed in boxes, not publicly and pompously.[80]

In Venice in 1420, a law entitled *Pars Nuptiarum* fixed the dowry on a sliding scale determined by the perceived need for incentives to attract a spouse. Patrician daughters, for instance, were allowed a dowry of only 1,600 ducats as their eligibility, and hence desirability was deemed incentive enough. Only a third of this dowry could be spent on the trousseau. However, the dowry for the daughters of those who, only under certain circumstances, could marry into patrician families, were allowed a dowry of up to 2,000 ducats. As for lame women or women blind in one eye, they were exempt altogether.[81]

In Genoa, in 1449, a sumptuary law decreed that no trousseau was to exceed one-fifth of the dowry and severe restrictions were placed upon the contents of the trousseau.[82] In 1488, the Genoese went further and forbade any trousseau to a bride. However, acknowledging that the husband would then have to assume the burden of supplying his wife with clothes, this law provided that, if the dowry had to be restored due to death, he should have one-fifth of it if restitution occurred within the first six years of marriage, one-eighth if it occurred within twelve years, and one-tenth if over twelve years.[83] In Gubbio in 1469 a sumptuary law made detailed distinctions in

79 Gregorio, 'Leges somptuariae', 529: 'Ut cum homines ipsius civitatis, qui hactenus in superfluo mulierum ornatu, nec non in immoderatibus dotibus inter se dandis ad invicem, ultra quam eorum exegerint facultates, gravabantur quamplurimum, & depauperabantur totaliter, itaquod nisi opportuno remedio sibimet succurrissent, depauperationis, & totaliter, inopie periculis subjacebant, super moderandis ornatibus mulierum, & dandis dotibus supradictis, & aliis eorum circumstantiis infrascripta statuta duxerint ordinanda, confirmare statuta ipsa de benignitate Regia dignaremur.'

80 Ibid.

81 ASV, Senato, Delib. Miste, Reg. LIII, fo. 953 and Reg. LV, fo. 101 and Newett, 'Laws of Venice', 271–2: 'Mariti vero dominarum que essent claude atque de uno oculo non viderent, si per virum et proximiorem parentem per sacramentum affirmatum fuerit ita esse, non subiaceant presenti parti.'

82 Pandiani, 'Vita privata genovese', 193.

83 Ibid. 198.

total cost of the clothing allowed to women based on the value of their dowries. Women with dowries valued at less than 100 florins were not to have ornaments and clothes worth more than half of the dowry. Women with dowries worth more than 100 florins were not to spend more than one-fifth of this sum on adorning themselves, although the wives of knights, gentlemen, and doctors could spend up to the value of half of their dowry.[84] Similarly, and more simply, in Ferrara in 1447, the sumptuary law of Marquis Leonello forbade more than one-third of the dowry to be spent on a woman's clothing. In 1453 Borso d'Este placed restrictions on 'the prodigality of fathers who allowed exorbitant dowries for their daughters at the expense of their sons who would have to succeed them in the burdens of the family'.[85] In Siena in 1424, not only was the level of the dowry limited, but it was decreed that the husband was not to spend more than 20 florins per 100 of the dowry on clothing and ornaments for his wife, and for a year after the wife had entered her husband's house, she was not to have any new dresses made.[86]

Clothing and dowries were not the only subjects of laws designed to encourage marriages. The expenses required for wedding festivities could also be considerable and laws were passed all across the peninsula which imposed limits on all aspects of a wedding celebration: the number of attendants for both bride and groom; the value of gifts to be given to those attendants; the number of guests; the number and content of courses at any wedding banquet; the value of the wedding presents presented by guests, and so on. A series of provisions in the Ferrara statutes of 1287 provide an early example of this kind of law,[87] but other good examples can be found in the laws of Venice and Siena.[88]

As well as restrictive laws, some legislators provided incentives for men to marry. In Lucca in 1454 it was decreed that no man could exercise public office if, aged between 27 and 50, he was unmarried. In addition, marriage brokers were to receive a reward from the *Cassa del Comune* of 1 florin of gold per cent on the dowry of the marriage contract concluded by them.[89]

[84] G. Mazzatinti, 'Di alcune leggi suntuarie eugubine dal XIV al XVI secolo', *Bollettino della Regia deputazione di storia patria per l'Umbria*, 3 (1897), 293.

[85] ACF, Archivio segreto del Magistrato, libro 6, n. 20 and Frizzi, *Memorie di Ferrara*, iv. 25.

[86] Casanova, *Donna senese*, 81–2.

[87] W. Montorsi (ed.), *Statuta Ferrariae anno MCCLXXXVII* (Ferrara, 1955), 399–400.

[88] Newett, 'Laws of Venice', 255, 261–2, 268–70; Casanova, *Donna senese*, 74–7.

[89] Bongi (ed.), *Bandi lucchesi*, 379. Some twenty years later, in 1476, this law concerning rewards for brokers was abolished, perhaps because, as the reward was in direct proportion to the dowry contracted, it encouraged brokers to arrange higher dowries thereby exacerbating rather than remedying the problem.

Included in a Brescian sumptuary law of 1477 was a similar decree. This declared that,

> Due to the circumstances that have occurred in marriages contracted by the hands of brokers and other unsuitable persons, to the great damage of many families and their kin and to the whole city, and as there are still many marriages that have not been made that would have been made if there had been some honourable persons intervening, it is provided to elect through our council a suitable citizen for each quarter of Brescia, so that by many actions in such an office they can intervene, with all diligence and every ingeniousness, to make marriages between the citizens of this city, to which the aforesaid, elected men must give their oath to do their utmost with complete diligence, solicitude and vigilance to search, think, and work to contract all possible marriages as much in their quarter as for the whole city of Brescia . . . and for every marriage that they secure, they shall have 1 ducat for every 200 of the dowry.[90]

Incentive was also provided for the husband or father to police women in the means chosen for enforcing the sumptuary laws. In all cases the man of the woman's household (whether husband, father, brother, or uncle) was responsible for payment of any fine and nearly always the laws specified that the money for this fine was to come from the woman's dowry.

In their efforts to encourage marriages through laws against clothing and dowries, however, legislators saw a further problem. Young women, they argued, needed to look attractive in order to find a husband, and married women needed to look attractive in order to keep their husbands faithful. Cities varied in their opinion as to which status of woman required most assistance in the matter of dress, some giving girls relative freedom in dress, others giving married women the privilege, and some changing from one policy to the other. In Bologna, for instance, in 1289, it was specified that no married woman was to ornament her clothing with devices known as *frixis* or *gramitas*. An unmarried woman, on the other hand, was allowed to ornament her clothes with four *frixis* and was allowed to wear one *bracchia* of *frixos* up to the value of 2 Bolognese *soldi*.[91] A century later, though, the government leaned in the opposite direction. Now it was forbidden for women under 40 to ornament their plaits with gold threads, while women over 40 were given complete freedom in the matter.[92] Similarly in Bergamo in 1491, in a statute with many exemptions based on status, it was decreed that no nubile girl, whatever her status, was to wear or even possess more than two pairs of silk sleeves.[93] Either way, one's married position marked

[90] Cassa, *Funerali*, 78–9. [91] Frati, *Vita privata*, 272.
[92] Ibid. 276 ff. [93] Pinetti, 'Limitazione del lusso', 61.

a watershed in one's sumptuary status. Such awareness of the often opposing effects of dress upon marriage (as an element of attraction, as well as an economic deterrent), meant that legislators found it hard to devise an effective sumptuary policy. To condemn excess, and yet allow for sufficient luxury to attract the opposite sex meant that, as with so many aspects of a sumptuary policy, legislators found themselves striving for an elusive 'golden mean'. The result was a seeming lack of clear direction in their policies, with unfortunate results for the efficacy of their laws.

Restrictive and moralistic in tone as they often were, all the sumptuary laws described in this chapter had a reasoned, productive intent. Seriously concerned to protect and encourage two resources essential to their survival—money and people—city rulers used sumptuary laws not as a useless, rhetorical exercise in moral catharsis, but as a practical means of dealing with practical problems. In what follows we shall see how sumptuary measures were also used as a means to social and political control.

4

Ambition and Social Order

For those who are either of princely birth to begin with or able by their own qualities to win office what could be more disgraceful or injurious than moderation?

Plato

The justification for the sumptuary laws dealt with in the previous chapter was one of economic and demographic regeneration. On numerous occasions, however, governments used sumptuary laws as a conservative or even repressive force; as a means of providing order in society, both structural and behavioural, and of denying opportunities to the politically ambitious. These regenerative and conservative aims of sumptuary policy, though seemingly opposed, were, in fact, intimately connected. The economic expansion experienced by the Italian towns from at least the eleventh century continued to gain pace throughout the period of this study. This, coupled with the dramatic fall in the population levels, contributed to a large-scale movement of people from the countryside into the cities, and within the cities these same factors allowed for some measure of social mobility.[1] As Cosimo de' Medici was succinctly, if ironically, to express it: 'a gentleman can be made with two yards of pink cloth'.[2] At the same time this social fluidity and the fiscal burdens faced by most governments created a fertile bed for political upheaval. It is with the attempts by governments to tackle the wide variety of problems presented by these changes as well as to cope with the problems of public order experienced by any state, no matter how stable, that this chapter is concerned.

[1] The extent and nature of this social mobility, however, should not be overemphasized; see e.g. P. J. Jones, 'Economia e società nell'Italia medievale: La leggenda della borghesia', in *Storia d'Italia, Annali*, i (Turin, 1978), 185–372.

[2] This has often been misquoted as 'scarlet' rather than 'pink' cloth. However, Machiavelli, who is the original source for this, relates Cosimo as saying: 'come due canne di panno rosato facevono uno uomo da bene'. See the *Istorie fiorentine*, 7. 6, in *Opere di Niccolò Machiavelli*, ed. E. Raimondi (Milan, 1966), 708.

I

In seeking to control the everyday behaviour of their citizens, a particular concern of Italian governments was a moral one, that of modesty in the outward apparel, and the avoidance of any clothing that might lead to, or encourage, immoral activities. In this area, unlike most others dealing with clothing, men were dealt with as frequently and as sternly as were women, nor were legislators in the least bit prudish in their terminology. Only one city, Lucca, seems to have been troubled by displays of complete nudity, for an addition to the statutes of 1342 prohibited those over the age of 14 from showing themselves nude in the streets.[3] More common was a concern with the depth of women's décolletage and the shortness of men's doublets. The 1375 sumptuary law of Aquila instructed that no one was 'to dare to wear a doublet so short that the genitals remain uncovered'.[4] In Bergamo in 1491, all women, no matter what their age or status, and under threat of a fine of 50 imperial lire, were told that they 'must wear the bodice of their clothing or jacket or other similar dresses so high that their breasts are and shall be completely covered'. Nor was any tailor, under penalty of 25 imperial lire, to cut or make a garment that was insufficiently high-cut. Finally, no man was to wear any clothing so short as to leave his private parts (*pudibunda*) exposed, under threat of a fine of 6 gold ducats.[5] The Florentines were also concerned with the length of men's garments but not to the extent that they were unwilling on occasion to make money out of such immodest clothing. In the 1373 list of *gabelle* is one declaring that any man over 10 years of age who wished to wear *pannos curtos* (defined as any garment which did not cover at least half of the thigh when the wearer was standing upright), could do so if he paid a *gabella* of 10 gold florins, farm workers exempted.[6]

Women's immodesty also came under attack in Florence. In 1449 necklines cut 'in the French style' were forbidden and were to be cut instead 'in an honest manner',[7] while in 1463 a provision complained that women in

[3] Bongi (ed.), *Bandi lucchesi*, 374.

[4] M. Piacentino, 'Gli statuti in Abruzzo', *Bullettino della deputazione abruzzese di storia patria*, 5th ser., 9–11 (1947–9), 21: 'nullus audeat portare pandos curtos ut eorum genitalia remaneant discoperta'.

[5] Pinetti, 'Limitazione del lusso', 62–3: 'portare teneantur et debeant captita, seu busta investituram, seu zachetarum, vel aliarum similium vestium suarum tam alta, quod in totum illarum mamillae cooperiantur et cooperitae sint'.

[6] Rainey, 'Legislation in Florence', 204. In the revised sumptuary law of 1377, however, such clothes were forbidden outright although farm workers were still exempt, see ibid. 214–15.

[7] Ibid. 449.

mourning were not sufficiently respectful, wearing exceedingly long trains on their cloaks and, beneath these cloaks, dresses with low necklines which exposed too much flesh.[8] In similar general terms the Brescian Council of *Anziani* in 1497 deplored the abuse of wearing 'immodestly cut clothes' and unanimously decided that the officials of the commune should devise such an efficacious provision that all clothes of this type would be 'extirpated [*estirpati*]'.[9]

Some cities tried to approach the question of décolletage with more precision. The Genoese in 1488 instructed all women to cover their chests and shoulders so that 'the two bones in front of the throat' were covered. Furthermore, women were not to use this law as an opportunity for the display of finery rather than flesh, for the law went on to specify that the fabric used to cover this area was not to be crimson fine wool, or Dutch silk—all highly prized fabrics.[10] In Perugia in 1342, no woman was to wear a dress cut away below the 'fork of the throat'. In 1472 the Perugians gave women ten days to refashion any clothes they possessed that revealed the chest, specifying that all clothes made in the future had to be modest from neck to foot and not reveal any nudity. Now, however, the cut of necklines was allowed to be to the width of one finger below the 'fork of the throat'. In 1475 this measure was extended minimally to that of two fingers. However, in 1485 the Perugians drew back and instructed that low necklines were to be covered up completely with cloth of wool, silk, damask, velvet, or satin of whatever colour the woman wished so long as no ornament was added, and that any cutting away over the shoulders was to be covered with linen of such a thickness that it was not transparent.[11]

Governments also tried to suppress, not only provocative clothing, but also clothing that could disguise the perpetrator of immodest acts. In this respect, the most frequently targeted objects were masks, veils, and cloaks. The attitude towards veils was not a straightforward one, however. Whereas Cardinal Latino, in 1279, as the papal legate for the Romagna, believed that it was immodest for a woman to keep her head uncovered and instructed all women in the region to veil themselves modestly, most other legislators were of the contrary opinion that the use of veils and similar coverings for the face and head encouraged immodest behaviour. In Lucca in 1337, for instance, it was forbidden for any woman of whatever status, except for lay sisters, nuns, and other Religious, to go about in the city and environs with the hoods of

[8] Ibid. 530. [9] Cassa, *Funerali*, 88.

[10] Belgrano, 'Vita privata dei genovesi' (1866), 218–21.

[11] Fabretti, 'Statuti suntuari', 166, 203, 205, and 209.

their cloaks over their heads. Women were allowed to wear hoods, however, when it was raining and on the day of their husband's funeral. A law in Perugia of 1416 complained that 'one cannot distinguish good and honest women from bad and dishonest women'. Consequently no 'woman, prostitute, dishonest woman of bad repute, of whatever status, residing in the city or countryside, whether citizen or foreigner, nor any priest's concubine or servant of other Religious', was to wear a mantle that extended below the knees or to wear a mantle over her head. The only exceptions to this law were for widows and the Religious. This was a very rigid law as it meant that mourners other than the wife could not demonstrate their grief by covering their heads and that women who wished to cover themselves in the rain or snow did so at the risk of sacrificing their honour. Not surprisingly, this law was modified within twelve days to extend the exemptions to family members in mourning, women over 40, and women out in inclement weather.[12]

To avoid scandalous behaviour in Gubbio in 1507 it was decreed that no one, male or female, was to wear a mask or to hide his or her face in any way, nor was anyone to wear clothing of the opposite sex, nor the laity to wear clothing of the Religious.[13] A similar preoccupation was evidenced in Brescia. In 1466 a law forbade anyone, male or female, from going about the city with the face covered with fabric or with veils of silk, linen, or any other cloth in such a way that they could not be recognized, and in 1481 the Brescians passed a law against the use of carnival masks whose use was 'as much against God as against good customs', as well as forbidding the use of masks to disguise oneself in any imaginable guise.[14] In Pisa, too, in 1350, no woman was to go through the city or its environs with her face veiled at any time or on any day, although it was permitted for women to wear veils when on horseback.[15] In Ferrara in 1476 the covering of one's face was forbidden on the grounds that it made it easier for dishonest women, and men dressed as women, to act badly.[16] Venetian men were forbidden to wear clothing of the opposite sex in a law of 1443,[17] as were both men and women in a Florentine law of 1325.[18] The latter law also prohibited a game known as the 'game of the Old Man of the Mountain', in which youths dressed up as

[12] Fabretti, 'Statuti suntuari', 180–1.

[13] Mazzatinti, 'Leggi suntuarie eugubine', 296.

[14] Cassa, *Funerali*, 67–8.

[15] L. Simoneschi, *Ordinamenti suntuari pisani per gli anni 1350, 1386* (Pisa, 1889), 13.

[16] ACF, Archivio segreto del Magistrato, libro 9, n. 31, and also Frizzi, *Memorie di Ferrara*, iv. 41.

[17] ASV, Senato, Terra, Reg. 1, fo. 105, and also Newett, 'Laws of Venice', 266.

[18] Rainey, 'Legislation in Florence', 55.

old men, on the grounds that it was 'highly suspect' and played by men of ill will, and also forbade any other game in which 'anyone transformed himself'.[19]

Most of these rubrics restricting immoral acts and encouraging modesty seem to have emanated simply from a desire to foster decency in the daily behaviour of the citizens. As the Florentine law of 1427 expressed it, the *Signoria* was anxious 'to restrain and hinder the unbridled excess of women's clothing and ornaments' not only to reduce immoderate expenses but 'so that respectability and modesty might shine more brightly'.[20] In all these laws immodest clothes were forbidden because they were deemed 'dishonest'.[21] While this description implies a certain religious and moral framework, religious motives are, perhaps surprisingly, rarely explicitly expressed in this context. Indeed it is only occasionally that these clothes are condemned on the grounds that they are sinful and displeasing to God, and it is significant that the city that did emphasize this aspect of immodest clothing was Perugia, a city under the domination of the papacy. In 1460 when under the papal governorship of Bartolommeo Vitelleschi, bishop of Cornetto, the Perugians passed a law condemning immodest and expensive clothes because from their use results 'first, grave offence to the Divine name, then destruction of those who spend more than their means, third the worst example which from one or a few is transmitted to many'.[22] In 1472 a law passed under the governorship of Angelo Lupi, bishop of Tubertino, expressed the fear that the new custom of women wearing 'indecorous clothing' would lead to iniquity and be 'the cause of sin [*causa peccandi*]', and in 1485 another law aimed to 'restrain and modify the dishonest deportment of women, to avoid much offence to God and other inconveniences'.[23]

[19] Ibid.

[20] Ibid. 431–2.

[21] See e.g. Milan 1396 against 'inhonestam voluptatem' (Verga, 'Leggi milanesi', 9); Perugia 1402 desiring to 'refrenandum et moderandum inhonestas et sumptuosas expensas a certo tempore citra ex male et dampnosa consuetudine in et pro vestimentis mulierum in dicta civitate inducta, pro bono et pacifico statu dicte civitatis' (Fabretti, 'Statuti suntuari', 177–8); Venice 1505 forbidding 'foze et habiti nuovj, bruti, et deshonesti' (ASV, Senato, Terra, Reg. xv fo. 77 and Newett, 'Laws of Venice', 248); Gubbio 1484 'Circha ornamentum mulierum et inhonestam portaturam earumdem' (Mazzatinti, 'Leggi suntuarie eugubine', 295).

[22] Fabretti, 'Statuti suntuari', 193: 'Ex quibus resultat primo gravis offensa divini nominis, deinde destructio eorum qui super facultates expendunt, tertio peximum exemplum quod ab uno vel paucis in multo transmictitur'.

[23] Ibid. 203 and 207.

II

Far more frequent than rubrics dealing with modest deportment and dress, however, were those concerned with behaviour at public occasions such as weddings, funerals, christenings, and feasts in general. While immodest clothing could be forbidden in a few short sentences, and the reasons for doing so were fairly apparent, the possibilities for disorderly behaviour during public ceremonial occasions were greater and the rubrics restricting them reveal a multiplicity of related concerns. On the most basic level, all of these rubrics expressed a simple desire to prevent general disorderly behaviour, a concern of any government. Beyond this, however, was a fear, implicitly or explicitly expressed, that such public disorder could lead to, or provide the occasion for, the expression of disaffection with the current political regime. Still further, the opportunity that such occasions provided for the display of family strength, both in terms of wealth and numbers, could allow unfocused political disaffection to become focused upon a particular person, family, or faction.

Simple expressions of concern at public disorder are found most often in wedding and banqueting laws. A law from Venice in 1336, for instance, announced that, 'Since many follies are committed at wedding feasts and elsewhere, no person is allowed to ask ladies to supper between Michaelmas and Easter, except his near kinswomen.' This decree was re-enacted in 1339, and in 1356 the Venetian *Maggior Consiglio* again expressed concern at the 'foolish things' done on the evening of wedding feasts, and instructed that no one was to keep any person at a wedding feast or in his or her house after the third hour of the night.[24] More stern, if proverbial, in tone was the 1366 feasting law of Perugia. This law prohibited banquets in the city at night giving as its reason: 'Because it is written that the evildoer hates light, and many scheme, as they may be able, to offer late banquets to ladies to provide opportunities for malefaction.'[25] This law did allow, however, for feasts to be held at night if one only invited relatives up to the third degree, or if one was hosting a wedding. Further, for banquets held during the day or night, one was not to invite more than twenty men, excluding blood relatives up to the third degree. This law also gave detailed instructions as to the types and quantity of food that could be served in each course and instructed that anyone hosting a party with more than six people present (excluding relatives) was, under pain of a fine of 25 *lire di denarii*, to send for

[24] Newett, 'Laws of Venice', 265–6.

[25] Fabretti, 'Statuti suntuari', 170: 'Quia scriptum est qui male agit odit lucem, et multi ut possint volentibus male facere dare tempus student convivia de sero facere dominarum.'

the sumptuary official or his notary to check that all the courses were in accordance with the law.[26]

In Milan in 1396, a law decreed that nuptial feasts were not to last more than one day, and after that day guests other than the immediate family were not allowed to be present in the bride and groom's houses, nor was the feasting to be resumed within a few days.[27] In Florence a wonderfully descriptive law of 1330 restricted the courses served at a feast to three in order 'to restrain riots and ambitions of the throat', while at banquets held in honour of newly dubbed knights no more than three types of food were to be offered although 100 platters could be used to serve this food.[28] In Venice in the fifteenth century, lawmakers became increasingly concerned at the excessive behaviour of the feasting societies known as the *compagnie delle calze*—so-called because of the fantastic hosen worn by members of these societies. In 1459 expenses at feasts for high-born youths were limited to half a ducat per head, a law re-enacted in 1465, and in 1472 the number of courses to be offered at feasts was limited to three excluding dessert, which had to be small *confetti* only. Pheasants, peacocks, partridges, and doves were all banned and no torches or candles were to be used that weighed more than 4 lb.[29] In Genoa in 1449, an unusual wedding law instructed that, as the parents of the bride had got into the habit of staying to eat with the bride after she had entered her husband's house, thereby prolonging the feasting, such guests were to be served only soup and eggs.[30]

Other laws tried to prevent disturbances at weddings. A rubric in the 1375 law from Aquila specified that no one was in any way to impede the formal journey of a bride to the house of her husband (the *transductio*). Similarly in Genoa in 1440 a provision prohibited anyone, either in jest or seriousness, secretly or openly, from taking a new bride from her husband's home, and in Lucca in 1362 no one was 'to spoil nor occupy the bed of the spouse or in truth seize the bride or groom against their will'.[31] In contrast to such frolics, the Lucchese were faced with a different problem. In 1362 a stern law forbade any person of whatever status on the occasion of a ring

[26] Ibid. 170–1.

[27] Verga, 'Leggi milanesi', 37.

[28] Giovanni Villani, *Cronica*, 10. 153; Rainey, 'Legislation in Florence', 73.

[29] ASV, Senato, Terra, Reg. IV, fo. 133; Reg. V, fo. 149; Reg. VI, fo. 193, and also Newett, 'Laws of Venice', 273.

[30] Pandiani, 'Vita privata genovese', 201.

[31] Piacentino, 'Statuti in Abruzzo', 76; M. Staglieno, 'Le donne nell'antica società genovese', *Giornale ligustico di archeologia, storia e belle arti* (1878), 296. Staglieno suggests that this could be referring to a custom known as the *serraglio*; C. Minutoli (ed.), 'Sommario della storia di Lucca dall'anno MIV all'anno MDCC', *Archivio storico italiano*, 1st ser., 10 (1847), 102: 'Né guastare o occupare lo lecto dello spozo, o vero pilliare lo spozo o la spoza contra loro volontade.'

ceremony from 'giving one or more punches or blows to the head, or hitting with anything else, or doing any other indecent thing to the fiancé making his betrothal or to any other person making the betrothal [on his behalf], or to anyone gathered there for the said occasion'.[32]

Other provisions restricted the level of noise at public ceremonies. A Sienese law of 1343 directed that when a groom formally greeted his bride at a wedding ceremony he was to do so with no more than two trumpeters (*tubatores*) and one kettledrum (*naccherarium*), or with one tambourine (*tamburellum*) and one shawm (*ciaramellam*) or trumpet (*trombettam*). Similarly when the wife was led to his house she was to be accompanied by no more than two trumpets and one kettledrum or tambourine or shawm or similar instruments.[33] A Florentine wedding law of 1349 specified that at all wedding feasts there were to be only two jesters, two heralds, and one drummer.[34] Much more restrictive was a Pisan law of 1350 which not only forbade the bride from any dancing on the day of her *transductio* and the night when she was formally led back to her father's house, but disallowed any trumpeters, instrumentalists, singers, or any sort of instruments.[35] In 1362 in Lucca, at the feast celebrating either a ring ceremony (*anellamento*) or the formal *transductio* of a bride, or indeed at any other feast where women were gathered together, there was to be no jester or buffoon, or any player of an instrument. However, on the day of the ceremony, before the feast, it was permitted to have one or more instrumentalists who could play until the woman was betrothed or 'led', but not after the ceremony. The instrumental playing had to be outside the fiancée's house in the case of an *anellamento* and outside the groom's house in the case of the *transductio*, and not anywhere else. Furthermore, on the first day of any wedding celebrations it was permitted to have an instrumentalist in or outside the house who could play as he pleased so long as his instrument was not a tromba, trumpet, kettledrum, or the type of bagpipe known as a cornemuse. At the feast celebrating the customary return of a bride to her father's house, however, there were to be no instruments, jesters, or buffoons. While professional music was permitted to some limited degree in Lucca in 1362, spontaneous amateur celebratory noises were absolutely forbidden. In this same law, no one at the time when a woman went to her husband's house nor for three days afterwards was to 'make any noise, or "play" on pots and pans

32 Minutoli (ed.), 'Storia di Lucca', 95–6.

33 Casanova, *Donna senese*, 65–6.

34 Rainey, 'Legislation in Florence', 87.

35 Simoneschi, *Ordinamenti pisani*, 19–20. Any bride who danced was fined 10 Pisan *lire di denarii* while any man who accompanied her in this activity was fined 25 Pisan *lire di denarii*.

or bells or boards [*taule*] or any type of metal, or to play a horn, or throw stones at the doorway or, in truth, at the house of the husband receiving his wife, or in truth to throw or place anything else at the house or habitation of the husband'.[36] In the Milanese sumptuary law of 1396 one rubric specified that, on the feast of Saint John the Baptist, people must not 'fiant cantegore'. While the meaning of this expression is not precisely clear, Verga feels that it refers to the celebratory singing that often degenerated into a din.[37] Nor was excessive noise at weddings and other occasions the only sort of pollution that concerned legislators. A chapter in the Bolognese law of 1289 instructed that no one on the occasion of a wedding was to throw at the couple 'snow, bran, sheets of paper, saw dust, seeds, and other similar rubbish'.[38]

Marriage ceremonies, however, represented much more than festive occasions that could sometimes become too rowdy. At a time when family power and political power were intimately connected, marriages were important opportunities to cement advantageous relationships, make new alliances, or reaffirm old ones. It is this context that makes sense of the fact that the majority of wedding laws devoted most of their rubrics to limiting the numbers that could attend each of the stages of a new marriage alliance and specifying who was allowed to be included amongst the guests.

One of the earliest examples of such restrictions comes from Perugia. Here in 1266 it was forbidden for the citizens of the city of Perugia or its district to gather together publicly for a betrothal or wedding ceremony without first announcing their intention to do so to the *podestà* or the *capitano del popolo* and obtaining a marriage licence. To either of these ceremonies the groom was to be accompanied by no more than six of his blood relations, or by six friends if he had no relatives.[39] Other thirteenth-century laws were more lenient in terms of the number of guests that could be invited. Padua in 1277, Bologna in 1289, and Venice in 1299 all passed laws allowing up to forty guests to be invited, twenty from each side of the alliance,

[36] Minutoli (ed.), 'Storia di Lucca', 98–102: no one to 'fare alcun romore, o sonare bacini o campanelle o taule o alcuna maniera di metallo, o corna sonare, o gittare pietre all'uscio o vero alla habitagione del marito che menera mollie, o vero altra cosa gittareo ponere alla casa u vero alla habitagione del marito'. The Sienese were also concerned to restrict the presence of jesters and in 1343 forbade any jester from a wedding feast, even if he were invited. All jesters had to go to the 'secundas mensas', see Casanova, *Donna senese*, 55. To put this Lucchese law in a wider context, and for a detailed discussion of the custom of *mattinate* in Italy (the boisterous, noisy displays when a widower married a widow), and their control by statute see C. Klapisch-Zuber, 'The "Mattinata" in Medieval Italy', in ead., *Women, Family, and Ritual*, 261–82.

[37] Verga, 'Leggi milanesi', 39.

[38] Frati, *Vita privata*, 50.

[39] Fabretti, 'Statuti suntuari', 156–7.

although in some laws fewer were permitted to attend the accompanying feasts.[40] To aid enforcement of the Bolognese law, the betrothed couple, or their relatives acting on their behalf, were to make public a list with the names and surnames of all their guests.[41] Similarly in Modena, in a wedding law compiled between 1327 and 1336, the couple or their parents, or other relatives on their behalf, were to come before the *podestà*'s notary on the day before a betrothal ceremony and give him a list of all those who would be attending (up to twelve from each side) together with 25 Modenese lire as a security payment.[42] In the Lombard rural commune of Riperia d'Orta, in the fourteenth century, no couples could invite to their wedding any relatives above the third degree, and in nearby Orzinuovi no women in the commune were to visit a newly espoused woman in groups of more than four.[43] In the Mantuan sumptuary law compiled between 1302 and 1310, the bride was not to be accompanied by more than six maidens and the groom was not to be accompanied by more than twelve married women when receiving her.[44] In Aquila in 1375, no man was to go to his betrothal ceremony with more than twelve men, and no woman was to go with more than six women (excluding her domestic servants). After this ceremony the fiancée's family were not to invite anyone to a feast except for the fiancé with two of his companions. On the day of his wedding, no groom was to have more than thirty-two people to feast in his house and no more than eight extra servants. Of this number only six women were to have been invited by the groom and four by the bride (excluding her two personal companions).

Many wedding laws added further clauses to prevent wedding ceremonies providing the opportunity for groups of friends and supporters from outside the immediate district gathering together. In the same law of Aquila from 1375 mentioned above, no couple was to invite to their wedding celebrations anyone from outside the quarter in which they lived except for close relatives up to the third degree who could come with five companions at most. If anyone was contracting a marriage with someone from outside the city and its immediate environs, then they could take with them twenty-four men on horseback but no more.[45] This last restriction

[40] Bonardi, 'Lusso di altri tempi', 9; Frati, *Vita privata*, 272–3; Newett, 'Laws of Venice', 261.

[41] Frati, *Vita privata*, 274.

[42] C. Campori, 'Del governo in Modena', 399.

[43] Toubert, 'Statuts communaux', 503 n. 3.

[44] M. Vaini, *Dal comune alla signoria: Mantova dal 1200 al 1328* (Milan, 1986), 270.

[45] Piacentino, 'Statuti in Abruzzo', 73–6.

was echoed by the Sienese law of 1343 which decreed that when any woman married outside the city of Siena she could be accompanied by no more than twelve horsemen each of whom could have two equestrian companions, and likewise when she returned to her father's house within the city. In addition, when any woman was returning to her father's house her husband was not to send with her any of his own male relatives.[46] Looser restrictions on the same subject can be found in the Florentine statute of 1322–5. In this no more than ten men were to be invited by either side of the alliance from outside the *sesto* in which the ceremony took place (blood relatives exempted). However, as each guest could bring one companion with him to the feast, and as knights, judges, and physicians could bring two companions with them, the numbers allowed, if one includes relatives, were still large. This law continued by allowing a bride to ride on horseback on the day of her wedding accompanied by two horsemen, and more if she was travelling from outside Florence or from Florence to somewhere outside the city. But she was not to be accompanied by more than ten women.[47]

Funerals more than weddings, though, were the occasions that provided for the arousal of passions that could lead to political unrest. Repeatedly across the peninsula, laws were devised which sought to prevent the great grief and public emotion that a funeral could arouse from degenerating into something more threatening. The acute perception of city rulers in this matter is evidenced in the words of Francesco da Carrara that preceded the Paduan funeral legislation of 1398. Francesco warned that piety towards the dead 'degenerates when it is overpowered by vain and damaging ambition, that manifests itself in the excess of funeral display'.[48] This law specified that, on the occasion of someone's death, no bells were to be rung without the permission of the *Consiglio del Signore*; that only a single order of mendicants and the parishioners of the church in which the corpse was to be buried could follow the bier (or in place of the monks, the chapter of the cathedral, and a small group of priests); that no more than four torches were to be carried in the procession, and each of these was not to weigh more than 4 lb; that only the inhabitants of the deceased's house and his mother, sisters, and daughters could wear scarves (*fazzoletti*); and that no one was to dress in mourning except the wife and children of the deceased.[49]

[46] Casanova, *Donna senese*, 66.

[47] Rainey, 'Legislation in Florence', 58.

[48] Bonardi, 'Lusso di altri tempi', 12: 'quando è soppraffatto da vana e dannosa ambizione, che si manifesta nell' eccesso delle pompe funebri'.

[49] Ibid. 11. Although *fazzoletto* usually means a kerchief, when worn by women fine silk or linen *fazzoletti* were tucked into, or worn over, the lower necklines of dresses and hence I have translated this as 'scarves'. See Herald, *Renaissance Dress*, 216.

In most of the funeral legislation the overriding desire seems to have been to bury the body as quickly as possible with the minimum of fuss. Thus the Reggian law of 1277 instructed that once a body had been taken from the house the coffin was not to be placed upon the ground but had to be taken to the church without delay and likewise, once the church ceremony was over, the coffin was to be buried in its grave without delay.[50] In Aquila in 1375 it was forbidden for anyone to carry the body of a deceased man outside the city walls,[51] and in Milan in 1396 a rubric specified that no one was to conduct funeral rites for any deceased person whose body was not present under pain of a ferocious fine of 200 lire.[52] Nor was a funeral procession to be announced by the loud ringing of many church bells or by loud verbal announcements. In Modena the funeral law compiled between 1327 and 1336 decreed that on the occasion of a funeral no one was to ring bells by hand 'as for concerts' but only by a cord and this only in the church where the deceased was to be buried. Furthermore, no bells were to be rung on the anniversary of anyone's death.[53] More lenient was the Pisan law of 1350 which prohibited bells to be rung on the occasion of a death but allowed those of the chapel of the deceased, the church where he was to be buried, the churches of his *quartiere*, and the churches passed on the way to his burial to be rung.[54] In the Florentine statute of 1322–5 a family could hire a herald (*bannitor*) to announce publicly a death but he had to be a professional crier who had posted a bond with the commune of 100 lire. This crier could be paid no more than 10 lire, was to announce only one death at a time, and had to make his announcement during the day. Anyone who cried out to announce a death who had not posted bond was to be considered outside the law.[55]

Perhaps most frequent of all in funeral regulations was the ban upon excessive wailing, weeping, tearing of hair, and beating of palms, particularly by women. Presumably the reasoning here was that such open displays of grief would serve to arouse passions and unite mourners around a common cause, thereby serving the interest of the politically ambitious. In the Bolognese law of 1276 women were forbidden to cry out or tear their hair or clothes or in any other way abandon themselves to grief.[56] In Siena in the law compiled between 1277 and 1282, no one was to cry, plaint, or lament

50 Cerlini (ed.), *Consuetudini reggiani*, 46.

51 Piacentino, 'Statuti in Abruzzo', 79.

52 Verga, 'Leggi milanesi', 47.

53 Campori, 'Del governo in Modena', 475. See also Lucca (1308), Minutoli (ed.), 'Storia di Lucca', 90 and Bologna (1289), Frati, *Vita privata*, 267 ff.

54 Simoneschi, *Ordinamenti pisani*, 28.

55 Rainey, 'Legislation in Florence', 60.

56 Frati, *Vita privata*, 59.

with a high voice.[57] In the Modenese statute compiled between 1327 and 1336, it was forbidden for anyone to cry loudly outside the house of the deceased or to beat the hands or palms.[58] In Aquila in 1375, the law forbade people to tear their hair or clothing.[59] In Forlí in 1359 no female relative was to lament or cry in the streets or in the church either on the day of the funeral or the weekly or annual anniversary of the death or on any other anniversary commemorating the dead man.[60] In the rural Lombard commune of Isola d'Orta, it was forbidden for women to participate in the funeral cortège with 'loud manifestations of their sorrow'.[61] Alone of all these laws was that of Brescia in 1277 which showed some sympathy towards the feelings of the mourners. For, while this specified that no man or woman was to weep or lament pitifully, nor to beat their hands or chest or other part of their body, it went on to say that 'weeping without clamour and ostentation, however, shall be permitted for everyone'.[62]

Loud laments were not the only excessive manifestations of grief that legislators targeted. The wearing of mourning and other external symbols of grief by more than strictly close relatives and for long periods was frequently forbidden, and the cost of these clothes was also restricted. In Aquila in 1375, for instance, male relatives close to the deceased were allowed to remain unshaven and grow a beard but only for a period of ten days.[63] In Florence the statutes of 1322–5 forbade a woman from wearing black unless she were a widow.[64] In Bologna in 1276 no widow was to wear a black veil for longer than eight days.[65] In Brescia in 1473 'to avoid damaging expenses and useless customs' the wearing of mourning clothes was severely restricted.[66] And in Lucca in 1308 no women except for the mothers and wives of any deceased were to wear mourning; grieving mothers were permitted to wear such clothing for thirty days and wives for a period of two months.[67]

The public demonstration of grief was a role traditionally assigned to

57 Mazzi, 'Leggi senesi', 140.

58 Campori, 'Del governo in Modena', 474.

59 Piacentino, 'Statuti in Abruzzo', 77.

60 E. Rinaldi (ed.), *Statuti di Forlì dell'anno 1359* (*Corpus statutorum italicorum*, 5; Rome, 1913), 329–30.

61 Toubert, 'Statuts communaux', 503 n. 3.

62 Cassa, *Funerali*, 36.

63 Piacentino, 'Statuti in Abruzzo', 78: 'et quod proximior mortuo debeat dare licentiam radenti portantibus barbam occasione predicta elapsis decem diebus'.

64 Rainey, 'Legislation in Florence', 62.

65 Frati, *Vita privata*, 59.

66 Cassa, *Funerali*, 38–9: 'Ad evitandas damnosas expensas et inutiles consuetudines'.

67 Minutoli (ed.), 'Storia di Lucca', 89–90.

women, which helps to explain why women so frequently were excluded from funeral processions and instructed to stay inside.[68] Sharon Strocchia suggests that this segregation of the sexes at funerals was a relatively new innovation, probably dating to the late thirteenth and early fourteenth centuries. Her principal source for this is an anonymous chronicler from Pavia writing in the early fourteenth century who notes that women had only recently been excluded from the funerary procession.[69] That the primary motive for such restrictions was probably political is suggested by the fact that it was often permitted for women to follow the corpse if it was that of a woman or a child, both politically impotent groups. In Siena, for example, in the funeral provisions of 1277–82, if the deceased was a woman, then up to six women were allowed to accompany the body to its place of burial.[70] Again in Siena in 1343, although no woman was allowed to precede or follow a body when it was carried to the grave or through the public streets, if the body was that of a woman of any age or of a boy aged 10 or less, up to six women could accompany the bier.[71]

For related reasons, funeral laws, like wedding laws, also heavily restricted the numbers of people of either sex who could gather together for any part of the mourning ceremonies. Occasionally such restrictions applied even before a man was completely dead. In Pisa in 1350, for instance, no more than ten laymen other than members of the family were to be present at the sacrament of extreme unction.[72] In the Bolognese funeral law of 1276 there were to be no reunions of people nor the receiving of any presents in the house of the deceased before he had been carried to the grave; the bier was to be accompanied by no more than ten men and eight priests only as far as the door of the church and the number of torches and crosses that could be carried was also limited. After the burial, only members of the immediate family were to attend the wake.[73] Similarly in 1289 the Bolognese decreed that no one should gather at the deceased's house after the burial except relatives up to the fourth degree, no more than eight priests were to assist at the burial, and no one was to pay his respects to any deceased with more than ten men except in cases where the deceased belonged to one of the guilds or was a member of the knightly order, in which case all guild members or fellow knights could be present.[74] In Milan in 1396 it was decreed that no more than ten men from the surrounding countryside were to attend any funeral

[68] See e.g. Aquila (1375), Piacentino, 'Statuti in Abruzzo', 77 and Bologna (1276), Frati, *Vita privata*, 59.

[69] Strocchia, *Death and Ritual*, 10 ff.

[70] Mazzi, 'Leggi senesi', 140.

[71] Casanova, *Donna senese*, 56.

[72] Simoneschi, *Ordinamenti pisani*, 23.

[73] Frati, *Vita privata*, 59.

[74] Ibid. 267 ff.

rites and, if any did so, then a fine of 100 *soldi* was to be paid by whoever had invited them.[75] In the Modenese statute of 1327–36 it was laid down that, on the day of the burial and for a period of eight days after, no man, except for the father, sons, or brothers of the deceased, was to drink in the deceased's house nor stay with members of the immediate family outside the house under the portico.[76] In Siena in 1411, funeral feasts were banned altogether and when in 1473 they were once more permitted it was with the proviso that only close relatives were to dine and that the only meat consumed was to be lamb, cow, kid, or wether.[77] In Lucca in 1308 there were to be no more than twelve men and ten women at any weekly remembrance of any dead man.[78] More detailed were the instructions contained in the Florentine statute compiled between 1322 and 1325. This laid down that non-family members who had accompanied the bier in the funeral cortège were to return to their homes immediately after the burial and were not to go to the deceased's house to continue mourning. There were to be no gatherings on subsequent days at the church where the body had been buried except for groups of the immediate female relatives. Nor were torches or candles to be burned in memory of the deceased man in the streets at night. If, on the night her husband died, a widow wished to return to the home of her family then, this statute firmly instructed, this should not provide the occasion for a mass demonstration of excessive public mourning. Only ten men and six women were to accompany the widow, and only a single torch weighing no more than 6 lb was to light their way. Furthermore, there were to be no gatherings for the funeral of anyone being buried outside Florence and if the mass for any dead man was to be held outside the city or *contado* then only two non-family members were to accompany the relatives.[79] This desire to keep mourners to a minimum and to keep an eye on their whereabouts was also stressed in the 1375 law of Aquila which instructed that 'close relatives of the dead man or any other people at the time of mourning are to stand or sit in one place and not to walk about here and there'.[80]

Some rubrics were concerned that no extra distinction be conferred upon the dead man himself. In the Florentine statute of 1322-5 it was decreed that the corpse be dressed simply in plain wool lined with linen and a cloth cap also lined with linen and not to wear any clothes of silk, gold, or

75 Verga, 'Leggi milanesi', 47.

76 Campori, 'Del governo in Modena', 475.

77 Mazzi, 'Leggi senesi', 142.

78 Minutoli (ed.), 'Storia di Lucca', 92.

79 Rainey, 'Legislation in Florence', 61.

80 Piacentino, 'Statuti in Abruzzo', 78: 'statutum et ordinatum est quod consanguinei affines mortui vel quicumque alius tempore luctus ipsius stent vel sedeant in uno loco et non vadant huc et illuc ambulando'.

silver, nor have his coffin draped in cloth of gold.[81] Although this and similar injunctions from other cities can partly be explained in economic terms—that is, that the lawmakers wished to prevent wasteful expenditure on such fabrics—it should also be remembered that to display wealth was also to incite ambition and display potential political power. As the preamble to a Paduan law of 1504 expressed it, excessive funerary pomp occurred because 'no one wants to appear inferior to his companion, and many are constrained to do more than their condition can support'.[82]

Lawmakers also restricted what could be said on the occasion of a funeral, perhaps fearing that an impassioned oration could arouse mourners to action. In the funeral provision devised sometime between 1200 and 1277 in Brescia, no one was to make a speech near the body. The only words allowed were 'ite et recedite cum Domino'.[83] In the Faenzan law of 1410 it was decreed that when mourners returned from the church to the house of the deceased, no one was to sit down but rather immediately one of them was to say to everyone present, 'quod recedant cum Domino', at which point everyone was to leave at once. If, however, the deceased was an eminent citizen, then a brief sermon was allowed to be given by a Religious or other worthy man concluding with the words 'quod recedant cum Domino', and then everyone but six of the closest relatives was to leave the house.[84] More lenient was the Milanese funeral law adopted by the citizens of Bergamo in 1343 when under the Visconti. This allowed a eulogy to be given once the corpse had arrived in the church but once this was over all laymen were to leave the church except for the pall-bearers and immediate relatives.[85]

Some laws were even more explicit in their intention to prevent political unrest and opportunities for political alliances to be forged. The Pisan law of 1350 decreed that the *podestà*, *capitano del popolo*, or any member of their respective official households were not to go to any obsequies for the dead except in cases where, at the time of his death, the dead man was a foreigner, an official of the Pisan commune, or an *anziano* of the Pisan people.[86]

[81] Rainey, 'Legislation in Florence', 62–3.

[82] Bonardi, 'Lusso di altri tempi', 13: 'E questo intervien che niun vuol apparer inferiore del compagno, e molti sono costretti a far più de quelo porta la sua condictione.' For a discussion of this issue in relation to Florence and 'new men' see also Strocchia, *Death and Ritual*, 70–5.

[83] Cassa, *Funerali*, 35: 'Et nullus ad corpora dicat aliqua verba arrengando. Liceat tamen cuique volenti dicere; "ite et recedite cum domino".'

[84] G. Rossini (ed.), *Statuta Faventiae* (L. A. Muratori (gen. ed.), *Rerum italicarum scriptores*, 28/5; new edn., Bologna, 1929), 349–50.

[85] Pinetti, 'Limitazione del lusso', 50.

[86] Simoneschi, *Ordinamenti pisani*, 29.

Clearly the aim here was to prevent anyone with political power from identifying himself too closely with the interests of a specific individual or family.[87] Similarly in Aquila in 1375 the citizens were forbidden to invite knights of the city's captain (*milex capitanei*), judges, and public notaries to the celebrations for the *transductio* of a bride, or to any feast in any place, nor were knights of the captain or any of his official family, nor the treasurer (*camerarius*) or the notary of the statutes (*notarius capitulorum*) or any of his official household to be asked as godparents for anyone's children.[88] This same law also restricted the number of godparents to three godfathers and three godmothers,[89] while the Paduan law of 1277 allowed for no more than two godfathers and two godmothers at any baptism and forbade gifts to the godchild of more than 12 *grossi* with the customary linen.[90] More extreme in its desire to prevent advantageous alliances being encouraged and cemented in baptismal ceremonies was the Pisan law of 1350 which specified 'that citizens of Pisa may only choose poor people to stand as godparents for their sons and daughters'. 'The poor' were defined as those who possessed less than 50 lire of Pisan *denarii*, and spiritual sponsors were not to be prelates or Religious, neither priest nor cleric.[91]

Recognition of the potential political influence of the Religious indicated at the end of this Pisan baptismal law was common in sumptuary laws. Not only did many of the funeral laws limit the numbers of Religious who could participate in the rite and specify from which church or religious order they could come,[92] but many other laws forbade large gatherings or the giving of expensive gifts on the occasion of someone entering a religious order. In Modena the statutes compiled between 1327 and 1336 prohibited the entertainment of anyone entering a religious order, a tertiary order, or singing his first mass. Nor was anyone to bring on such occasions gifts or torches, wax or candles, or anything else except for one small *denarius* which could be offered on the altar.[93] In Perugia, too, the law of 1366 laid

87 An exception to this was the Bolognese law of 1289 in which, although no more than ten men were to pay their respects to the corpse at any one time, if the deceased had been a member of the 'societatibus artium et armorum', then homage was allowed to be paid to him by all the members of his guild. See Frati, *Vita privata*, 267 ff.

88 Piacentino, 'Statuti in Abruzzo', 72.

89 Ibid. 75.

90 Bonardi, 'Lusso di altri tempi', 9.

91 Simoneschi, *Ordinamenti pisani*, 30: 'Et quod nulla persona de civitate pisana possit habere pro filio vel filia aliquam personam in conpatrem vel in commatrem nisi pauperes. Et intelligantur pauperes qui habent in bonis minus valentia librarum quinquaginta danariorum pisanorum et spirituales qui non sint prelati seu religiosi, nec presbiteri vel clerici.'

92 See e.g. Bologna 1276 (Frati, *Vita privata*, 59); Aquila 1375 (Piacentino, 'Statuti in Abruzzo', 77); Faenza 1410 (Rossini (ed.), *Statuta Faventiae*, 345).

93 Campori, 'Del governo in Modena', 477.

down that no one in the city or its district, whether male or female, in public or in private, was to give any gifts, torches, wax, or any other item to any cleric, Religious (of either sex), or any woman about to be married or entering a monastery, or to any cleric or Religious saying or singing mass. People were allowed, however, to give to all Religious in the above situations 10 *soldi di denarii* or 1 lb of wax, and women were allowed to give to the Religious one tablecloth.[94] In Bologna in 1289 no one, small or great (*parva vel magna*), was to give to any Religious wax, candles, unleavened bread, or any other gift, on the occasion of their entering their religious order.[95] In Pisa in 1350 no one was to give 'to those who hold an archbishopric or bishopric either personally or to others on their behalf more than one ecclesiastical girdle worth 20 *soldi* of Pisan *denarii* or less, or a belt and bag of leather'.[96] Nor were gifts to the Religious to be given too expansively on the occasion of a funeral. In Brescia, for instance, in 1277, those paying for a funeral were not to give anything to priests, clerics, or members of religious confraternities unless such Religious were members of the church where the deceased was to be buried.[97]

The giving of gifts in general, of course, provided further opportunities, not only for mere wasteful expenditure, but also for the display of wealth and hence potential or real power both by the giver of the gift and the receiver, and was, further, a means of showing one's support and friendship. The most open acknowledgement of this can be found in the Perugian law of 1366 in which no person, either secretly or openly, was to give any woollen or linen fabric or any other material, cord, money, meat, wax, or any other gift to an associate (*affigliato*).[98] But gift-giving was also heavily restricted for the lay participants in weddings, baptisms, and, less frequently, funerals. Gifts given on the occasion of weddings were most often the target of legislators, probably because the traditional scope for gifts on such occasions was very large, given the number of guests and the different stages of the ceremony. Not only were gifts from the bride and groom to each other restricted, but also gifts from the guests. Such laws ranged from complete prohibitions (Como 1335; Aquila 1375; Bologna 1398; Treviso

[94] Fabretti, 'Statuti suntuari', 172. See also the laws of 1318 and 1342, ibid. 165 and 167.

[95] Frati, *Vita privata*, 270.

[96] Simoneschi, *Ordinamenti pisani*, 30: 'quam teneret coram archiepiscopo vel episcopo, vel alii pro ea recipient ultra cordonem unum valoris soldorum viginti denariorum pisanorum et ab inde infra, vel cintulum et bursam de corio'.

[97] Cassa, *Funerali*, 37. See also Pisa 1350 (Simoneschi, *Ordinamenti pisani*, 26).

[98] Fabretti, 'Statuti suntuari', 170.

1432)[99] to laws which allowed moderate gifts up to a specified value (Bergamo 1491; Bassano 1259; Pisa 1350).[100] In the case of christenings, gifts were restricted or forbidden outright not only to the baby but also to the godparents. The Florentine law of 1345 forbade any gifts to be given at baptisms, while the law of 1377 forbade anyone on the occasion of a baptism from giving any gift worth more than 1 gold florin to any godparent or to anyone else present at the ceremony.[101] In Lucca in 1362, no one was to give anything to a godfather or to a godmother, although the child's nurse or the woman who carried the child to the christening was allowed to be given gifts or money up to a value of 20 *soldi di piccioli*. When the child was being dressed again (*al tempo del rivestimento*) one could give it a baptismal robe (*battimale*) of linen provided there was no gold, silver, pearls, gems, or precious stones on it, a candle of 2 lb weight in wax or a little belt of silk, but nothing else. Furthermore no woman was to give any sweetmeats to any women who came to visit her during her confinement.[102] The Genoese lawmakers prohibited the giving of gifts to any newborn baby in 1449.[103] The Perugians restricted gifts to a first-born child to a value of 4 florins in 1460,[104] and in Treviso in 1432 a sumptuary law forbade the giving of cradles or cradle furnishings to a newborn baby.[105] The rare provisions restricting gifts to lay people on the occasion of a death are mainly concerned with food brought to the house. The Bolognese law of 1289, for instance, specified that no one was to bring any cooked or raw food to the deceased's house before the body had been buried nor for a period of eight days after the burial.[106] Other more unusual prohibitions on gift-giving, such as that of Florence from 1330 prohibiting gifts to buffoons and jesters from a knight on the occasion of his investiture,[107] still had at their base a desire to limit occasions for the display of largesse, wealth, and influence.

Two other laws deserve mention in this context of the display of family power. In Milan in 1396 no one in a funeral procession was to carry the

99 G. Manganelli (ed.), *Statuti di Como del 1335 volumen magnum*, 2 vols., i (*Reale deputazione di storia patria per la lombardia sezione di Como*; 1936), 141; Piacentino, 'Statuti in Abruzzo', 74–5; Frati, *Vita privata*, 278; and F. Stefani, *Legge suntuaria circa il vestire degli uomini e delle donne ordinata intorna all'anno 1432 dalla città di Treviso: Tratta de un vesto Latino a penna del secolo* XI (Venice, 1880), 27.

100 Pinetti, 'Limitazione del lusso', 62; Fasoli (ed.), 'Statuti di Bassano', 134; Simoneschi, *Ordinamenti pisani*, 20.

101 Rainey, 'Legislation in Florence', 221 citing Ammirato, pt. 1, vol. i. pp. 492–3.

102 Minutoli (ed.), 'Storia di Lucca', 103.

103 Pandiani, 'Vita privata genovese', 201.

104 Fabretti, 'Statuti suntuari', 192.

105 Stefani, *Legge di Treviso*, 27.

106 Frati, *Vita privata*, 267 ff.

107 Villani, *Cronica*, 10. 153 and Rainey, 'Legislation in Florence', 73.

banners of the deceased man's family or flags or use drapery on horses (presumably all with the family's device upon them). This prohibition was repeated in 1498 with the added injunction that no family shields embroidered in gold were to be attached to the torches carried in the procession.[108] Similarly in Brescia in 1477 no one of any status was to wear stockings or clothing on which were 'the device of any other person whatever the status, grade, and pre-eminence of the person whose device it was'. However, it was permitted for people to wear family devices if the person belonged to the family's immediate household or was a true soldier 'actually exercising the profession of a soldier'.[109]

III

All the laws examined above demonstrate a concern at disorderly behaviour in society. Legislators were also concerned, however, with the fundamental structure of society. Sumptuous clothing, elaborate ceremonial, and expansive gift-giving were all visual symbols and indicators of one's wealth and status in society. At a time of increasing social change and instability, the strict regulation of such symbols was a means to reimpose order, or, alternatively, to introduce a new order into society. The importance of such items in determining one's status and the extent to which lower orders were popularly seen to be assuming airs and graces to which they had been unaccustomed can be seen in an anonymous poem from Genoa:

> So well dressed, in fine gear
> Every man resembles a marquis.
> Their servant girls and their squires
> Seem indeed ladies and knights,
> And the ladies so well adorned
> Resemble queens in truth
> Furnished with such grand clothes
> That it cannot be told nor recounted.[110]

[108] Verga, 'Leggi milanesi', 44 and 70.

[109] Cassa, *Funerali*, 79–80: 'de diguisa de alguna altra persona cujuscumque status, gradus et preheminentia existat cujus fuerit divisa'; 'li soldati veri e feriti che exercitano el mestier del soldo attualmente'.

[110] Pandinai, 'Vita privata genovese', 119 citing *Rime genovesi*, Arch. glott. it., 10, p. 111: 'Pe ben vestir, de bello arneise | Cascaun par un marcheise. | Lor camairere e lo scuer | Paren pur done e cavaler, | E le done si ben ornae | Paren reine in veritae, | Si fornie de gran vestir' | Che no se po contar ne dir.'

The ease with which the lower classes were wearing clothes traditionally worn by their social betters can also be seen in a chronicle from Brescia. Writing in 1439, the author of this chronicle attributed the war and pestilence that plagued his city to the luxury of women's clothing, especially that of the lower classes:

builders, blacksmiths, pork-butchers, shoemakers, and weavers dressed their wives in crimson velvet, in silk, in damask and finest scarlet; their sleeves, resembling widest banners, were lined with satin or with marten, fitting only for kings, on their heads pearls and the richest crowns glittered, crammed with gems; I myself saw wives of shoemakers wearing stockings of cloth of gold and dresses embroidered with pearls, interwoven with gold, silver, and silk with marvellous skill.[111]

While the impact of the new middle classes in the period has been exaggerated[112] and while the majority of the population was still living humbly, nonetheless there was more money available to some classes than previously. There were new industries and new trading possibilities which gave unprecedented opportunities to a lucky few and which encouraged people to move from the countryside into the towns, transforming the more static order of society into something altogether more unpredictable. These structural changes in society created problems for governments of all political persuasions. The royal regime in the south, and the ducal regimes in the very north of Italy, faced the threat of a powerful, discontented aristocracy. The republican regimes in the northern communes faced the task of pursuing the ideal of republican virtue while, as in Florence, keeping the disenfranchised but powerful magnates content. And the despotic regimes faced the difficult task of maintaining a sufficiently magnificent court to generate respect, enough public festivities to keep their powerless subjects happy, and yet adequate restrictions to keep the wealthy families from gaining too much power. To all these regimes sumptuary law seemed a logical way to tackle these problems to the extent that they were represented by and generated by the outward expressions of wealth.

As mentioned earlier, historians have based most of their work on sumptuary laws on those enacted by republican regimes. This has led some to conclude that sumptuary legislation must be linked not only with the

[111] Cited in Cassa, *Funerali*, 61–2: 'fabbri, ferrai, pizzicagnoli, calzolai e tessitori vestivano le mogli di velluto cremisino, di seta, di damasco e scarlatto finissimo; le loro maniche, somiglianti ad amplissimi vessilli, erano foderate di raso o di martora, che ai re soli s'addicono, sulla testa splendevano perle e corone ricchissime, zeppe di gemme; io stesso viddi spose di calzolai portare calze di panno d'oro e vesti ricamate con perle, con mirabil arte intratessute d'oro, d'argento e di seta'.

[112] See Jones, 'Leggenda della borghesia', 185–372.

development of republican regimes, but with the very ideals of those regimes.[113] Although it is true that republican regimes passed many more laws than their royal and despotic counterparts, sumptuary legislation was by no means their exclusive domain. In Chapter 2, the number of royal governments enacting sumptuary laws was discussed briefly, what now needs to be added to that list is the number of despotic rulers who passed sumptuary laws. The cities, so far known, that passed laws when under despotic rulers, are listed in Table 4.1. From this table it is obvious that a thesis based on the idea that sumptuary law and republicanism in Italy were in some way linked faces considerable difficulty in trying to account for the great number of royal and signorial decrees which, in many cases, pre-dated those from republican cities. Even without these examples, a thesis based on the new assertiveness of the *popolo* encounters other difficulties. Diane Owen Hughes's claim that the *popolo* were eager to 'fetter the aristocrat' echoes that of the Marxist art historian Antal who, writing three decades earlier, said that the laws, in Florence at least, were 'originally aimed at the aristocracy and their imitators'.[114] The fact is, however, as will be seen, that communal governments frequently made exemptions for those of higher status and made the law hit hardest at the *popolo*. Rather confusingly, Antal seems to take this fact into consideration when, a few pages later, he changes tack and claims instead that the laws were instruments of class conflict and class oppression and were principally directed towards the petty bourgeoisie who sought their repeal.[115] This theory founders too, however, when it is discovered that the government which Antal believes was dominated by the petty bourgeoisie did not abolish the laws but in 1355 actually instituted more stringent restrictions.[116] Indeed, the irony is that it was the monarchies of Italy, France, and Spain, and many of the despotic regimes of Italy who all passed some of the earliest legislation with the express intention of 'fettering the aristocrat', while the statutes of urban governments in northern Italy were quite lenient towards the aristocracy and most severe with those of lower status.

Many laws, passed by all three types of government, applied to all citizens no matter what their social status. In these cases it was usually specified that the law applied to all 'great and small', or to all 'no matter what

[113] See the discussion of this in Ch. 2 above.

[114] See Owen Hughes, 'Sumptuary Law and Social Relations', 74 and F. Antal, *Florentine Painting and its Social Background* (1948; Boston, 1965), 19 n. 43.

[115] Ibid. 22 n. 59.

[116] Cf. M. Meiss, *Painting in Florence and Siena after the Black Death* (Princeton, 1951), 52 n. 156.

TABLE 4.1. Despotic regimes which enacted sumptuary provisions

City	Year of law	Description of regime
Bergamo	1331	John of Bohemia's Lordship (1331–3)
	1343	Under Milanese domination
	1353	
	1374	
	1391	
	1482–91	
Bologna	1352	Under the Visconti
	1357	
	1453	Law of papal legate approved by Bentivoglio
	1474	Under Bentivoglio supremacy
Brescia	1200–76	Under a succession of signorial regimes from 1258
	1277	
	1442	
	1466	
	1473	
	1477	
Camporotondo	1322–66	Subject to the Lords Varano of Camerino
Castel Fiorentino	1305	Subject to Viterbo
Faenza	1410	Communal statutes approved by Giovanni Galeazzo Manfredi
Ferrara	1287	Under Este domination throughout
	1420	
	1434	
	1447	
	1453	
	1456	
	1460	
	1467	
	1476	
Gubbio	1469	Under Federico da Montefeltro
	1484	Under Guidubaldo I
Lucca	1337	Communal law approved by Alberto and Mastino della Scala
Mantua	1302	Under the Gonzaga
	1430/2	
Milan	*c.*1343	Under Visconti and Sforza regimes
	1351	
	1396	
	1421	
	1498	

TABLE 4.1. *Continued*

City	Year of law	Description of regime
Modena	1327–36	Approved by Obizzo and Niccolò d'Este
Padua	1398	Under Francesco Novello da Carrara
Parma	1258–65	Under virtual signorial regime of Giberto da Gente (1253–9) and then Pallavicino (1263–9)
	1316	Under virtual signorial regime of Giberto di Correggio
	1422	Under Filippo Maria Visconti
Savona	1325	Genoa under King Robert of Naples
	1430	Visconti in the city
Verona	1295 } 1328 }	Under the *de facto* signoria of the Della Scala

status, grade, or pre-eminence' a person had. The majority of laws, however, contain some class distinctions to a lesser or greater degree. Before discussing the possible reasons governments may have had for singling out particular social groups, it would be helpful to establish exactly which groups were isolated. Table 4.2 shows the results of a survey of the categories of profession exempted from all or some prescriptions of the sumptuary laws of this study. The aim was to be as comprehensive as the available material would allow but some points need to be made. First, although knights were often exempted from the law because they were magnates, some laws specify magnates as a category distinct from knights, and so these have been given an entry of their own. Secondly, in Venice the doge and his family were always exempt from the sumptuary laws regulating clothing, but as this was only mentioned in the initial sumptuary law, and was thereafter understood but not specified, it has been counted only once under the heading 'rulers of the city'. Similarly in other cities, such as Ferrara, one can be fairly certain that the ruling and/or noble families were exempted from the laws, but unless this was specified in a law, it has not been factored into the table. Where wives and families of certain groups were singled out by legislators they have been included with their husband's group. Finally, the term *licenziati* refers to teachers of medicine, grammar, and philosophy.

What is immediately apparent from the table is that only a few groups were singled out repeatedly for favourable treatment. Furthermore, the majority of sumptuary laws did not work to uphold an order of society that would be recognizable as the traditional three-tiered medieval one of those

TABLE 4.2. Categories exempted from sumptuary prohibitions

Category	No. of exemptions
Knights	46
Doctors of medicine	30
Doctors of civil and canon law	23
Judges	12
Nobles	9
Magistrates and communal officers	4
Lawyers	5
Counts	5
Gentlemen	5
Individual dispensations	4
Rulers of the city	4
Licenziati	3
Mercenaries	3
Magnates	3
Doctors of the statutes	3
Marquises	3
Honourable citizens	2
Jurists	2
Advocates of the Milanese college	2
Members of the silk guild	2
Notaries	2
Clothiers	2
Bankers	2
Barons	1
Experts in science	1
Juriconsults	1
Fiscal auditors who are doctors	1
Senators	1
Those who have studied for five years	1
Lettered men	1
Priors	1
Abbots	1
Canons	1
Provosts	1
Prelates	1
Bishops	1

who fight, those who pray, and those who work the soil. Not only did exemptions for professions such as notaries, bankers, and clothiers marginally outnumber those for abbots and barons, for example, but only seven of the 300 laws studied here express a detailed class structure that in any way resembles the sumptuary laws of Spain, France, and England examined in Chapter 2: that of Sicily and Puglia in 1290, Milan in 1396 and 1498, Faenza in 1410, Piedmont in 1430, and Bologna in 1453 and 1476. Of these, two were devised by monarchical regimes, one by a long-established signorial regime, and two by papal legates who perhaps had a more traditional Aquinian view of the world order. The Sicilian law of 1290 was authorized by the two vice-regents of Charles II of Anjou and was aimed almost exclusively at nobles.[117] It restricted what could be served at the daily table of counts, flag-bearers, barons, knights, or others holding land owned by the *Curia*, or having obligations towards the king. Further, it forbade any of the aforementioned, or anyone else other than the royal family, from lining their clothes with costly or rare furs, using more than a certain value of purple, gold, silken, or woollen cloth for more than two items of clothing a year, having long trains on dresses, and renewing saddles more than once a year.

Similarly the Piedmontese law passed by the ducal family of Savoy in 1430, as would be expected, placed the ruling family at the head of its hierarchical order, although it did specify that the clothing that family members chose to wear should at least be 'honest' in that it should neither trail on the ground nor be too short, nor be superfluous nor immoderately sumptuous. Duchesses in the ducal household were not to wear dresses with trains longer than a palm nor to wear high headdresses. Wives and daughters of others in the ducal household were on no account to surpass the luxury of the duchesses' clothing. This law then continued with minute prescriptions for the free men in the ducal employ and in particular for squires (*scuderi*). These were especially instructed to guard against immodesty in the length of their clothes and were forbidden the use of velvet or other silken clothes, furs such as ermine and vair, the use of silver signs other than military ones, and objects of gold or gilt other than money and rings. After these came a series of graded prescriptions for barons, bannarets, *valvassori*, doctors, and knights 'who do not use arms', noble doctors, doctors in law, teachers of law and medicine, treasurers, magistrates, citizens and *borghesi* who lived off their own income, and finally those who engaged in commerce out of the country, other citizens of the middle rank and merchants, manual workers, *contadini* and their wage

[117] Del Giudice, 'Legge del 1290', 3–4.

labourers. To these were added additional prescriptions concerning head-dresses for the women in the households of all these different categories.[118]

Interestingly the Milanese laws of 1396 and, more especially, 1498, were designed to reserve privileges, not just for members of the ruling family of the city, but for all the noble and eminent citizens of the city as well. The law of 1396 under Gian Galeazzo Visconti had exemptions from the restrictions on clothing and ornaments for the wives of knights, doctors of law, judges, advocates at the Milanese college, and lawyers, while knights, judges, doctors, and the rulers of the city were exempted from the funeral prohibitions.[119] The preamble to the law of 1498 explicitly states that it was necessary to reintroduce the sumptuary laws in the city after so many years because of complaints by nobles and other eminent citizens that their privileges were being eroded.[120] This later law had many more grades of nobles included in the exemptions than that of 1396, perhaps indicating an increased aristocratization of Milanese society. Now added to those exempt from clothing and jewellery regulations were wives of senators, barons, counts, marquises, juriconsults, physicians, and teachers; exempt from the laws regulating post-partum practices and the use by women of carriages were the wives of senators, counts, marquises, barons, magnates, lawyers, and fiscal auditors who were also doctors; exempt from the funeral restrictions were counts, barons, marquises, doctors, and knights; and exempt from the limits on the number of crosses that could be carried in the cortège were marquises, barons, counts, and their wives, friars, nuns, regular canons, doctors, knights, and their wives.[121]

The funeral law from the Faenzan statute of 1410, sanctioned by Giovanni Galeazzo Manfredi, bears many similarities to the Milanese funeral provisions of 1498 and, if anything, goes even further in its class stratification.[122] This law has five different levels of social categories which are outlined at the beginning of the law, with specified funeral practices that become less sumptuous as the levels descend:

1. Magnates, nobles, knights; bishops, abbots, priors, *preposti* (provosts), canons; doctors, *licenziati*, experts in canon or civil law or those who have studied for at least five years in a university, and physicians.
2. Experts in law who have studied for less than five years, or who have studied out of a university; lawyers, surgeons, rhetoricians; relatives of

[118] C. B. Borelli, 'Della prammatica o sia regolamento sopra il sontuoso vestire degli huomini e donne, e sopra le larghe spese dei convitti e funerali', *Editti antichi e nuovi di sovrani principi della Real Casa di Savoia* (Turin, 1681).

[119] Verga, 'Leggi milanesi', 9 ff.

[120] Ibid. 56.

[121] Ibid. 48 ff.

[122] Rossini (ed.), *Statuta Faventiae*.

those in the first category; ecclesiastical clerics of a grade inferior to those in the first category.
3. Citizens belonging to the *corporazioni delle Arti*.
4. Simple citizens of an inferior condition to the preceding categories.
5. Women and inhabitants of the *contado*.

The last two laws with a detailed class structure are the two from Bologna, both devised by papal legates. As the first of these, that of Cardinal Bessarion in 1453, will be dealt with in Chapter 6, and as the second is virtually identical to this in its class structure, no more will be said of them here except to note their existence.

Many other laws which specified that they applied to all citizens, no matter what their status, did, however, make an extra distinction concerning servants and slaves. One of the most detailed laws in this respect was that of Lucca in 1337. This law contains numerous paragraphs restricting various aspects of clothing, ornaments, and gift-giving which applied to all women of any status and, overall, are quite lenient. However, servants are dealt with severely and are kept very much in their place. For instance, no maid or servant was to wear any headdress which contained another's hair or silk, nor was any maid to wear dresses with necklines cut lower than the fashion which was proper to her estate, nor made of cloth worth more than 4 lire of Lucchese *denarii* a length, or of more than one colour, nor was she to have gold or silver in any belt, any bag of silk, any buttons of gold or enamel, or any slippers or high-heeled shoes bordered with gold, silver, or pinchbeck (tinsel).[123] The Florentine law of 1318 forbade servant girls and wet-nurses from wearing dresses that touched the ground and hoods over their heads.[124] The Pisan law of 1350 instructed that no female slave, servant, or wet-nurse was to wear a dress with a train, any high-heeled shoes, any ornament, or a mantle.[125] The Modenese statute of 1327–36 forbade servants or women of 'parve conditionis' to wear dresses with trains, or false plaits of silk on their heads.[126] Another Lucchese law, this time of 1308, made a distinction between types of servants. This forbade servants and domestic staff from wearing certain ornaments and instructed that, if any violated this regulation, not only would they be subject to a fine but that any citizen was allowed to strip the offending items off their backs. Such molestation was not allowed, however, in the case of domestic concubines who were also

[123] Bongi (ed.), *Bandi lucchesi*, 47–54.
[124] Rainey, 'Legislation in Florence', 55.
[125] Simoneschi, *Ordinamenti pisani*, 14.
[126] Campori, 'Del governo in Modena', 470–1.

servants.[127] These women were seen, apparently, as being one grade higher than the average domestic and perhaps also possessed clothing and ornaments of some value that were gifts from their masters. Occasionally residents of the *contado* were also discriminated against. In Ferrara in 1447, *contadine* were forbidden the use of silk clothes, ornaments of gold, silver, or pearls, and were instructed to dress in either linen or wool.[128]

As indicated earlier, it was republican regimes which most often made exemptions for those of higher status. But unlike the royal and signorial laws cited above, which had a multi-tiered system, republican laws tended to single out only a few groups repeatedly for exemption, and then applied the restrictions uniformly to everyone else. Moreover, of the four groups that fell into this favoured category, three were professional: doctors of medicine, doctors of canon and civil law, and judges. This recognition of the honour due to those who had spent many years in study acquiring skills that would benefit the city distinguishes these laws from those of Spain, France, and England, and from the royal decrees of Naples and Piedmont. In this context, the fact that knights were the most frequently exempted category, by a large margin, might seem somewhat anomalous. There are several factors, however, which may account for this.

The first is one relating to the anti-magnate legislation of the thirteenth century. The arrogance, violence, and factionalism for which the magnate families became notorious led to their exclusion from participation in the government of many cities, and it was the possession of knighthood which was used most often as a means to distinguish magnates. Having rendered them politically impotent, there was no longer the potential for magnates' lavish clothing, weddings, banquets, and funerals to make a dangerous political statement. Indeed, if anything, such privileges were now necessary in order to keep magnate families content with the severe curtailment of their political role. Having subdued the magnates, the new concern became one of ensuring that wealthy *popolani* families, who played a major role in government, did not try to imitate the habits of their magnate neighbours. This concern was clearly expressed in the Florentine statute of 1322–5. In the introduction to the section of this statute dealing with the size and cost of weddings, the lawmakers explained that regulation in this area was necessary 'because so many Florentine citizens and artisans do not wish to live modestly or according to their means or station [*ad rationem*], but rather they prefer to live in the

[127] Bongi (ed.), *Bandi lucchesi*, 373.
[128] Frizzi, *Memorie di Ferrara*, iii. 502.

style of magnates [*ad similitudinem magnatum*], incurring great loss in their expenses'.[129]

The second factor which may explain the exemption of knights is an extension of the diminished internal political role of magnates. For, while magnate knights could no longer serve in government, they were often chosen to represent the commune as ambassadors. In this function it was important that they should be dressed magnificently, for this was seen to reflect on the wealth and power of the city they represented. This role, indeed, seems to have been more important than that of their traditional function as military defenders of the city. Unlike the French, Spanish, and early Sicilian laws, the concern of city rulers, whether republican or signorial, does not seem to have been one of keeping the populace steeled for war, and this despite the constant warfare of the period. Perhaps this is because fighting was increasingly dominated by foreign mercenary soldiers in the employ of the commune rather than by a local fighting force led by the city's own knights. The accoutrements of battle seem in some instances to have been delegated to a ceremonial status. For instance in Imola in 1334, a law forbade the use of gold in personal ornaments to most citizens, but allowed knights and doctors to have gold on their swords, spurs, bridles, and saddles.[130] Moreover, on three occasions, cities made exemptions from the sumptuary regulations for mercenary soldiers: Siena in 1343, Florence in 1373, and the latter again in 1377.[131] Perhaps in these instances mercenaries were demanding as their condition of work the favourable treatment accorded to the fighters they had supplanted, or perhaps the city used such measures as an extra bonus to attract mercenaries into their employ.

This idea of the proper measure of luxurious clothing redounding to the honour of the state is a common theme in sumptuary laws, and is referred to obliquely even in the very first Genoese provision of 1157 which allowed for forbidden furs to be worn by ambassadors or visitors to the papal and royal courts.[132] In Pisa in 1350 the law restricting the numbers of men one could invite to a banquet to twenty, and limiting the food served to two courses and two confections, did not apply in the case of banquets held to honour foreign ambassadors visiting the city.[133]

A similar desire to honour the city explains why the doge and his family

[129] Rainey, 'Legislation in Florence', 66–7.

[130] Gaddoni (ed.), *Statuti di Imola*, 223–4.

[131] For Siena see Casanova, *Donna senese*, 55 and for Florence Rainey, 'Legislation in Florence', 205 and 211 ff.

[132] Niccolai, 'Antichi brevi', 125–6.

[133] Simoneschi, *Ordinamenti pisani*, 16–17.

were exempt from all Venetian sumptuary regulations. The idea here was not so much to accord a favourable treatment to the members of the family, but rather to enable them to sustain with appropriate lustre and décor the transitory quality of the family of the reigning prince. The privilege ceased as soon as the doge died and then the symbols of the honour of the state were transferred to another family. The Venetians also required that the six councillors who sat on the bench with the doge should not wear mournful clothing when discharging their official duties except when they were in mourning for a near kinsman. On 30 October 1433, the Venetian Senate stated that when these councillors 'leave the palace dressed in lugubrious clothing, and so dressed go through the city, this is diminishing the honour of their office and of our government'.[134]

Montaigne saw such social and political exemptions from sumptuary law as evidence for the hypocrisy of city rulers and suggested that the fastest way to ensure adherence to the law would be to remove such favouritism and thereby remove any cause for envious emulation.[135] But such an opinion fails to see one of the important functions of such laws. City rulers never desired to stamp out luxury per se. Luxury performed many useful functions within the city and it was precisely because of its symbolic importance that legislators were concerned to ensure the strict regulation of its use.

[134] Newett, 'Laws of Venice', 249: 'quam cito recedunt a palatio induunt vestes lugubres, et sic induti vadunt per civitatem, quod est in diminutionem honoris Consiliare et Regiminis nostri'.

[135] 'Of Sumptuary Laws', in *Essays of Montaigne*, ed. W. C. Hazlitt, trans. C. Cotton, 5 vols., ii (London, 1923), 149–52.

5

The Church and Sumptuary Law

> Instead of perfume there will be rottenness; and instead of a girdle, a rope; and instead of well-set hair, baldness; and instead of a rich robe, a girding of sackcloth; instead of beauty, shame.
>
> Isaiah

When discussing the revival of sumptuary laws in medieval Europe, historians have frequently included the Church councils among those passing laws directed towards the laity. Invariably cited as evidence for this inclusion is the lone statement by Ricordano Malespini that, at the Council of Lyons in 1274, Gregory X 'forbade superfluous ornaments for women throughout the Christian world' ('vietò i soperchi ornamenti delle donne per tutta la Cristianità').[1] Malespini's testimony has been cited so frequently by historians, and those citations themselves so frequently cited at second hand by other historians, that the existence of this conciliar pronouncement has come to be accepted without question. It is one of the 'facts' in the history of European sumptuary law. In this chapter, however, the existence of this conciliar pronouncement will be called into question as will historians' interpretation of Malespini's evidence. Whilst the detailed examination of a single statement by Malespini might seem mere antiquarianism (and I apologize for the detailed exegesis that follows), its significance for the historiography of sumptuary law is larger than may at first appear. Indeed, the existence or otherwise of conciliar sumptuary law is important in clarifying the position and influence of the Church in the revival and passage of secular sumptuary legislation in late medieval Italy.

I

Given the Church's generally condemnatory attitude towards luxury, as formulated by Tertullian and reiterated by Cyprian, Jerome, Augustine, and other early theologians, it is not surprising that the Church hierarchy

[1] *Istoria fiorentina di Ricordano Malespini coll'aggiunta di Giachetto Malespini e la cronica di Giovanni Morelli* (Florence, 1718), pp. 181–2, cap. 199.

issued cautions to its own ministers against indulging in sumptuousness throughout the medieval period. Apart from the decrees of early ecumenical councils outlined in Chapter I, four other ecumenical councils addressed the problem between the thirteenth and fifteenth centuries: the Council of Montpellier in 1216,[2] the Council of Vienne (1311–13),[3] the Council of Paris (1323),[4] and the Council of Constance (1414–18).[5] Common to all these pronouncements was an exclusively moral character and clerical focus. Absent in the ecumenical conciliar and synodal documents, indeed, is any decree concerning the luxurious habits of the Church's lay members. More pertinently, there is no sumptuary pronouncement—clerical or secular—in the documents of Gregory X's second Council of Lyons as given by Mansi and by Schroeder. So how is Malespini's assertion of the existence of a secular sumptuary enactment in this council to be explained?

It is conceivable that there was a sumptuary pronouncement but that the document containing it has been mislaid. As Schroeder points out: 'There were published in this council decrees which not so long after their publication became lost, and consequently never found a place in any collection.'[6] Even so, the decree would have been unique in the history of the ecumenical councils, and it is therefore remarkable that Malespini's would have been the only reference to it, no matter how dubious the authenticity of his chronicle.

Some have noted the absence of a sumptuary enactment in the documents of this council and have offered an alternative account based on Simone della Tosa's *Annals*. Levi Pisetzky, citing Biagi's use of Della Tosa,[7] and Rainey, citing Davidsohn's use of the same document,[8] claim that Gregory's was not a conciliar pronouncement but, rather, a Lenten edict. This Lenten edict, they claim, was pronounced, not in 1274, but in the following year, 1275. In the words of Della Tosa: 'by the will of the Pope, it was forbidden for women to wear pearls, and certain clothes with designs of birds, and ornaments of gold or of silver were forbidden, and the length of the trains of their dresses was brought back to a length of half a *braccio*' ('di volontà del Papa fue tolto alle donne le perle, e certo vestire d'uccelli, e vietate fregiature d'oro, o d'ariento,

[2] Canons 1, 2, and 3, cited in Bistort, 'Magistrato alle pompe', 245.

[3] Schroeder, *Disciplinary Decrees*, 387 ff.

[4] Mansi (ed.), *Sacrorum conciliorum*, 25. 730.

[5] Schroeder, *Disciplinary Decrees*, 455.

[6] Ibid. 329.

[7] G. Biagi, *Fiorenza fiore che sempre rinnovella* (Florence, 1925), 26 cited in Levi Pisetzky, *Storia del costume*, i. 259.

[8] Rainey, 'Legislation in Florence', 88 n. 5 citing Davidsohn, *Storia di Firenze*, iii. 213.

e recati i loro panni a misura di mezzo braccio trarre dietro').[9] We would seem, then, to have two conflicting accounts. Either there was a conciliar pronouncement against women's ornaments in 1274, or there was a Lenten edict against them by Gregory in the following year, 1275. Whose account are we to follow? Because of the additional details supplied in Della Tosa's account, and the earlier date of his work, he would appear to be a more reliable source than Malespini. Perhaps, then, Malespini was aware of some pronouncement on the matter, referred to it in brief, and got both the year and the occasion wrong.

However, if we place Malespini's statement in the context of the chronicle as a whole and examine the sources he used, and do the same for Della Tosa, we find that historians have unwittingly misrepresented both chroniclers and that, in fact, they both tell the same story. We shall see shortly that an examination of Della Tosa's sources does not bear out historians' interpretation of the crucial passage. In the meantime, if we look at the passage itself, it does not support the view that the Lent referred to is that of 1275. The first point to be noted is that Della Tosa places his description of Gregory's edict not in 1275, as is claimed, but in the section of his work dealing with 1274. The confusion of years by those citing him seems to have arisen because of a misunderstanding of his use of the word 'prossima'. After recounting the events of the 1274 Council, Della Tosa continues: 'Ed in quell'anno, la Quaresima prossima di volontà del Papa fue tolto alle donne le perle.' 'Quell'anno' is clearly 1274, and 'prossima' simply indicates that the Lent referred to fell shortly after the Council. However, taken out of context, 'prossima' has been understood to mean 'following', in other words, the Lent of the following year. But Della Tosa's entry for 1275 follows this passage, quite clearly, a sentence later. Simone della Tosa, then, was describing a Lenten edict of 1274.

What, then, are we to make of Malespini? If we follow Charles Davis' analysis of the sources used by Malespini,[10] chapter 199, in which the description of the Council occurs, was derived from a source called simply the *Anonymous*.[11] Now, according to Davis, the *Anonymous* was a condensed version of Giovanni Villani[12] and, if we look at book 7, chapter 43, of Villani's chronicle, he describes the Council of Lyons called by Gregory X and then writes: 'And they made many other useful constitutions and

[9] Simone della Tosa, 'Annali di Simone della Tosa', in D. M. Manni (ed.), *Cronichette antiche di varj scrittori del buon secolo della lingua toscana* (Florence, 1733), 145.

[10] Davis, 'Buon tempo antico', 45–69.

[11] Ibid. 57. The MS of the *Anonymous* is in BNF, II, I, 252.

[12] Davis, 'Buon tempo antico', 57.

decrees for the Church, and he forbade superfluous ornaments for women throughout the Christian world' ('E molte altre costituzioni e decreti utili per la Chiesa vi si feciono, e vietò i soperchi ornamenti delle donne per tutta la cristianità').[13] The last phrase is identical to that used by Malespini, and its position within Villani's chronology and account of events is also the same as that of Malespini. So, Malespini derived his information concerning Gregory's edict from Villani, via the *Anonymous*.[14] This, however, would seem to raise further problems regarding Simone della Tosa's account, for, although there is some dispute over the dating of Villani's chronicle, it certainly preceded that of Della Tosa (Villani died in 1348 and Della Tosa's *Annals* were completed no earlier than 1346).[15] Was there a conciliar edict after all?

If we trace the sources used by Villani and by Della Tosa, the picture becomes clearer. According to Green, for the relevant section of his chronicle, Villani employed, among other sources, the *Gesta Florentinorum*,[16] the same source used by Simone della Tosa. If we examine this thirteenth-century chronicle, as compiled by Schmeidler, we find that, like Della Tosa, it describes Gregory's statement as a Lenten edict of 1274. All three chroniclers, Villani, Della Tosa, and Malespini, derived their information from this thirteenth-century source. Moreover, if we place both Villani and Malespini's statements in their context, it is soon apparent that they conflict neither with the *Gesta* nor with Della Tosa. Both Villani and Malespini begin their relevant chapters with an account of the Council of Lyons and its principal achievements. Both then conclude that 'many other constitutions and useful decrees for the Church were made'. It is after the conjunction 'and', that they both mention Gregory's ban against female clothing and ornamentation. Villani (and through him, Malespini) summarized the information contained in the *Gesta*, and his condensation of the two events was unfortunately to mislead later readers to believe that he was still referring to the Council of Lyons. Villani does draw some distinction between the two events by employing the plural 'vi si feciono' when referring to the achievements of the Council, and the singular 'vietò'

[13] *Croniche storiche di Giovanni, Matteo e Filippo Villani*, ed. Gherardi, i. 375.

[14] Davis feels that probably Malespini had no direct knowledge of Villani, see 'Buon tempo antico', 59.

[15] See L. Green, *Chronicle into History: An Essay on the Interpretation of History in Florentine Fourteenth-Century Chronicles* (Cambridge, 1972), 161.

[16] Ibid. 155–64. The original text of the *Gesta Florentinorum* has been lost but has been reconstructed by Schmeidler from other sources in Schmeidler (ed.), *Die Annalen des Tholomeus von Lucca in Doppelter Fassung: Nebst Teilen der Gesta Florentinorum und Gesta Lucanorum* (*Monumenta Germaniae Historica Scriptores*, NS 8; Berlin, 1930), app. 1, pp. 243–77.

when referring to the Lenten edict but, unless one is familiar with the original source of the *Gesta*, it is easy to condense his account into one event.

Further indirect evidence for assigning this edict to 1274 may be found in the *Annales Ecclesiastici* compiled by Baronius. This reveals that the habits and customs of the laity were in Gregory's thoughts in this year. We read that in 1274 Gregory instructed that if students of Christ wished to please God they should be temperate in matters of food, drink, and, more significantly, dress themselves not in finery but in virtue.[17]

All this might seem to be pedantic. However, the establishment of the precise nature of Gregory X's pronouncement is crucial to an understanding of the Church's attitude towards, and involvement in, the passage of secular sumptuary laws. For if, as was thought, Gregory's statement was a precept of an ecumenical council, then it would represent a dramatic change of ecclesiastical policy and one requiring explanation. But if instead, as has been argued, Gregory's statement was no more than a Lenten edict, it can be seen to fit in neatly with the Church's approach to excess throughout the span of this study, and to be no more than another in a long line of condemnations that seemed to cluster around the Lenten season.

The Church's attitude towards luxury underwent some refinement and elaboration in this period. The position established by Tertullian, Cyprian, Jerome, Augustine, and others had been formulated with a specific audience in mind, namely young virgins in the pastoral care of the writer. With the great increase in the availability and consumption of luxury goods during the late Middle Ages, the Church was concerned to clarify its attitude to luxury. In particular theologians were concerned to establish whether excess in personal ornamentation was sinful and, if so, sinful to a venial or to a mortal degree.

The hard line, that such ornamentation was mortally sinful, was taken by Alexander of Hales, whose arguments were analysed and repeated with approbation by the Franciscan friar Orfeo de Cancellari.[18] Cancellari concluded that costly clothing, false hair, and make-up were all sinful if employed to feign greater beauty than that bestowed by God ('ad fingendum maiorem pulchritudinem'). Moreover, they were evidence of personal vanity, could lead to the ruin of others through lustful provocation, and could cause public scandal through offensive immodesty. Cancellari did, however,

[17] C. Baronius, *Annales ecclesiastici denuo excusi et ad nostra usque tempora perducti ab Augustino Theiner*, 37 vols., 22 (Paris, 1870), p. 335, col. 38: 'quod sibi cibos, potus et vestes temperent, est se illis studentes placare Deo non in ornatu vestium, sed virtutum'.

[18] See Denholm-Young and Kantorowicz, 'De Ornatu Mulierum', 328–9 citing the unedited tract of Orpheus de Cancellariis in the Bodleian Library, Oxford, Antiq, e, I 1526/4.

admit that the measure of extravagance was tied to personal circumstances and that a rich woman could wear certain items without the taint of sin where a poor woman could not. But, he cautioned, if a rich woman's intention was evil or if, for instance, her clothing was purchased with ill-gotten money, was unsuited to her rank, or likely to impoverish her, then she too sinned mortally.

A more moderate line was taken by Aquinas. In the *Summa Theologica, secunda secundae, quaestio* 169 entitled 'Of Modesty in the Outward Apparel', Aquinas considered two questions: whether there can be virtue and vice in connection with outward apparel; and whether the adornment of women is devoid of mortal sin. To Aquinas, the key to determining the morality of ornate clothing and make-up lay not in the nature of the clothing but in the nature of man: 'It is not in the outward things themselves which man uses, that there is vice, but on the part of man who uses them immoderately.'[19] He claimed that costly apparel had many functions, not least among which was its use in ecclesiastical rites as a means to worship God;[20] that it was a relative concept dependent upon 'the customs of those among whom one lives';[21] and that its lack, indeed, could be sinful if the reason for wearing coarse clothing was ostentation or pride.[22] Inordinate attachment to finery, however, whether through vainglory, lust, or oversolicitousness was not, he warned, devoid of sin.

Aquinas's analysis of the degree of sinfulness engendered by overattachment to finery again stressed intention and paid particular, though not exclusive, attention to women's clothing. A woman could adorn herself without sin if her intention was to please her husband and thereby prevent him from falling into adultery.[23] Aquinas also allowed that extra finery may be required in order to signify a person's rank. Unmarried women, however, could not adorn themselves without sin. If their intention was one of 'provoking others to lust', then they sinned mortally; if they did so 'from frivolity, or from vanity for the sake of ostentation', their sin was not always mortal but was certainly venial.[24] Regarding make-up, Aquinas agreed that as falsification used for sensuous pleasure or in contempt of God it was sinful.[25] If, however, make-up was employed to hide illness or disguise a disfigurement, then it was perfectly lawful.[26] Aquinas also considered the moral status of those involved in the garment trade. Here he reserved his criticism only for those creating excessive or novel styles.[27] Otherwise, the practice of 'an art the products of which may be employed by man either for

[19] *Summa Theologica*, 2–2 q. 169a, 1st article. [20] Ibid.
[21] Ibid. [22] Ibid. [23] Ibid., 2nd article.
[24] Ibid. [25] Ibid. [26] Ibid.
[27] Ibid.

a good or for an evil use, such as swords, arrows, and the like' was not sinful.[28]

The position taken by Aquinas is important if we are to understand why the ecumenical councils were so silent on the matter of secular adornment. The personal possession of fine clothing by the clergy could never be condoned, and was, moreover, a matter completely within the Church's jurisdiction. Hence the councils could condemn it without qualification. But if, so far as the laity were concerned, such finery could be put to good or bad use according to the intention of its owner, then the Universal Church could not condemn finery as a matter of general policy. Further, from the early thirteenth century, the Church could see that secular governments were increasingly concerned with the problem of excess and were attacking it through legislation far more suited to the problem than conciliar edicts, for their legislation could be constantly revised in an effort to keep pace with the changing face of fashion and they had greater scope for enforcement. If secular governments were already actively involved in an area appropriate to their jurisdiction, it was not in the Church's political interests to enter the ring, pass edicts applicable across state boundaries, and risk unnecessary conflict.

II

Of course there were several sumptuary laws passed by churchmen but, on examination, none of them conflict with the premiss regarding general Church policy. First were those approved and/or devised by papal legates for enforcement within Papal States. For instance in 1279 Nicholas III's papal legate, Cardinal Latino, imposed a law on all the women of the papal territories of Lombardy, Tuscany, and the Romagna, forbidding them to wear dresses longer than one palm on the ground, with trains longer than one and one half of a *braccio*, and ordering them to veil themselves modestly.[29] His ordinance was notified in the Church as a precept and no priest was to absolve any woman who disobeyed it. In 1371, in Gubbio, a sumptuary law was confirmed by Cardinal Albornoz, although in this case there was no penalty of excommunication.[30] In Perugia in 1445, 1475, and again in 1485, apostolic legates and papal governors devised sumptuary laws with

[28] *Summa Theologica*, 2–2 q. 169a, 2nd article.

[29] The text of Latino's decree, 'De habitu mulierum', is in Mansi (ed.), *Sacrorum conciliorum*, 24. 252. See also the account in Salimbene de Adam, *Cronica*, ed. G. Scalia, 2 vols., i (Bari, 1966), 246 and 632.

[30] Mazzatinti, 'Leggi suntuarie eugubine', 287.

or without the cooperation of local magistrates.[31] In Bologna, in 1453, the papal legate, Cardinal Bessarion, passed a sumptuary law restricting clothing according to a person's estate which also carried the penalty of excommunication,[32] and in Genoa in 1484 a decree restricting revelry at banquets was approved which had been devised by the delegates of Cardinal Paolo Fregoso, archbishop and doge of the city.[33] All these laws were passed in cities or territories where the Church was not just spiritual but also secular lord. Here, where there was often no other government to do the job, the papal legates, or the doge, as secular overlords, could quite appropriately take on the task. The same situation applied in Rome once the papacy returned there from Avignon. In 1429, Martin V passed a sumptuary edict,[34] followed in 1469 by a law regulating dowries, weddings, and funerals under Paul II,[35] one in 1473 under Sixtus IV,[36] and one in 1487 restricting clothing, dowries, weddings, and funerals under Innocent VIII.[37]

An area with more potential for conflict between Church and State authorities was that of episcopal sumptuary constitutions. Here churchmen were acting in a sphere quite appropriate to their jurisdiction as such laws were in keeping with the bishops' responsibility to prescribe and preserve an ordered Christian life among those under their pastoral care. However, there are not a great number of episcopal sumptuary laws and the few examples one can find were nearly always absorbed into, or superseded by, secular regulations. This is probably due to the fact that city governments were already so active in the area. The bishops could see that city rulers were passing laws along much the same lines as the episcopal laws would have proceeded and that they were, moreover, in a better position to enforce their laws than were the bishops.

The earliest episcopal constitution that we know of is that of Federigo Visconti, archbishop of Pisa. Although this constitution is not extant, it must have been drawn up sometime between 1254, the year of Visconti's

31 Fabretti, 'Statuti suntuari', 187, 205, and 207.

32 The text of Bessarion's edict is in F. C. Saccus, *Statuta civilia et criminalia civitatis Bononiae* (Bologna, 1735) and in G. B. Comelli, 'Di Nicolò Sanuti primo conte della Porretta', *Atti e memorie della reale deputazione di storia patria per le province di romagna*, 3rd. ser., 17 (1899), 148–52.

33 Belgrano, 'Vita privata dei genovesi' (1866), 171.

34 This law is unedited in the Archivio Capitolino, *Fondostorico*, credenzone XV, tomo 45, cc. 93ʳ–96, cited in M. L. Lombardo, 'Abbigliamento e moda a Roma nel secolo XV: Fonti documentarie', in *La famiglia e la vita quotidiana in Europa dal '400 al '600: Fonti e problemi etc. . . .* (Rome, 1986), 325.

35 This is edited by E. Narducci in his edn. of M. A. Altieri, *Li nuptiali* (Rome, 1873).

36 E. Rodocanachi, *Histoire de Rome de 1354 à 1471* (Rome, 1922), 247.

37 Lombardo, 'Abbigliamento a Roma', 325.

election to the archbishopric, and 1277, the year of his death. Significantly, all we know of it is what we are told in a Pisan *Breve consulum curiae mercatorum* of 1305 which instructed tailors not to make any dress for women contrary to the constitutions of the 'venerable Father Federigo'.[38] Pisa was one of the earliest centres of luxury trade and consumption in Italy, yet its government seems to have been comparatively tardy in legislating against it. Despite the moderation of his approach to luxury, as evidenced in his sermons,[39] Visconti may well have felt that he should take on the responsibility for legislating against its excesses. Once the commune became involved, however, the bishops seem to have ceded this responsibility and, as this 1305 *Breve* and later Pisan sumptuary law attest, Visconti's constitution was taken over by the city and then elaborated as circumstance required.[40]

Similarly in Florence, apart from two examples, only one of which is extant, sumptuary regulations were not a feature of episcopal law. The 1310 episcopal constitution of Bishop Biliotti of Florence[41] included several rubrics concerned with women's apparel, wedding celebrations, and funeral expenses. Biliotti's regulations were similar to, though not as comprehensive as, the commune's regulations of the period which were incorporated into the 1322–5 statute[42] (although his measures for enforcement also included excommunication). But the constitution promulgated by Biliotti's successor in 1327 contained no sumptuary provisions.[43] The only other Florentine instance is a constitution of Bishop Acciaiuoli of 1351 which serves to confirm the general picture. His constitution does not survive, but in April 1354 there was a curious provision of the Florentine commune making all previous ordinances concerning apparel and ornaments null and void and enforcing in their stead the prohibitions contained in Acciaiuoli's 1351 episcopal constitution.[44] This rare adoption of episcopal legislation by the commune has been explained by Rainey in the context of a series of jurisdictional disputes between bishop and commune in the years from 1342 to 1355.[45] In 1354, in fact, the year in which this provision

[38] Simoneschi, *Ordinamenti Pisani*, p. x.

[39] Visconti actually misrepresented the Pauline position on female adornment by quoting only the words 'Women should adorn themselves' and omitting the end of this sentence which reads in full: 'Women should adorn themselves modestly'; see A. O. Murray, 'Archbishops and Mendicants in Thirteenth-Century Pisa', *Stellung und Wirksamkeit der Bettelorden in der städtischen Gesellschaft*, Band 3, Ordensstudien 2 (1981), 37.

[40] See Simoneschi, *Ordinamenti pisani*, *passim*.

[41] This is published as an app. in R. C. Trexler, 'Synodal Law', *Studi e Testi*, 268 (1971), 227–87.

[42] See Rainey, 'Legislation in Florence', 131–4.

[43] Ibid. 135.

[44] Ibid. 127.

[45] Ibid. 137 ff.

was enacted, Acciaiuoli placed the commune under an interdict for executing a priest who had broken municipal law.[46] During the resultant controversy, and perhaps in an effort to encourage the pope to lift the interdict, the commune enacted a number of provisions as conciliatory gestures, suspending all communal laws considered to be against ecclesiastical liberty. So it is possible that the adoption of an episcopal statute was another conciliatory gesture.[47] Significantly, once a new bishop was appointed in 1355, the *Signoria* commissioned a revision of the commune's statutes resulting in a new compilation of provisions including a concise and entirely new rubric on women's ornaments, baptisms, and weddings enacted by the *Signoria* in August 1355.[48]

Although bishops seem tacitly to have allowed city governments to take the dominant role in legislating against excess, city statesmen were quite prepared to enlist the help of their bishops, as spiritual leaders, in the enforcement of their laws. The most common instance of this was the addition of the punishment of excommunication to the usual monetary fine for disobeying a sumptuary law. In Bologna, as early as 1250, the penalty of excommunication was added to a monetary fine in a law curtailing wedding festivities.[49] In 1266, a wedding law in Perugia also called upon the bishop to excommunicate transgressors.[50] In Pisa, in 1286, a *Breve* restricting women's clothing instructed the *capitano del popolo* and the *podestà* that they were obliged to come to an agreement with the archbishop whereby he would 'hurl a sentence of excommunication against the disobedient'.[51] In Bologna, in 1289, a funeral law with many rubrics, each with an individual monetary fine, added the further penalty of excommunication to any woman, other than the immediate female relatives of the deceased, who returned to the deceased's house after the funeral.[52] In Perugia, in the reforms to the statute carried out between 1318 and 1342, the rubric concerned with men and women's ornaments also instructed the *priore de l'Arte* that he was to ask the Bishop of Perugia to excommunicate any offender, and that he in turn was to ask all rectors in the district of Perugia to do likewise.[53] In Perugia again in 1485 women who had broken the sumptuary regulations were not only liable to excommunication but were not

[46] Ibid. 137–8.
[47] Ibid.
[48] Ibid. 137.
[49] Fabretti, 'Statuti suntuari', 158.
[50] Ibid. 157–8.
[51] Simoneschi, *Ordinamenti pisani*, p. xii: 'furono obbligati a intendersela sollecitamente con l'arcivescovo, onde questi fulminasse sentenza di scomunica contro le disubbedienti'.
[52] Frati, *Vita privata*, 269, there was also a monetary fine of 10 Bolognese lire to be paid from the dowry.
[53] Fabretti, 'Statuti suntuari', 167.

able to have their confessions heard until they had paid 1 gold ducat to the Hospital of the Misericordia. If a woman failed to do this and a priest subsequently heard her confession then he too was subject to excommunication.[54]

Even closer involvement was called for by the legislators of Florence, Faenza, and Venice. In Florence, the statute of 1322–5 required parish priests to maintain a copy of the regulations regarding wedding and funeral practices and to have them read out in their churches at least once every two months. The priests were to notify the *capitano del popolo* of any violations of the law and any who failed to do so were to be fined. Finally the Priors were to ask the bishop, or the cathedral chapter in the bishop's absence, to excommunicate offenders. This is the only instance in the Florentine statutes of the commune requiring parish priests to publish civil legislation from the pulpit,[55] but it was not without precedent in other cities. In Faenza's funeral law contained in the statute of 1410,[56] parish priests were instructed, under pain of a fine of 100 *soldi*, to deliver a sermon every six months in 'a loud voice so that all can understand it well'.[57] Similarly, in Venice in 1480, a law proscribing women's head ornaments ordered the patriarch to give notice of the law by means of his confessors and to preach against the abuses that women wearing the forbidden ornaments committed.[58]

One unique use of the clergy, presumably in an effort to have someone of greater impartiality, was attempted in Florence. Here in April 1345 a monk was put in charge of the money that was to be spent on food for the Priors so that expenditure could be decreased. The chosen monk had to sleep and eat in the *palazzo dei Priori* for the full six-month term of office. The records do not relate, however, whether expenditure decreased with this new system.[59]

III

Church and State, then, could collaborate closely in enforcement. There is no reason to doubt the sincerity of preambles like that of Parma (1316–25)

[54] Fabretti, 'Statuti suntuari', 209.

[55] See Trexler, 'Synodal Law', and also Rainey, 'Legislation in Florence', 65.

[56] Rossini (ed.), *Statuta Faventiae*, p. 349, rubric 35.

[57] 'et saltem omni semestri i sua congregatione et concione legi facere publice et alta voce vulgari sermone, ita quod omnes possint bene intelliger, sup pena 100 sol. bon. si contrafecerint vel neglexerint in aliquo'.

[58] G. Giomo, 'Il lusso: leggi moderatrici—pietre e perle false', *Nuovo archivio veneto*, NS 31, 16/1 (1908), 105: 'prescrivere la tenuta dei capelli; ordina al Patriarca di avere notizie per mezzo dei confessori, e di far predicare contro gli abusi che si commettevano'.

[59] Rainey, 'Legislation in Florence', 80.

which declared the law was for 'the honour or God';[60] that of Venice in 1360 which saw immoderate expenses as 'gravely offending God';[61] that of Bologna in 1398 desiring 'above all to please God';[62] that of Venice in 1472 which feared the excesses of the city would so agitate God's goodness that he would seek to correct them by means of 'many wars and tribulations'.[63] The alliance, though, was not a comfortable one. Having called upon the city's bishops to excommunicate offenders, city councillors found themselves beset by a far graver moral problem. Rather than deterring their citizens from indulging in excess, such punishments seemed merely to lead to an inordinate number of excommunicates—a situation potentially more offensive to God than indulgence in luxury. In fear of even greater retribution, and also in response to protests from their citizens, governments found themselves in the humiliating position of requesting the pope to lift the excommunications imposed at their own request by their own bishops.

This situation came to a crisis in the mid-fifteenth century and our main evidence for it is a series of petitions to the papacy written by, or on behalf of, women.[64] The earliest are those of some Venetian noblewomen. In 1437, the Venetians, suffering badly in their war with the duke of Milan, appealed to God for assistance by propitiatory processions, charitable offerings, and a sumptuary law devised by Lorenzo Giustiniani, head of part of the Venetian diocese and bishop of Castello. For infractions of this severe law directed exclusively at the luxury of women, the penalty was excommunication.[65] This law was approved by the Venetian Senate[66] which at first seemed well pleased with the bishop's involvement. But soon the government regretted its decision for rather than end the vice of luxury it seemed merely to lead to an accumulation of excommunications. Nor apparently did this law meet with complete support from other clergymen. According to the biography of Lorenzo Giustiniani written by his grandson Bernardo, Lorenzo had to enter into a public theological dispute with 'a prelate of great reputation residing in Venice' the subject of which was 'The constitution of the holy Bishop against the luxury and immodesty of women'.[67] Gallicciolli records that the Venetian government sent two ambassadors to

60 A. Ronchini (ed.), *Statuta communis parmae ab anno MCCCXVI ad MCCCXXVII* (Parma, 1859), 261.

61 Newett, 'Laws of Venice', 269.

62 Frati, *Vita privata*, 275.

63 Newett, 'Laws of Venice', 277.

64 These petitions are discussed further in Ch. 6 below.

65 Bistort, *Magistrato alle pompe*, 69–70, citing Gallicciolli, *Memorie*, I n. 407.

66 Ibid. 70 for the full text.

67 Ibid. 70 n. 2, *Vita di S. Lorenzo Giustinianio* (Venice, 1712), 83 ff. Bistort was unable to find any more information about this dispute from any of the other numerous lives of this saint.

Pope Eugenius IV requesting a licence permitting Venetian women to wear the forbidden items free from the threat of excommunication.[68] According to Bistort, Gallicciolli was probably alluding here to the petitions sent to the pope by a group of patrician women. The first of these was that of Cristina Corner.[69] She informed the pope that she possessed many fine clothes which she had been unable to wear since Giustiniani's constitution. She begged His Holiness that she, Cristina Corner, born of noble blood, be allowed to wear the forbidden items for the honour of her parents, because of her great beauty, and also because such clothing had been customary in the city before this constitution was observed. For the payment of 4 ducats and 1 *grosso* to the papal treasury, Cristina was granted a licence to wear such items for three years.

Five other Venetian women, less audacious than Cristina, grouped together in another petition to the pope. They too stressed their nobility but did not bring forward reasons of personal beauty in their defence. Rather, they pointed out that Venice was famous among all Italian cities for the distinguished impression she made upon the eye ('Cum civitas Venetiarum, interalias Italiae civitates insignia et famosa ac opibus') not just because of her endowments but also due to the customary adornments of her women. These ladies too were granted a licence after payment of the same sum that Cristina Corner had paid.[70]

In 1471 another group petition was presented to the pope by Venetians. Andrea Gritti wrote to Sixtus IV on behalf of twelve women all related to him by blood or by marriage. He begged that they be allowed to wear long trains, platform shoes, and false hair because the married women among them wished to please their husbands, and the single women wished to wear such items for reasons of propriety not vanity—in other words, to attract a husband. Once again a licence was granted.[71]

What is significant in all these petitions is that, apart from Cristina Corner's plea of personal beauty, all the reasons for the women to be allowed their finery fell into the various categories outlined by Aquinas of lawful personal adornment, without the taint of sin: Cristina Corner and the other five noblewomen stressed reasons of customary usage,[72] honour,

[68] Cited ibid. 71.

[69] C. Foucard, *Lo statuto inedito delle nozze venetiane nel 1299* (Venice, 1858), 23–4; Bistort, *Magistrato alle pompe*, 71–2; Newett, 'Laws of Venice', 259–60.

[70] Foucard, *Nozze venetiane*, 24–5; Bistort, *Magistrato alle pompe*, 72–3; Newett, 'Laws of Venice', 259–60.

[71] Bistort, *Magistrato alle pompe*, 74–5.

[72] Aquinas, *Summa Theologica*, 2–2q. 169a, 1st article.

and their estate;[73] Andrea Gritti stressed the chaste intentions of the women in his care—the married women wished to prevent their husbands from straying into adultery and, while the unmarried wished to attract husbands, Aquinas allowed that such an intention was venial and not mortal.[74] With such reasons placed before him, the pope had to concede that these women ostensibly wished to put luxury to a legitimate use and that they could not be subject to the penalty of excommunication.

With the establishment of apostolic legates in Perugia from 1445, excommunication was also introduced as a punishment for infraction of sumptuary laws. In the Lent of 1468 many women obviously repented of their excesses and begged Pope Paul II for absolution. On 25 March the pope gave the bishop of Perugia permission to grant absolution. But the women's repentance cannot have lasted for long because the following Easter women begged for absolution again. Once more it was granted and once more it was followed by more excommunications and more requests for absolution. This situation led Paul II to question the appropriateness of the law itself. On 1 August 1469, he instructed Girolamo Lando, archbishop of Crete and governor of Perugia; Giacomo Vanucci, bishop of Perugia; the dean of the cathedral; and the abbot of the monasteries of Saints Peter and Benedict to examine whether the law needed to be corrected or changed. They confirmed the substance of the law but moderated the fine and lifted the threat of excommunication from anyone who went to confession.[75] It is doubtful whether they felt that by reducing the threat of punishment they would secure closer adherence to the law, but such a drawing back by ecclesiastics is again indicative of the influence of the Thomistic position on luxury and the inappropriateness theologically of applying excommunication across the board.

Nor was excommunication limited to the consumers of luxury goods. In the Perugian law of 1472, tailors who made forbidden clothes were themselves subject to a fine of 25 *lire di denarii* and excommunication without absolution. Further, all priests were instructed to be vigilant in the confessional, especially when hearing the confession of tailors. Once again, however, the city rulers realized that they had been too hasty, not to mention harsh, in asking the bishops for this additional penalty. In 1474 the new municipal magistrates begged the new papal governor to free from excommunication all those citizens who had received it, a request to which he agreed in February of this same year.[76]

[73] Ibid.
[74] Ibid.
[75] Fabretti, 'Statuti suntuari', 197–8.
[76] Ibid. 203–4.

While the Church, on the whole, seems to have been prepared to leave the sumptuary legislative process to state authorities, conflict could also occur when ecclesiastics felt that areas, properly their own, were being infringed upon by city legislators. This did not occur with most laws but, in the case of funerary restrictions, the line of demarcation became more obscure. From the mid-fourteenth century, it became a fairly common practice for laws against funerary excess to restrict the numbers and categories of ecclesiastics who could participate in the rite. For instance, in Bergamo in 1343, the funeral *capitoli* from a Milanese law were approved. These restricted the number of ecclesiastics who could assist at the funeral according to the place where the deceased was to be buried. If he was to be buried near the house of some order of mendicant friars, than all the brothers of that religious house could attend together with three chaplains or parish priests and four brothers from each of the other two convents of friars. The number was restricted to four friars from each convent and three chaplains, parish priests, or canons if the burial was near the presbyteries of S. Alessandro and S. Vincenzo, and was reduced still further if he was to be buried in some chapel of the city or district.[77] In Pisa in 1350 a sumptuary law also restricted the number of clerics taking part in the rite.[78] In Aquila in 1375 the number of clerics participating in a funeral was limited to those of the deceased's parish.[79] In Padua, in 1398, a law decreed that only an *ordine* of mendicants and the parishioners of the Church in which the corpse was to be buried could follow it to its place of burial, or, in place of the mendicants, the chapter of the cathedral and a *fraglia* of priests.[80] In Faenza in 1410 the lengthiest and most detailed provision of the newly revised statutes was devoted to the subject of funerals. In this case, the number of Religious who could attend was restricted according to the status of the deceased.[81] In 1473 in Brescia a law decreed that no more than twenty-four Religious were to attend any funeral, excluding those bearing crosses.[82]

Despite the constant interference by secular governments, in this century and a half of such funerary legislation there were only two instances of ecclesiastical protest. The first occurred in Parma in 1421. In this year, Filippo-Maria Visconti ordered a reform of the city's statutes. Among the new rubrics was a funeral disposition which, unfortunately, has not survived.

77 Pinetti, 'Limitazione del lusso', 48–9 n. 4.
78 Simoneschi, *Ordinamenti pisani*, 25.
79 Piacentino, 'Statuti in Abruzzo', cap. 560, and also p. 37 of her introd.
80 Bonardi, 'Lusso di altri tempi', 11.
81 Rossini (ed.), *Statuta Faventiae*, 345 and 351, rubric 35.
82 Cassa, *Funerali*, 39.

However, its infringement of ecclesiastical liberty created such an outcry that the duke ordered the *Collegio de' Giudici* to examine the funeral rubric and reform it appropriately. The new disposition was then approved by Filippo-Maria on 20 December. It decreed that, whatever the status of the deceased, his bier was not to be carried through the streets nor to be paid homage to in the church with more than a certain weight of candles, only clerics of the parish were to participate in the service and these with only one cross, and only the bell of the parish church was to be rung. In addition this reform restricted excessive expenses made for a priest's first mass and for the taking of the veil by nuns.[83] No more is heard of this dispute so, despite the severity of even this reform, we must suppose that the monks of Parma were placated.

More vitriolic was the situation in Brescia in the early sixteenth century. In 1505, a funerary provision decreed that, no matter what the status of the deceased, no *scuola* could intervene in the funerary rite except that to which the deceased himself had belonged, nor was it permitted for the members of the *scuola* to be preceded or followed by paupers (presumably seeking alms) ('nè fosse lecito far gli stessi precedere o seguire da poveri *vestibus indutis*'). Many priests, in particular the friars of San Domenico, were outraged by this law and, perceiving it as a violation of ecclesiastical liberty, they refused absolution to anyone who observed it. Their opposition became so severe that in 1506 a special council passed a provision allowing anyone to give whatever alms they wished for the souls of the deceased. But, in a meeting of the General Council, five citizens were elected to inspect the offending statute and give their measured opinion as to whether it infringed ecclesiastical liberty or not. Having decided in the negative, the statute in its final version of 1507 concluded: 'sub rubrica de funeribus, bonum et sanctum et non contra libertatem ecclesiasticam', and the five elected inspectors were given full power to defend the statute.

However, the friars of San Domenico, not to be outdone, sent a petition to the pope. In this they expressed their deep disapproval of excess funerary pomp and the ruin it often engendered. But this statute, they claimed, interfered with ecclesiastical liberty and, as a result, they had been beset with demands from the faithful desiring to know whether, by obeying the statute, they would incur excommunication. Could His Holiness resolve the dispute and determine a path to follow such that, without diminishing the liberty of the Church, families would not be impoverished and would be able to provide for the material welfare of the religious? Julius II delegated the bishop

[83] Pezzana, *Storia Parma*, ii. 202 and 239–40.

of Brasco and the vicar-general to give the supplication mature deliberation. On 21 July 1507, the sentence, pronounced by the archbishop, was that the statute and the successive decree were to be approved and confirmed as just and valid because they were solely concerned with funerary excess and did not touch on spiritual matters. The decree, therefore, was not contrary to the liberty of the Church, and those who had established it did not incur excommunication of any sort.

The friars appealed to the pope again, this time using words found to be insulting to the honour and dignity of the city and to the archbishop who had declared the statute sound. As a result, on 9 October 1508, the prior of San Domenico was ordered before the government of the Veneto. Here he conceded that, notwithstanding their appeal against the decree, his confraternity and all the other religious orders of the city would stand firmly by the deliberation of the 'most faithful Council of the city'.[84]

Given the potential for such acrimonious disputes, it is not surprising that the most frequent involvement of the Church in secular sumptuary laws was an indirect one via her preachers. Excess in personal ornamentation became a regular theme with many preachers and was the subject of numerous pastoral tirades.[85] Here it is important to follow the lead of Bernadette Paton and distinguish between the attitudes of the conventual and the observant friars.[86] The conventuals, faced with their parishioners on a daily basis, were more concerned, in Thomistic style, with the motives of the wearer. As the Sienese friar Mariani declared, the ornamentation of women was either harmless, or sinful to a venial or mortal degree, according to the lust it was intended to generate.[87] The observant friars, however, tended to take a more ascetic stance and, like Tertullian and Cyprian, impose the standards expected of Religious upon laymen. One of the most

[84] The above account is from Cassa, *Funerali*, 42–8.

[85] See e.g. Bernardino da Siena, *Opera omnia*, ii (Florence, 1950): sermon 44, 'Contra mundanas vanitates et pompas', pp. 45–58; sermon 46, 'De multitudine malorum quae ex vanitatibus subsequuntur', pp. 73–85; sermon 47, 'Contra se fraudantes et capillos adulterinos portantes, atque contra feminas caudatas', pp. 86–99. Also sermon 28, 'Questa è la predica della vanità del mondo e massime ne le donne', in C. Cannarozzi (ed.), *Le prediche volgari*, 2 vols. (Florence, 1958), ii. 82–97. In a similar vein are those of Giacomo della Marca, sermon 4, 'De vanitate mulierum', in R. Lioli (ed.), *Sermones Dominicales*, 3 vols., i (Ancona, 1978), 107–26, and Bernardino da Feltre, sermon 38, 'De vanitatibus mulierum', in *Sermoni del beato Bernardino Tomitano da Feltre*, ed. P. C. Varischi da Milano (nella redazione de Bulgarino da Brescia), 3 vols. (Milan, 1964), i. 475–87 and sermon 100, 'De vanitatibus et pompus', ibid. ii. 121–31.

[86] See B. Paton, *Preaching Friars and the Civic Ethos: Siena, 1380–1480* (London, 1992). For the Sienese friars' attitudes to luxury and ornamentation esp. see ibid. 320–33.

[87] Ibid. 327–8.

fervent and influential of the observant friars in this respect was Bernardino of Siena who introduced the infamous 'bonfires of the vanities', one of the most enduring symbols of the Italian condemnation of luxury in this period. The first of such fires was in Siena in 1400.[88] There soon followed fires in Rome (1424),[89] Florence (1424 and 1497),[90] Perugia (1425),[91] and Brescia (1494).[92] Such theatrics together with the impassioned sermons of these seemingly inexhaustible peripatetic observants temporarily raised religious fervour, and had considerable influence upon secular legislators.

The earliest evidence of such influence is found in Bologna. As mentioned earlier, in 1233, Giovanni da Vicenza gave a series of sermons in the city. Amongst other things, he inveighed against women's head ornaments and instructed women to wear veils. So inspired was the government that, according to a contemporary chronicler, the statute books were given over to Giovanni to alter as he saw fit.[93] Similarly, in Brescia in 1442, seven preachers gave a series of sermons urging people to give over superfluous ornaments in their clothing for it signified nothing less than 'luciferiana superbia'.[94] Thus encouraged, the city councillors legislated against excessive ornamentation of clothing for both sexes, decreeing that all should dress honestly and decently.[95] The involvement of a preacher was spelt out in the Paduan sumptuary law of 12 May 1460. In this year, Jacopo della Marca preached in the city and the city councillors declared that, due to the 'exhortations of fra Iacopo della Marca against superfluous ornaments and expenses of pleasure sustained for women, they had realized the necessity of reform, not only to honour God with decency and honesty of costume, but to avoid a great ill'.[96] In Gubbio in 1507, the friar Battista da Mantova gave a Lenten sermon condemning superfluity in women's clothing, in particular

[88] Casanova, *Donna senese*, 27.

[89] Stefano Infessura, *Diario della città di Roma di Stefano Infessura scribasenato*, ed. Oreste Tommasini, *Istituto storico italiano fonti per la storia d'Italia* (Rome, 1890), 25.

[90] R. Trexler, *Public Life in Renaissance Florence* (New York, 1980), 381, and E. Polidori Calamandrei, *Le vesti delle donne fiorentine nel quattrocento* (Florence, 1924), 18.

[91] Fabretti, 'Statuti suntuari', 201, citing Graziani, *Cronaca*, in *Archivio storico italiano*, 16, 1a, p. 314.

[92] Cassa, *Funerali*, 82–3, the *Reggitori*, inspired by Bernardino da Feltre, ordered a fire on 22 Aug., they also asked Bernardino to come again the following Lent.

[93] Sorbelli (ed.), *Corpus chronicorum*, ii. 102: 'Item devedò che le donne non portasseno lo capo ornato de frange e de girlande; et tucti li statuti de Bologna li funo dati che li ornasse a suo arbitrio . . . Item commandò a le donne che portasseno li vili in capo.'

[94] A. Zanelli, 'Predicatori a Brescia nel Quattrocento', *Archivio storico lombardo*, 3rd ser., 15 (1901), 95.

[95] Ibid. 96, provision of 7 Mar. 1442.

[96] Bonardi, 'Lusso di altri tempi', 12–13, and app. 4 for the full transcription.

the wearing of *faldiglia* and lengthy trains. The friar spoke of the matter to Guidubaldo, *signore* of the city, who then wrote to the city's Council instructing them to restrain a situation which he considered to be 'of great detriment to the city' ('maximum detrimentum civitatis'). Accordingly, on 10 May, the Council, which had not passed a sumptuary law since 1484, proposed a law restricting the length of trains, and the wearing of *faldiglia*, masks, and clothes of the opposite sex or of the Religious.[97]

Nor was the influence of the observant friars restricted to secular legislators. The controversial sumptuary law of Cardinal Bessarion in 1453 was inspired by the Lenten sermons of Timoteo Maffei.[98] And in Perugia in 1472, the Lenten sermons of fra Battista da Montefalco against the depth of women's décolletage inspired Angelo Lupi, bishop of Tubertino and the stand-in for the apostolic legate, Giacomo Ammannato da Lucca, to publish a decretal forbidding women to wear any garment with a décolletage or indeed with any opening below what they termed the 'fork of the throat'.[99]

The frequency and influence of sermons, Lenten or otherwise, against excess brings us back to the Lenten edict of Gregory X. By now it will be apparent how anomalous this edict would have been had it been a conciliar pronouncement. As a Lenten edict, however, it was quite in keeping with the Church's general attitude towards the problem of luxury in this period. This attitude, moreover, was not as severe as has sometimes been supposed. Individual clerics, it is true, often held extreme views, but the Church as a legislative body was never as opposed to the use of luxurious commodities as were secular governments. The latter were prepared to utilize the Church's interest in the matter and its spiritual influence to bolster their own laws, but the driving force behind secular legislation was always separate from any Church policy. Further, whenever any conflict in the matter arose, the Church was always the first to step down in deference to secular governments. The latter felt that they had much to lose through their citizens' attachment to finery, while the Church stood to lose theological credibility if it did not recognize the subtleties of the issue and the priority of an individual's conscience and circumstances.

97 Mazzatinti, 'Leggi suntuarie eugubine', 295–6. I presume here that *faldiglia* is a local variant of *faldia* which, according to Herald, *Renaissance Dress*, 216, was an underskirt of linen held out by means of horizontal bands padded with cotton wool or wool fibre. This of course would also require extra fabric in the overgarment.

98 See Comelli, 'Di Nicolò Sanuti primo conte della Porretta', 119.

99 Fabretti, 'Statuti suntuari', 202.

6

Women and Sumptuary Law

and thus the immoderate appetite of women conquers the reason and good sense of men.

Giovanni Villani

Of all aspects of sumptuary law, women's clothing has attracted by far the most attention. This is partly, of course, simply because the majority of sumptuary laws were directed towards women's clothing. However, it is also because the regulation of women's clothing is the most complex, multi-layered, and, at times, puzzling aspect of the Italian sumptuary ethos. Though this book takes as its starting point the words of legislators themselves as explanatory statements, when it comes to laws against women these statements open up a range of issues that are not readily resolved without recourse to a more theoretical position. This chapter will explore what clothing represented in early modern Italy, why it was that women were overwhelmingly the target of clothing laws, and why the laws were expressed, at times, with such misogynist venom. The chapter will also look at the efforts of women to mitigate these laws which curtailed further an already highly regulated and restricted life.

Before exploring issues of gender in relation to clothing, it is important to consider clothing in general and what it signified in medieval and Renaissance Italy. We saw already in Chapter 2 that many more sumptuary laws were directed towards clothing than towards weddings, feasting, and funeral practices. Clothing was a target for legislators in the first place because of what it represented and encapsulated. Most fashion theorists would now modify Alison Lurie's definition of clothing as a language[1] for the reason that it does not have an explicit vocabulary, parts of speech, syntax, and dialogue, and nor can it be grammatically parsed.[2] But nor is it, as Finkelstein suggests, 'an arcane sign system'[3] nor, as Davis says, 'an "under-coded" form of communication'.[4] Clothing does require interpretation,

1 *The Language of Clothes* (London, 1992).

2 See F. Davis, *Fashion and the Construction of Identity* (Chicago, 1993), 5 and also J. Finkelstein, *After a Fashion* (Melbourne, 1996), 24.

3 *After a Fashion*, 30.

4 Davis, *Fashion*, 5.

and is not in that way explicit, but it is not arcane either, but public. The symbols of clothing are available for everyone to interpret, and so transparent are they that they are understood at some level even by the most inarticulate. In the early modern period clothing was used to signify a range of things to those who viewed it. At a single glance clothing could be used to display wealth, rank, profession, nationality, gender, and marital status. Moreover, clothing is visible, clothing is portable, and it can be changed with relative ease. In a nascent consumer society clothing was used as a potent sign system, and this usage was not lost on legislators.[5]

Clothing, however, proved a particularly problematic area for legislators and one that necessitated many more laws than other areas of consumption. Though the ultimate end of legislators may have been to proscribe luxurious clothing, in practice they had to identify such clothing by employing specific fashion terminology. Sumptuary legislation against clothing, then, was required to take the form of fashion legislation. This seemingly small point had major implications and, by identifying luxury with fashion, legislators found themselves beset with an insoluble problem. Fashion is, by its very nature, a phenomenon in constant flux. By the time legislators had formulated a law and governments had approved it, the fashion might very well have changed. So, rapid changes in fashion meant that the laws had to be constantly revised. Moreover, passing a law could itself precipitate a change in fashion. If, for example, silver buttons were outlawed people might wear instead silver hooks, thereby obeying the law but allowing luxury to continue unabated. Paradoxically this meant that often a law's success in restricting a particular fashion ensured its overall failure to contain luxury. This is partly why laws directed against clothing increased so dramatically. They arose to a great extent simply from the generative nature of the interaction between the law and what it sought to contain.

The difficulties of legislating against fashion helps to explain the great increase in clothing laws per se. However, over the period of this study clothing laws which had been fairly evenly divided between men and women's clothes increasingly and persistently came to target women only. In his study of the sumptuary laws of Renaissance Florence, Ronald Rainey found, not only that the majority of Florentine laws were aimed primarily at women, but that even when such laws contained measures concerning men, they still appeared in the documents under the rubric *ornamenta*

[5] C. Breward, *The Culture of Fashion* (Manchester, 1995), explores the link between fashion and consumption and argues that dress is one of the most reliable indexes for charting the growth of consumer society. See also Finkelstein, *After a Fashion*, 89.

mulierum, and the official responsible for the laws' enforcement, though he had jurisdiction over both men and women, was known as the 'official on women'.[6] Diane Owen Hughes, too, in her comparison of the laws of Bologna, Siena, and Venice passed in a period from the thirteenth to the fifteenth centuries, found a marked change in the direction of the lawmakers' attention in favour of women. While the earlier legislation in these cities divides fairly evenly between laws directed to the control of wedding and funeral practices as well as clothing for men and women, by the fifteenth century laws concerning ceremony and men's clothing had declined significantly in relation to those against women's clothing, and this despite the fact that expenses involved in ceremonies and feasts had risen steadily over the period.[7] Whilst it is not clear precisely how the figures which support these claims are arrived at,[8] the comparisons of laws which I detailed in Chapter 2 support Owen Hughes's general conclusions. There is indeed no disputing that by the late fifteenth century the overwhelming majority of sumptuary laws were directed against women's clothing.

So how is this great increase in legislation against women to be explained? In Chapter 3 we saw how lawmakers made a frequent connection between excessive expense on women's clothing and the unstable balance of the economy, the rapid decline in marriages, and the fall in birth rates. These concerns alone explain much of the legislation against women's clothing, but some additional factors were also at work. Whilst it was an age of luxurious clothing for both men and women, the acceptance of such clothing for the former and its close regulation for the latter was partly due to the structure of society and its theoretical underpinnings. It is uncontroversial that to a great extent medieval and Renaissance Italy was a patriarchal society in which women were excluded from the public sphere. This exclusion was legal, political, economic, and social. Despite the existence of what Kent and Simons have termed 'an informal *sottogoverno*' by means of which wealthy and well-connected women could act as intercessors and gain access to male-dominated centres of power,[9] the operative adjective is still *sotto*. And, although it is certainly true that women in monarchical and despotic cities had more opportunities for formal access to political power

[6] 'Legislation in Florence'. See also id., 'Dressing Down the Dressed-Up: Reproving Feminine Attire in Renaissance Florence', in J. Monfasani and R. G. Musto (eds.), *Renaissance Society and Culture: Essays in Honor of Eugene F. Rice* (New York, 1991), 218.

[7] 'Sumptuary Law and Social Relations', 84.

[8] e.g. one could take the 'number of restrictions' to mean one entire law or the various *capitoli* of a particular law which would produce an entirely different number.

[9] F. W. Kent with P. Simons, 'Renaissance Patronage: An Introductory Essay', in eid. (eds.), *Patronage, Art and Society in Renaissance Italy* (Oxford, 1987), 7.

than women in republican regimes,[10] they too could not escape the ambiguities and problems inherent in these roles, roles which they filled in any case only in the absence of a suitable male.[11] Overall, the situation of women in Italy was one defined by philosophical texts dating back to Aristotle;[12] to theological texts produced by Tertullian, Aquinas, and others;[13] and to legal texts as old as the *Digest*.[14] However much the reality of woman might differ from the theories about her, it was the latter that decided her legal, political, and social position in society. And, indeed, the paradoxes and ambiguities that resulted from the conflict between the reality and the theory probably fostered an increasing insistence upon the latter. As a result, Italian women, at least those wealthy enough to be affected by sumptuary laws, occupied for the most part a private sphere circumscribed by the confines of their father's or husband's houses, or by convent walls. Wealthy women usually emerged from these private confines into the public arena only for such harmless activities as daily mass in their local parish church, or for feast days, and on ceremonial occasions such as weddings, christenings, and funerals. Whilst Livy had rather condescendingly explained rivalry between women in displaying their finery by the fact that 'they have no political offices, no priesthoods, no triumphs, no gifts, no spoils of war to give them prestige',[15] he certainly pinpointed a social situation that was still relevant many centuries later to Italian women.

Men, by contrast, gained public recognition from their civil, professional, and military roles, and their elaborate clothing was easily justified by appeal to these same public roles. Indeed cities could deal quite sternly with men who seemed not to be visibly upholding the honour due to these public

[10] See the argument put forward by N. Z. Davis, 'Women in Politics', in ead. (ed.), *Renaissance and Enlightenment Paradoxes: A History of Women in the West*, iii (Cambridge, Mass., and London, 1993), 169–70.

[11] For a recent discussion of the problems facing women in power see N. Tomas, 'Alfonsina Orsini de' Medici and the "Problem" of a Female Ruler in Early Sixteenth-Century Florence', *Renaissance Studies*, 14/1 (2000), 70–90. See also P. Stafford, 'More than a Man or Less than a Woman? Woman Rulers in Early Modern Europe', *Gender and History*, 7 (1995), 486–90.

[12] See e.g. *De generatione animalium*, 1. 2 (716^a13); 2. 3 (737^a 27 and 838^a27); *Physics*, 1. 9 (192^a22); and *Politics*, 1. 13 (1260^a II).

[13] Tertullian, *De cultu feminarum*, 1. 1; Aquinas, *Summa Theologica*, 1a 92, I.

[14] *Digest*, 50. 17. 2 which debars women from all public offices, and also 1. 9. 5 which justifies this exclusion on the basis of woman's *levitas, fragilitas, imbecillitas*, and *infirmitas*. For additional texts that were used to underpin the Renaissance attitudes to women see I. Maclean, *The Renaissance Notion of Woman: A Study in the Fortunes of Scholasticism and Medical Science in European Intellectual Life* (Cambridge, 1980).

[15] Livy, *Rome and the Mediterranean: Books XXXI–XLV of The History of Rome from its Foundation*, trans. H. Bettneson (Harmondsworth, 1976), XXXIV. 7, p. 150.

positions. In Venice, in October 1433, as mentioned earlier, the city's councillors were ordered by a sumptuary law not to wear clothes of a mournful hue while dispensing their duties, but rather to wear the scarlet robe suited to their prominent public position. Fine clothes were seen in a positive light if they redounded to the honour and glory of the state. That men's luxurious clothing could be justified on the grounds of their public roles is also confirmed by the few occasions on which women were given exemption from sumptuary regulations. In Venice, for example, the ladies of the doge's family were exempt from the sumptuary laws for as long as the doge was in office so that they too could reflect his political honour. Again, in 1459 Venetian ladies were twice given dispensation from the sumptuary laws for a period of one day in order to impress visiting foreigners to the city.[16]

This limited way in which women could participate in the political life of the city was highlighted in the preamble to a Florentine law of 1433 which declared that 'the ornaments of women which are worn in a city, if they are worn in moderation, add to the honour and splendour of the city'.[17] But moderation was the key word here. If women exceeded what were deemed the bounds of propriety and moderation, then the opposite effect was achieved. As this law continues: 'if these ornaments are excessive, they lead instead to the city's disgrace and infamy, and these are usually attributed to the negligence and impropriety of those citizens who preside over the city's government'. The legislators found themselves striving for a delicate balance between excess in ornamentation on the one hand and its lack on the other, both of which served to detract from the city's honour.

Though, as Finkelstein reminds us, 'the public body, whether it is female or male, is always mediated through vestimentary codes',[18] women, I would argue, relied far more than men on these vestimentary codes. Whilst men could justify their garments by reference to their public roles, these roles in themselves gave men a public voice. Women, on the occasions that they appeared in the public sphere, were still predominantly silent. Their clothes gave them a voice, limited though that voice might be. This fact was recognized as much by women as by men. For instance, both Alessandra Strozzi and Lucrezia Tornabuoni gave their sons little more information

[16] ASV, Maggior Consiglio, Reg. Regina, XXX June 1459, fo. 23, and Senato, Terra, Reg. IV 25 Oct. 1459, fo. 126.

[17] Rainey, 'Legislation in Florence', 432, July 1433, and for original Latin see ibid., app. 9, passage 'A'.

[18] *After a Fashion*, 49.

about possible prospective brides than a description of the clothes that they were wearing.[19] Similarly, and more predictably, the future wife of Galeazzo Maria Sforza was described by his brother Tristano in 1468 solely in terms of appearance and her apparent physical capacity for childbearing.[20]

The public milestones of a wealthy woman's life were marriage, the birth of her children, and, often, widowhood. The first two of these stages were marked by ceremonial and increasingly elaborate and expensive clothing that served to demarcate publicly her new status. Widowhood, too, was marked by clothing, but of a deliberately subdued nature. In a patriarchal society, these marital stages and their accompanying clothing were means of identity enhanced by finery.

Moreover a woman's public 'voice' on these and all other public occasions was always linked to the male household and lineage to which she belonged. In other words, though clothing might give her a limited voice, she was speaking on behalf of men, not on her own account.[21] The message wealthy men required their women to convey through their clothing was multi-layered. On the one hand, given women's transient membership of a lineage, her clothing enabled her to be visually incorporated first into that of her father, and then within that of her husband's lineage. Further, men needed to demonstrate the financial and social success of their family quickly and visibly. Expenditure on dress was an excellent means to display such success, for apparel is always in evidence and so provides an immediate indication of the pecuniary standing of its wearer, or, more pertinently, of its owner. As Veblen described it, there are three cardinal principles to be adhered to if dress is successfully to demonstrate the wealth of its owner: expensiveness, novelty, and ineptitude (aesthetics may play some part, but it is certainly not required).[22] Renaissance women's dress fulfilled all these criteria: the yards of fine fabric ornamented with quantities of precious stones and embroidery demonstrated expense; the constant changes in fashion fulfilled the criteria of novelty and so afforded prima facie evidence

[19] See Polidori Calamandrei, *Vesti delle donne fiorentine*, 116, and also Alessandra Macinghi Strozzi, *Selected Letters of Alessandra Strozzi*, trans. and ed. H. Gregory (Berkeley, 1997), 154, letter of 17 Aug. 1465 and Lucrezia Tornabuoni, *Lettere*, ed. P. Salvadori (Florence, 1993), letter of 28 Mar. 1467.

[20] L. Collison-Morley, *The Story of the Sforzas* (London, 1933), 99.

[21] Strocchia, *Death and Ritual*, 68–9 provides further evidence for this in relation to the funerary exemptions which Florentine men were quite happy to purchase for their spouses, but only occasionally for 'good mothers', and very rarely for sisters or unmarried daughters who as yet did nothing to enhance the lineage.

[22] 'The Economic Theory of Women's Dress', *Popular Science Monthly*, 46 (1894-5), 204.

that a garment had only been worn for a short time; and the long trains, wide sleeves, and the ludicrously high platform shoes, or *zoccoli*, so favoured by Venetian women, clearly demonstrated that their wearer was incapacitated for any gainful occupation. As Veblen summarizes it, elegant dress 'not only shows that the wearer is able to consume a relatively large value, but it argues at the same time that he consumes without producing. It is, then, the "insignia of leisure".'[23] Renaissance women could be viewed as the ceremonial consumers of the goods that their fathers or husbands produced. If this were indeed the case, then by legislating against women's clothing, city rulers were partly attempting also to reduce rivalries between men and keep their ambition in check.

Women were also the agents by which a man's lineage could be extended through marriage alliances, and continued through the birth of his children. In this context, what families needed to demonstrate above all was that the women in their households were chaste. If there were any question about a woman's chastity then dishonour would be brought upon her family. Letta Sassetti, who dared to have an illicit liaison with Giovanni Porcellini, was spared, by her early death in the plague of 1383, further subjection to sentiments such as those of her kinsman, Paolo: 'May the devil take her soul, for she has brought shame and dishonor to our family.'[24] As Owen Hughes succinctly describes the situation: 'The conduct of wives and daughters was not a private matter. Men supervised it closely precisely because a woman's private shame, which might make her a public woman, could destroy a man's public honor, forcing him to retire to the private sphere.'[25] With any stain on her reputation, it was difficult for a woman to be transferred to another man's house in marriage and, if she were already married, then her husband could not be assured of the legitimacy of his offspring and hence that his lineage had endured.[26] Chastity is, however, a difficult quality to prove. Once more, it was often clothing that was used to proclaim the honourable status of a woman. Not surprisingly, modesty in clothing is a constant theme in sumptuary law, as already seen in Chapter 4.

[23] *The Theory of the Leisure Class: An Economic Study of Institutions* (1899; London, 1924), 171.

[24] From the diary of Paolo Sassetti, ASF, *Carte Strozziane*, series II, vol. 4, fos. 67^r–68^v, as translated by G. A. Brucker, *The Society of Renaissance Florence: A Documentary Study* (New York, 1971), 42.

[25] 'Invisible Madonnas? The Italian Historiographical Tradition and the Women of Medieval Italy', in S. Mosher Stuard (ed.), *Women in Medieval History and Historiography* (Philadelphia, 1987), 50.

[26] The *Digest*, 23. 2. 43 also upheld the importance of chastity as a guarantee of patrilinearity.

Though immodesty in men's clothing was also regulated, the language with which such laws were expressed was never more than factual and legalistic. Morally reprehensible though it might be, a man's immodest clothing had no practical implications for the honour of the household from which he came.

However, not only did unchastity in women have implications for the households to which they belonged, but it had deeper sexual resonances which some found troubling for society as a whole. Women were not to forget that it was Eve who had tempted Adam, Eve who was responsible for Original Sin, Eve whose actions led ultimately to Christ's death on the cross in atonement for that Original Sin. Eve's sin, moreover, was one peculiarly linked to clothing. Clothing did not exist in the Garden of Eden until Adam and Eve found it necessary to hide their new-found sense of shame. In this reading, expensive clothing was not the symbol of a successful society but was merely an elaboration on that original clothing. It was women who were to blame not only for wearing such clothing but for continuing the sin of Eve by tempting men to buy more of it.[27] When it came to immodesty in women's clothing, sumptuary laws on a few remarkable occasions used language altogether of a different kind to that used for men. The preamble to a Florentine law of 1420, for instance, states:

> Considering that the ornament of modesty, which is the chief ornament of a woman, is removed by unbridled excess in apparel, and since the way in which one dresses indicates the nature of one's mind, the priors want therefore to curb superfluous expense and excess in apparel, as well as to contain the 'fertile subtleties' of women through corrective measures.[28]

A law of 1427 refers to the 'lasciviousness of the female sex',[29] a Paduan law of 1504 talks of 'the nature and condition of the female sex, full of vanity and cause of many ills',[30] and in September 1433 the leading magistrates of Florence described the newly elected officials on women's ornaments as desiring 'to restrain the barbarous and irrepressible bestiality of women who, not mindful of the weakness of their nature, forgetting that they are subject to their husbands, and transforming their perverse sense into a reprobate and diabolical nature, force their husbands with their honeyed poison to submit to them'.[31] Less hysterical echoings of the same sentiments can be found in Siena's law of 1426/7 and that of Perugia in 1547.[32]

[27] See also Owen Hughes, 'Regulating Women's Fashion', 144.

[28] Rainey, 'Legislation in Florence', 455 and 500 n. 66, 27 Apr. 1420.

[29] Ibid. 577.

[30] Bonardi, 'Lusso di altri tempi', 13.

[31] Rainey, 'Legislation in Florence', 479.

[32] Casanova, *Donna senese*, 82: 'Item considerando i grandi desordini si fanno per le donne

The justification for these laws was here unequivocally laid in women's laps. Men assume the role of passive victims to the active sexual preying of the women in their households. These laws clearly argue that woman's fallen nature disposed her towards unbridled excess in apparel. They argue for a restoration to men of an active role, that of paternalistic regulation which, as a matter of necessity, would save women, but more especially their husbands, their fathers, and the city from their ruinous and sinful tendencies.

The language in these few preambles is so vitriolic, and women are so clearly viewed in them as sexual predators, that their existence should be underlined. It should still be noted, however, that undiluted misogyny, with no other reason given for legislating, proves to be exceptional rather than usual and this despite the claim that 'Most fifteenth century preambles state explicitly that women are the ruin of men'.[33] Indeed, of the 300 or so laws examined for this study, only these six overtly misogynistic preambles were found. Moreover, not everyone blamed women for the vice of luxurious dress. For instance the Sienese friar Salimbeni not only blamed men as well as women for the sin of superfluity in clothing ('homines et mulieres peccant in superfluo ornatu'), but went further and saw men as ultimately responsible for encouraging vanity in women. He castigated men as the greedy sons and slaves of Lucifer ('filii superbi et servi Luciferi') who adorn their women not just for their own pleasure and vanity, but so that they might have pride in their property.[34] As we shall see in a moment, the greater regulation of women's clothing, and the language with which such regulation was expressed, provoked increasing debate about women's clothing, which in turn became a springboard for a discussion of attitudes to women in general.

Overall, the response of women to these laws is hard to gauge. Certainly before the fifteenth century there is very little evidence for women's reactions and even then it is only indirect evidence provided by male chroniclers or male legislators. From the mid-fifteenth century, however, there is a marked change in the records. From 1437 onwards there is a series of petitions written by women, or by men on women's behalf. Whether this

ne' vestiri et portamenti loro, la qual cosa è grande disfacimento degl' uomini'; and Zanelli, 'Leggi pistoiesi', 211–12: the Pistoians lament 'che la città di Pistoia è generalmente aggravata da somma povertà ed indigenza, et in quella essere cresciuto l'orgoglio et avaro appetito delle donne talchè i mariti loro come prodighi, lasciandosi superare da quelle, non riguardando a quello che possano o debbono, condiscendano ad infinite superflue spese, divertimenti et ornamenti . . . nei quali cercando uno superare l'altro si incorre in gravi disordini'.

33 Owen Hughes, 'Sumptuary Law and Social Relations', 84.

34 I am indebted to Dr Bernadette Paton for this quotation.

merely represents an improvement in the keeping of records, or whether it is indicative of an increased assertiveness by women, or is part of a more general movement questioning the rights of governments to legislate in this area, is difficult to say. It should be pointed out, though, that these petitions appeared when the dowry market was high and as women brought larger dowries to their marriages perhaps their confidence and a willingness to assert themselves increased concomitantly.[35]

The earliest evidence of women's response to sumptuary legislation comes from Sicily when under the royal regime of the Anjou. In 1272 Charles I of Anjou approved sumptuary statutes for Messina which concentrated on the luxury of the city's women. However, the following year, 1273, the citizens of Messina sent a petition to the king asking him to revoke the law because the women in their households had refused to renounce their customary clothing. The king obligingly did so.[36] Almost two centuries later, in the despotic city of Modena, there was a curious instance of protest. In this year the reformers of the city statutes confirmed the law restricting the lengths of trains on women's dresses of an earlier statute. But very soon they were forced to alter this law. In its original formulation it applied only to *popolano* women. However, it seems that these women protested so strongly at having been singled out in this manner that the legislators decided, not to revoke the law, but rather to apply it across the board to women of all classes.[37]

The only other instance found of reactions to a despotic law comes from Ferrara. In 1467 the *Giudici dei Savi* were inundated with requests for exemption from the sumptuary law of 1460 which forbade, amongst other things, silk and ermine in any garment. As a result, the *Savi* published a declaration which permitted women to wear borders of silk, of any colour, and of ermine at the neckline and around the slashings of sleeves. These borders were not to exceed the width of a large finger. Otherwise the *Savi* confirmed the rest of the prohibitions on gold, silver, and silk. But it seems that even this concession was not considered sufficient, for in the documents it is followed by a series of dispensations, in response to individual petitions, to many noble and wealthy women allowing them to wear dresses of silk.[38]

[35] For a convincing discussion of this issue in relation to Venetian women see S. Chojnacki, 'The Power of Love: Wives and Husbands in Late Medieval Venice', in M. Erler and M. Kowaleski (eds.), *Women and Power in the Middle Ages* (Athens, Ga., and London, 1988), 126–48.

[36] Del Giudice, 'Legge del 1290', 120–2.

[37] Campori, 'Del governo in Modena', p. clx.

[38] Frizzi, *Memorie di Ferrara*, iv. 41.

As Table 2.1 demonstrated, republican governments passed many more sumptuary laws than other types of government. Not only were women under these regimes more closely regulated than elsewhere, but it seems that they also felt less able to express dissatisfaction with the law than their counterparts in other cities. Of all the petitions and protests that I found, in fact, not one was directed to a republican government. The only occasions on which women attempted to gain exemption from communal provisions were when the nobility were temporarily in power in the commune, or when some influential member of royalty was present in the city, or when the law was a lay sumptuary prohibition passed by an ecclesiastic. Otherwise, women under republican governments had to resort to subtler means to prevent the law from curbing their lifestyle.

The earliest instance of women under a republican government taking advantage of the temporary presence of a noble is from Siena. In December 1291, the women of Siena sent a commission to Robert, the count of Arras, who had just arrived in the city as the new *podestà* for January. This commission begged Robert to ask the *Signoria* to lift the restrictions on crowns and garlands of silver and gold set with pearls and precious stones. Robert requested this repeatedly until he finally gained a very temporary reprieve for the women. The crowns and garlands that had been prohibited were once again allowed but only until the next calends of January. As this deliberation was passed on 13 December, the women had only a few days in which to wear their head ornaments.[39]

Appeals to the nobility were also made by Florentine women. In 1325 the Florentine government approved their most comprehensive set of sumptuary measures to date. However, later that year the *Signoria* of Florence was given over to Charles, duke of Calabria, so that he could organize the city's defences against Castruccio Castracani. During his stay he and his wife, Marie de Valois, maintained a lavish court thought to set a bad example to the Florentines. Giovanni Villani reports that in 1326 some Florentine women then petitioned the duchess of Calabria for permission to wear various types of false tresses for their hair which had been forbidden by an earlier communal sumptuary law. The duchess approached her husband and he acceded to her request.[40] The Florentine women also persuaded the duke to interfere in enforcement of the law. In November of the following year, 1327, several women and a man complained that they had

39 Mazzi, 'Leggi senesi', 137–8 and Casanova, *Donna senese*, 51–2.

40 Villani, *Cronica*, 10. 11: 'Come alle donne di Firenze fu renduto certo ornamento.' The text of this earlier law has not been located, see Rainey, 'Legislation in Florence', 69.

been fined unjustly by the relevant magistrate for wearing forbidden ornaments and because several of the women had refused to give the names of their husbands when requested to do so. The duke ordered the magistrate responsible to re-examine the charges and, if they were found to be condemned unjustly, to drop the charges and return the fines which had been paid. (Unfortunately, we do not know the outcome of this retrial.)

In 1452, again in Siena, one woman sought exemption from the sumptuary laws. In this year the Emperor Frederick III and his fiancée, Leonora of Portugal, stopped in Siena on their way to their coronation and marriage in Rome. Battista Petrucci, the daughter of a professor of rhetoric, gave a Latin recitation in the couple's honour which so impressed them that they asked her to select a reward. She chose release for the city's women from all sumptuary regulations.[41] While the city's government had, reluctantly, to cede to this request or risk causing offence, it was granted for one day only.[42]

When women under republican government had no sympathetic aristocrat to appeal to, they had to resort to other methods to circumscribe the law's effects. A *novella* by Franco Sacchetti, based on a true story, vividly depicts women's ingenuity at working within the law to circumscribe it (it also underlines the difficulties of legislating against fashion). In this story, the newly appointed official for enforcement of sumptuary laws in Florence is brought before the government and reprimanded for his failure to secure any prosecutions. In his defence the official explains:

> when, obeying the orders that you gave me, I went out to seek the forbidden ornaments of your women, they met me with arguments the like of which are not to be found in any book of laws; and some of these I will repeat to you. There comes a woman with the peak of her hood fringed out and twisted around her head. My notary says, 'Tell me your name, for you have a peak with fringes'. The good woman takes this peak, which is fastened round her head with a pin, and holding it in her hand, she declares that it is a wreath. Then going further, he finds one wearing many buttons in front of her dress, and he says to her, 'You are not allowed to wear those buttons.' But she answers, 'Yes, Messer, but I may, for these are not buttons but studs, and if you do not believe me, look, they have no loops, and moreover there are no buttonholes.' Then the notary goes to another who is wearing ermine and says, 'Now what can she say to this?' And he prepares to write down her name. But the woman answers, 'Do not write me down, for this is not ermine, it is the fur of *lat-*

[41] Owen Hughes, 'Sumptuary Law and Social Relations', 86, citing Orlando Malavolti, *Historia . . . de' Fatti e Guerie de' Sanesi, cosi esterne come civili* (Venice, 1599), pt. 3, b, 38b.

[42] Casanova, *Donna senese*, 52, citing Tommasi Giugurta, *Seconda deca delle Storie di Siena*, pt. I, col. 737, ASS, *Biblioteca*, MS n. 22.

tizzi.' Says the notary, 'What is this *lattizzo*?' and the woman replies, 'It is an animal.'[43]

This ingenious use of the law was also demonstrated by the women of the Romagna. When Cardinal Latino, as papal legate, outlawed trains in 1279 and instructed women to veil themselves modestly, the women raised an outcry but then appeared in veils of the finest fabric worked in gold, appearing both more luxurious and seductive than previously.[44] Giovanni Villani provides another example, this time by Florentine women. In 1330, with the duke of Calabria gone, and hence no sympathetic noble to hear the complaints of the city's women, the Florentine *Signoria* passed severe sumptuary measures. As they were now not allowed to wear certain types of dresses, the women of the city compensated by purchasing even more of the permitted garments. According to Villani, the women sent to Flanders and Brabant at great expense for ornaments which they could no longer acquire at home. Though Villani recognized that this quite clearly broke the spirit of the laws, he hoped that by obeying the letter of the law women's field for indulgence would at least be narrowed.[45]

Sometimes, however, women expressed their displeasure more blatantly. In 1366 the Perugians passed a law dealing sternly with any women who refused to allow officials to examine their clothing, or who fled from officials, or refused to give their names to notaries.[46] This law does not seem to have had much success for in 1402 the Perugians felt constrained to repeat it, imposing a double fine on any woman obstructing officials. Similarly in Verona in 1441 a law was passed imposing fines on recalcitrant women and their husbands in cases where they abused or even assaulted enforcement officials.[47] And, of course, there were women who simply disobeyed the law. It seems that many women were wealthy enough to treat sumptuary laws as a form of luxury tax: in other words, break the law, face prosecution, pay the fine, and then carry on as before. In Venice the term 'pagar le pompe', or 'to pay the luxury fine', became such a common expression that it is found in dialectical dictionaries.[48]

43 Sacchetti, *Trecentonovelle*, no. 137. According to some dictionaries a *lattizzo* referred to a weasel-like animal similar to ermine but with milky white fur, whence its name.

44 Salimbene de Adam, *Cronica*, i. 246, ll. 10–29.

45 Villani, *Cronica*, 10. 153.

46 Fabretti, 'Statuti suntuari', 170: 'De recusantibus vel fugientibus vel celantibus se a dicto offitiali et eius familia nomen suum.'

47 Newett, 'Laws of Venice', 255. This was sanctioned by the Venetian Senate with a fine of 25 ducats allocated for injurious words and 50 ducats for injurious deeds.

48 See G. Boerio, *Dizionario del dialetto veneziano* (Venice, 1867), 520.

The final category of protest is that directed towards ecclesiastical prohibitions. Apart from the incident under Cardinal Latino already mentioned, all the reactions to ecclesiastical laws that we know of took the form of petitions and occurred in the mid-fifteenth century. The earliest are those of the Venetian noblewomen in 1437 which have already been discussed in the previous chapter, as has the group petition led by Andrea Gritti in 1471. What is interesting in all these petitions is that the women put forward the positive functions of luxury that were all recognized, not just by the Renaissance papacy, but by the legislators themselves and that were the main impediments to formulating an effective body of legislation. The various reasons put forward by Cristina Corner and the other women in 1437 all stressed one thing: honour. As outlined above, city governments recognized the role luxury played in demonstrating the power and prestige of the city. Luxury could confer honour, and this 'noble' function was also recognized by the Renaissance papacy. More significantly, the reasons put forward by Andrea Gritti indicate that women felt that luxurious clothing helped to attract rather than deter a husband and helped to keep him faithful once married.

It was the sumptuary law of Cardinal Bessarion, papal legate to Bologna, which provoked the most eloquent and lengthy response from a woman. On 24 May 1453, Bessarion promulgated a law which had been directly inspired by Timoteo Maffei who had given a series of Lenten sermons in Bologna that year.[49] In comparison with other laws passed in Italy this law was relatively lenient and, again unlike other laws, seemed more concerned with maintaining class structures by means of clothing. Despite opening with a sermon-like preamble deploring luxury itself, Bessarion devoted the bulk of his law to specifying which clothes were permitted to each class of women in the city. He gave precedence to families of knights, placing them above nobles in his sumptuary scheme. Next came women in the households of nobles, doctors, notaries, bankers, clothiers, and members of the silk guild. The next category was women in the households of workers such as carpenters, shoemakers, and builders. Finally came restrictions for peasant women. All the restrictions for each category of women in this law were comparatively mild but the penalty for infraction was excommunication.

Despite its comparative leniency, this law provoked a strong reaction from one of Bologna's most prominent noblewomen, the beautiful Nicolosa Sanuti, wife of Nicolò Sanuti, count of the Porretta, and lover of

[49] The text of Bessarion's edict is in Sacco (ed.), *Statuti di Bologna*, i. 363–8.

Sante Bentivoglio, the ruler of Bologna.[50] Shortly after the law was promulgated, Nicolosa sent a treatise to Bessarion demanding that his law be repealed. This treatise entitled 'Nicolosa Sanuti, Bolognese matron, to the most Reverend Father in Christ, the Bolognese papal legate, that ornaments be restored to women'[51] was, unlike the law itself, quite remarkable.[52] Sanuti's treatise was the lengthiest appeal against sumptuary law made during the period, and it was the only one to question the ideological underpinnings of sumptuary law. From this discussion, Sanuti used her treatise as a springboard to discuss the merits of women, and the merits of noblewomen in particular. What sumptuary law signified about society's attitude to women was not lost on Nicolosa Sanuti.

Since Sanuti was wealthy and beautiful, it might seem at first that her treatise was motivated by reasons of personal vanity, as in the case of the Venetian Cristina Corner. In the series of *novelle* by Sabadino degli Arienti, *Le Porretane*, set in the Sanuti's spa town of Porretta, Nicolosa is described as 'a most beautiful woman, more moral, charming, and graceful than any other Bolognese woman you could find today'.[53] Her love of finery is also confirmed in literary and notarial sources. In *Le Porretane* she is described wearing a gown of purple silk and a rose-coloured cloak lined with the finest ermine.[54] In 1475 we know that she possessed a necklace worked in gold,

50 For the details of Nicolosa's marriage, see Comelli, 'Di Nicolò Sanuti', 109 and for her relationship with Sante 101–61.

51 'Nicolosae Sanutae matronia bononiensis ad Reverendissimum in Christo patrem dominum d. Legatum bononiensum ut mulieribus ornamentur restituantur.' There are several extant MSS of Sanuti's treatise: Rome, Biblioteca Apostolica Vaticana, Fondo Ottob. lat., MS 1196, fos. 89^{r}–96^{r}; Biblioteca Apostolica Vaticana, Vat. lat. MS 6850, fos. 98^{r}–111^{v}; Paris, Bibliothèque Nationale, lat. 11313, misc. XV, fos. 53^{r}–64^{v}; Edinburgh, University Library, Edinburgh 119 (antea D 6.5.16) fos. 141^{v}–150^{r}; London, British Library, Sloane 2377; British Library, Harleian 2508, fos. 1^{r}–7^{r}; British Library, Harleian 3830, fos. 101^{r}–115^{v}; Vicenza, Biblioteca Civica Bertoliana, Fondo Principale, MS 7.1.83, fos. 1–22 (cited by Frati as Cod. G. 7.1.2; Miscellanee B. 205 and previously catalogued as 6.8.22). The text of the MS in Vicenza was transcribed by L. Frati as an appendix to the 2nd edn. of his book, *La vita privata di Bologna*. Although there are several errors in his transcription, for ease it is the text that has been used as the basis for this chapter.

52 I have discussed Sanuti's treatise more fully and issues of its authorship in ' "Heralds of a Well-Instructed Mind": Nicolosa Sanuti's Defence of Women and their Clothes', *Renaissance Studies*, 13/3 (1999), 255–82. Appended to this article is a translation of the treatise itself. For a fascinating discussion of Sanuti's treatise and the debate it engendered, and its probable influence on three orations produced in Viterbo in the 1460s see G. Lombardi, *Galiane in rivolta: Una polemica umanistica sugli ornamenti femminili nella Viterbo del Quattrocento*, 2 vols. (Rome, 1998), vol. i, pp. cxvi–cxxxviii. See also the discussion of Sanuti in J. Bridgeman, ' "Pagare le pompe": Why Quattrocento Sumptuary Laws Did Not Work', in L. Panizza (ed.), *Women in Italian Renaissance Culture and Society* (Oxford, 2000), 209–21.

53 *Le Porretane*, ed. G. Gambarin (Bari, 1914), *novella* 21, p. 109.

54 Ibid.

stones, rubies, and diamonds valued at more than 300 ducats,[55] and an inventory compiled after her death in 1505 registers a coffer containing 'twenty items of fine woollen clothing for the back of madonna Nicolosa'.[56] However, as Sanuti's husband was a doctor of law, a captain, and a senator, she was subject only to the mild restrictions of the first category of Bessarion's law, hardly enough, surely, to provoke such a lengthy and general protest. It was not, however, the specific limitations that seem to have bothered her. Rather she took issue with the very idea of depriving women of their ornaments, in particular, women of status, breeding, and virtue, such as herself. So, unlike the Venetian women, who all appealed for exemption on their own behalf, and unlike Battista Petrucci, who requested that all Sienese women be exempted, Sanuti's treatise was addressed to the cardinal on behalf of all the worthy women of the city and so is quite class-specific. Punning on *bononia*, she says: 'I come to your most Gracious Lordship with this petition in the name of every good/Bolognese woman.'[57] In a kind of rallying cry to other women she declares: 'who would be so torpid or idle, what woman so unlearned, what female so pusillanimous, that she would decline to speak in favour of the restoration, defence, and preservation of her ornaments?'[58]

The reasons advanced by Sanuti for rescinding Bessarion's law echo those heard earlier from other women, but they go further and are more forcefully and lengthily expressed. Her first argument is based (as was that of the Venetians before her), on customary usage: 'what could be more iniquitous or unjust than to infringe the perfectly equitable laws of ancient times and to discredit customs which have long been approved?'[59] Here it might seem that Sanuti is stretching the facts somewhat, for sumptuary legislation had been passed regularly in Bologna from at least 1233. However, the sumptuary law that pre-dated Bessarion's, that of 1398, had expressly exempted from all clothing restrictions the wives and daughters of knights and of doctors of medicine and of civil and canon law. For over half a cen-

[55] L. Frati, 'Lettere amorose di Galeazzo Marescotti e di Sante Bentivoglio', *Giornale storico della letteratura italiana*, 26 (1895), 319.

[56] Archivio Notarile di Bologna, among the deeds drawn up by Virgilio Gambalunga between 1501 and 1505 cited in Frati, 'Lettere amorose', 319.

[57] Sanuti, 'Treatise', 252: 'omnium matronarum bononiensium nomine ad te, humanissime domine, petitura adveni'.

[58] Ibid.: 'Quis item esset tam iners, aut desidiosus? Auae mulier tam indocta? Auae foemina tam parvi animi ut pro ornamentis restituendis, defendendis, conservandis causam non susciperit?'

[59] Ibid. 253: 'Verum quid est etiam injustius quam eo nos privare quod a maioribus est permissum diutissima consuetudine approbatum et sancitum lege atque confirmatum?'

tury, in other words, women in the upper ranks of Bolognese society had enjoyed complete freedom in dress. Bessarion's law, however slightly it might affect what they could wear, was the first direct restriction these women had experienced and was seen, if Sanuti's reaction is at all representative, as a serious slight. As she says, 'women of the first rank [should] differ from the less noble'.

Honour is the second, and more interesting ground of Sanuti's argument. Following classical models, she argues that finery is emblematic of honour. Then, adopting a Christian stance, she argues that, as striving for honour should be placed before a love of money, those in favour of the law on the grounds that too much money is wasted on finery are guilty of the sin of avarice. The law's repeal, therefore, would place an obstacle in the way of their sin: 'Take care', she says 'that the avarice of others should not weigh more with you than the greatness and distinction of the whole city.'[60] Though she feels that the maintenance of personal honour is important, it is to the honour of the city that she appeals here:

> [Since] almost all the peoples who rank below ours in fame and dignity employ these insignia of virtue, will it not be dishonourable and unjust for the Bolognese to lack these ornaments when they are the ones who most deserve them, while others are adorned, decorated, and ennobled by their use? If we excel others in virtue, ought we not at least to equal, even if we do not surpass them, in that attire which is the proof of virtue?[61]

This argument depends on classical notions of virtue, especially political virtue, rather than on Christian notions of spiritual virtue. Vanity was a vice for the ancients also, of course, but for them display appropriate to greatness was not vanity but proper pride.[62] It is especially in the classical tradition of political virtue, in which virtue contributes to the greatness of the city, that Sanuti's argument operates. Though women were denied an active role in the political life of the city, Sanuti suggests that by wearing finery women too can participate in, and acquire, political virtue (albeit passively).

60 Ibid. 262: 'Providete, nec plus apud vos valeat aliquorum avaritia, quam totius civitatis amplitudo et gloria.'

61 Ibid. 259: 'omnes fere populi quibus hic noster clarior est et prestantior, his virtutum utuntur insignibus nonne indignum erit et iniquum Bononienses qui haec maxime meruere, his ornamentis carere, quibus caeteri ornantur, decorantur, illustrantur? Si virtute caeteris praestamus, non hoc cultu, qui virtutis argumentum est, alios si non superare, at saltem aequare debebimus?'

62 See *Nichomachean Ethics*, $1107^{b}23$. The case is different in the Christian tradition where office is concerned. The glory of some secular or religious office might be displayed outwardly, but here it is display unrelated to the personal virtue of the office bearer.

Even if luxurious display advertises and reflects the 'fame and dignity' of the city, Sanuti has yet to establish that by this fact alone women are as entitled as men to lay claim to political virtue, and that they contribute as much as men to the honour of the city. Accordingly, the bulk of the treatise is devoted to an enumeration of the virtues of women, and here again Sanuti departs from her predecessors. In standard humanistic style, she begins by referring to a formidable array of classical examples to support her view that men would not have advanced very far if women were less than she claims. According to Sanuti's reading of antiquity, women were responsible for revealing the use of letters to men, discovering the cultivation of the soil, the use of wool, spinning, weaving, numbers, the olive tree, chariots of war, and the cultivation and harvesting of grain. Moreover, women were chaste, loyal, faithful, liberal, modest, constant, and well versed in letters.[63] Sanuti then moves on to contemporary examples, all of whom 'excelled the women of old, I shall not say just in modesty, prudence, fortitude, constancy, liberality, piety, and learning, but also in integrity and holiness'.[64]

When it comes to discussing virtue in women it is not Christian humility, as personified by Mary, that Sanuti stresses, but rather the striving for glory, as exemplified by the ancients and revived by humanist scholars. As she says: 'I could not believe that anyone could be so humble as not to be affected, at least in some degree, by the love of glory.'[65] Though Sanuti lacked humanist training herself, she recognized that the accomplishment most worthy of praise amongst her male contemporaries and most likely to lead to glory was learning and she places all men in women's debt in this regard. The first gift from women to men that she describes is letters, and when she moves on to contemporary examples of virtuous women, the first quality she stresses is learning. The argument of the treatise is that women not only brought letters to men, but have been actively involved with learning ever since. The reward that Sanuti seeks for such glorious achievement in learning is, of course, exterior adornment. As one of her opening rhetorical questions asks: 'Does not everyone know that gold and such adornments and all decoration are testimonies to virtue and heralds of a well-instructed mind?'[66]

[63] Sanuti, 'Treatise', 253–6.

[64] Ibid. 256: 'quae omnes non dicam pudicitia, prudentia, fortitudine, constantia, liberalitate, pietate et doctrina; sed eiam integritate ac sanctitate priscas excellerint'.

[65] Ibid. 252: 'Amens quidem et insanus is erit qui ea contempserit, quae ullo modo ad eius gloriam pertinere videbuntur. Nec ullum unquam extitisse tantae humilitatis crediderim qui aliqua saltem ex parte amore gloriae non sit affectus.'

[66] Ibid.: 'Et aurum et hujusmodi insignia, ac ornatus quem latebat virtutis testimonia et bene institutiae mentis eam praeconia?'

Sanuti's treatise clearly sets out to demonstrate that, in the past, 'if women did not surpass men, they at least showed themselves their equals',[67] and that therefore 'it is just to let what is permitted men be deemed proper for their wives, and that it [is] unjust for women to be denied the rights accorded to their husbands'.[68] In the conclusion to her work, however, Sanuti reveals no desire to share in men's active roles. She is not asking that the status quo be disrupted but rather that women be granted proper recognition, honour, and glory for the virtues and accomplishments that they have in abundance. With a nice twist to the injunctions of the *Digest* she declares:

> Let virtue attain her reward. Let not the rights of the humbler sex be snatched away by the injustice of the more powerful. State offices are not allowed to women, nor do they strive for priesthoods, triumphs, and the spoils of war, for these are the customary prizes of men. But ornaments and decoration, the tokens of our virtues—these, while the power is left us, we shall not allow to be stolen from us. Amen.[69]

Sanuti's treatise, eloquent and impassioned though it was, failed to achieve its stated purpose. Cardinal Bessarion did not reply to Nicolosa and he personally ensured that his sumptuary law was enforced. A few months after its promulgation, Sante Bentivoglio married Ginevra Sforza. The women in Ginevra's bridal cortège, however, wore dresses that violated the sumptuary prohibitions. Bessarion informed the canons of the church of San Petronio that they themselves would incur excommunication if they allowed Sante's marriage to take place there. Consequently the bridal party was turned away when it arrived at the doors of the church, and was forced to head for the church of San Giacomo. The Augustinians of this church agreed to marry the couple but they were then excommunicated by Bessarion. Sante, however, pleaded with the Cardinal who subsequently absolved the friars.[70]

[67] Ibid. 254: 'inveniemus eas si non superasse viros, at saltem aequasse'.

[68] Ibid. 262: 'Quod mihi nihil aliud sentire voluisse videtur nisi ut aequum ostenderet, quod viris permittebatur uxoribus non disconvenire, et injuste his mulieres privari quae maritis concedebantur.'

[69] Ibid.: 'Sinite virtutem sua proemia consequi. Permittite benemerentes suis insignibus uti. Quod inferioribus permittitur, dignioribus injuria non eripiatur. Magistratus mulieribus non conceduntur: sacerdotia, triumphi, bellica spolia et ipsae non contendunt, quia hujuscemodi dona virorum esse solent. Ornatus autem et cultus, quia notrarum sunt insignia virtutum a nobis eripi quoad poterimus non patiemur. Amen.' Here Nicolosa is obviously drawing from the Roman *Digest*, 50. 17. 2: 'Women are excluded from all civil and public offices; and thus they may not be judges, nor magistrates, nor advocates; nor may they intervene on another's behalf, nor act as agents.'

[70] Ady, *Bentivoglio of Bologna*, 50.

A little disappointingly, Sanuti herself did not have the moral fibre to hold her ground. Despairing at the loss of her lover on the eve of his marriage to Ginevra, Sanuti wrote a melodramatic letter to Sante declaring herself on the brink of suicide. Now she admitted that 'clothes, gold, pearls, and charming ornaments with other precious and expensive things were of such great delight to me for no other reason if not because they made me more magnificent and noble and rendered me more gracious in your eyes'.[71] She then declared that the opinions expressed in her treatise 'I now confess were false, the arguments of no value and that all that I brought to our defence and help was sophistry and against sustained and defended truth. Alas! In this very moment I recognize my great stupidity, my beastliness, my haughtiness'.[72] Sanuti did not speak again on the subject.

However, Sanuti's treatise was distributed in humanist circles and a minor debate on the regulation of women's clothing ensued. Matteo Bosso was the first to enter the ring. He was a pupil of Timoteo Maffei whose sermons had inspired Bessarion's law in the first place. His reply took the form of another treatise,[73] dry in tone, uninspired, and relying principally on assertions of virtuous and devout character as proof that Bessarion and Maffei were correct in their positions. His treatise, however, led to a far more lively and charming response from the great Guarino da Verona, then more than 80 years old. In a letter addressed to his friend, Sante Bentivoglio, Guarino criticized the opinions of Maffei, Bessarion, and Bosso, accusing them of trying 'to design a way for the human race easier in word than in deed'.[74] His letter then continues:

On this subject, since I was born of a woman, and she most virtuous, and see so many beloved children, so many dear pledges born of my wife by God's will, and for this I rejoice in my God, I should seem undutiful and ungrateful if to the best of my

[71] Frati, 'Lettere amorose', 334: 'I vestimenti, l'oro, le perle e gli ornamenti leggiadri co l'altre preciose e care cose non per altra cagione m'erano di gran dilecto se non perche facendomi più magnifica e prestante più mi rendessono graziosa a gli occhi vostri.'

[72] Ibid. 335: 'ora confesso ch'erano false, gli argumenti di niun valore e quello tutto ch'io recava in difesa et aiuto di noi era sufisticamente e contro il vero sostenuto e difeso. Oymé! Che pur testè ricognosco la mia gran sciocchezza, la mia bestialità, la mia baldanza'.

[73] 'Matthaei Bossi Veronensis canonici regularis ne feminis varia ornamentorum luxuries indigne ad irreligiose restituatur ad d. B[essarionem] cardinalem Tusculanum Bononie legatum', in *Opera varia* (Bologna, 1627), 156–65.

[74] R. Sabbadini (ed.), 'Epistolario di Guarino Veronese', *Miscellanea di storia veneta*, 3rd ser., 14 (Venice, 1919), letter 982, ll. 57–61, p. 528: 'Dura sane provincia praesertim contra eos suscipienda, qui vitae severitate et censorio quodam supercilio innituntur et quasi Catones saevi magis quam severi humano generi viam verbo potius quam re facilem struere conantur.' I wish to acknowledge the assistance of Janet Kovesi Watt in the translation of Guarino's correspondence.

poor wit I should suffer the cause of women to be neglected and them to be condemned with their case unheard, and not to embrace the heritage of women to the best of my ability.[75]

Guarino, however, did not take quite the same line as Sanuti. Where Sanuti had tried to argue that women deserved fine clothing as a reward for their inner virtue, he argued that clothing was not to be given any specific meaning. Instead he criticized these men for judging people from their external appearance rather than valuing their internal virtues:

It is not then the wearing of fine clothes, not indulgence in gold and pearls, not permission for adornment which engenders wantonness, as these Catos insist, since our disciplined rule of life, our disposition of uprightness, our eagerness for honours, our fear of shame, together with our constancy in a chaste way of life, are the things which have instructed and shaped our character.[76]

This letter must have had wider circulation than its addressee alone, for Matteo Bosso responded directly to it.[77] Yet again, however, Bosso did not have any real argument other than to praise the saintliness of Timoteo Maffei and to criticize anyone who tried to oppose such a devout man 'and his holy pulpit'.[78] Other minor scholars entered the debate also, including Sanuti's own notary, Cesare Nappi, who wrote two poems on the subject.[79]

This debate was not just a local matter. It was indicative of the wider debate amongst humanists as to the proper place of women in society. Interestingly, though, only one other woman entered the fray, and then only several decades later in her private letters. In a letter entitled 'Curse against the ornamentation of women'[80] Laura Cereta put a different twist on

75 Ibid. ll. 105–13, p. 529: 'Qua in re cum e muliere natus sim et ea quidem honestissima et e muliere tot mihi dulcissimos filios, tot "pignora cara nipotes" auctore deo germinasse videam et proinde in deo meo glorier, impius sane ingratusque videar, si, quantum virium exiguo est in ingenio, desertam esse mulierum causam patiar easque indicta causa damnari nec pro posse mulierum patrocinium amplectur.'

76 Ibid. ll. 161–6, p. 531: 'Haud ergo vestimentorum usus, non auri aut unionum licentia, non expolitionis concessio libidinem ingenerat, ut isti Catones volunt, cum castigata vivendi norma, cum probitatis habitus, cum honorum aviditas, cum infamiae timor, cum castii moris assiduitas ingenium mentem instruxit exercuit conformavit.'

77 *Miscellanea di storia veneta*, 3rd. ser., 11 (Venice, 1916), letter 906, pp. 650–1.

78 Ibid. 650.

79 Biblioteca Universitaria, Bologna, Cesare Nappi, *Zibaldone*, cc. 267 and 270, in which he preserved a poem entitled 'Ipsa Bononia mater loquitur contra garrulam querimoniam a quibusdam filiabus eiusdem factam de ornatu correcto'. And to which he himself replied with a poem entitled 'Medusa nomine honestissimarum mulierum Bononiensium eiussororum respondet Bononiae ipsarum matri, quae conatur tueri provisionem ornatus mulierum'.

80 A. Rabil, *Laura Cereta: Quattrocento Humanist* (Binghamton, NY, 1981), 82–3, 12 Feb. 1487.

Guarino and Sanuti's positions. Unlike Sanuti, Cereta did not believe that clothing was the reward for virtue and the symbol of a woman's honour. Like Guarino she believed that honour and virtue need not be linked to external appearance. However, unlike Guarino she felt that this meant that luxurious clothing was not merely incidental but was, rather, positively detrimental to society's perception of women. 'Was it for this . . . that we were begotten?' she asks. 'We should seek the adornment of honor, not vulgar display, and we should pursue this life mindful of our mortality.'[81] Cereta, then, believes that women, insofar as they are concerned with elaborate clothing, are themselves partly to blame for society's attitude to them.

Perhaps if Sanuti had been more limited in her request she would have been more successful. Hers, in fact, was the only appeal that failed to gain even a temporary reprieve from sumptuary regulations. Though all these protests demonstrate that women did not always accept sumptuary laws passively, none of them, even the most sustained, managed to change the general commitment of governments to sumptuary regulation. Indeed it was not until the eighteenth century that sumptuary laws were finally abandoned as an integral part of governmental policy.

[81] Rabil, *Laura Cereta*, 82–3, 12 Feb. 1487 and cf. also 67, letter of 1 Jan. 1486.

7

Problems of Enforcement and the Failure of Sumptuary Law

Italian governments enacted over 300 sumptuary laws in a span of three centuries. Yet, at the end of this period expenditure on luxurious commodities was no more restrained and was, if anything, on the increase. Sumptuary legislation, then, clearly failed, a fact acknowledged by the legislators themselves in the preambles to successive laws.[1] The number of laws and their overall failure has led many to assume that governments could not have been committed to the enforcement of their laws, for if they had been, there would have been no need to enact new laws and revise old ones in such great number. Thus: 'Prosecutions faded and ceased with the law still shouting from the books.'[2] And: 'these ordinances, so frequent in the Middle Ages, remained dead letters'.[3] Again: 'Enforcement . . . may not have been the primary goal of legislators. . . . Sumptuary laws, like sex and gambling laws, proclaim our collective devotion to moral values by defining immoral behaviour as a crime. It need not follow as a consequence, however, that we will therefore change our habits and forgo our pleasures by enforcing these bans vigorously.'[4] And again: 'the general impression is that execution of such laws was impossible from the outset'.[5] What is surprising

[1] See e.g. Florence, Apr. 1384: provision authorizing priors and advisory colleges to review the pragmatica of 1377 and to alter, correct, or add to it so that observance of it might be strengthened and so that 'the cheating which takes place daily against the spirit of these laws might be eliminated' (Rainey, 'Legislation in Florence', 227 citing ASF, Provv. Reg. 73, fo. 20^{rv}); Siena 1412: 'non obstante che per gli ordini vecchi fusse assai pienamente proveduto, bene chome si vede non sieno observati' (Mazzi, 'Leggi senesi', 143 n. 1); Venice 1495: 'Tanto è moltiplicata l'innobedienza, e più presto disonesta forma che Pompe nelli nobili et Cittadini nostri circa el vestir et ornamenti delle donne sue poco curando le grandissime pene nelle lezze et sanctissimi ordini nostri' (ASV, Compilazioni leggi, Busta 305, Pompe-Magistrate Filza T, c. 319).

[2] Vincent, *Costume and Conduct*, 133.

[3] Simeoni (ed.), 'Statuto suntuario a Verona', 235.

[4] Brundage, 'Sumptuary Laws and Prostitution', 353.

[5] Denholm-Young and Kantorowicz, 'De Ornatu Mulierum', 334. See also Stefani, *Legge di Treviso*, 5: 'Rinnovate secondo le occorenze dei tempi, e, in generale, poco osservate e presto dimenticate'; A. Zanelli, 'Di alcune leggi suntuarie pistoiesi dal XIV al XVI secolo', *Archivio storico italiano*, 5th ser. 16 (1895), 206: 'Furono vani sforzi, che acuirono anche più l'innata

about all these assertions is that they have been made with little, if any, consultation of Italian judicial records. While much archival work remains to be done, there is a sufficient number of prosecutions so far known from several cities to enable us to query this view. Moreover, the minute detail provided in the laws for procedure of enforcement together with the strong protests from citizens subject to the law leads one to conclude that the legislative process was not a sterile exercise. The failure of the laws, indeed, lay more in what they sought to contain than in any deficiency of commitment. This chapter will examine the provisions made for enforcement of the law, the instances of prosecutions that have so far been discovered, and the possible reasons for the ultimate failure of sumptuary legislation.

I

One of the strongest factors in favour of a view that the legislators were committed to their laws is the great detail provided for the laws' execution. Italy is unique in early modern Europe for such detail in sumptuary laws, as can be seen if we contrast Italy with two other European countries also legislating against luxury: England (which had the least provisions for enforcement) and Switzerland (which made more effort than others). In England the sumptuary law of 1363 only threatened to confiscate offending garments with no indication as to how this was to be done or by whom. It was not until 1463, a century later, that a scale of fines was included in an English sumptuary law, graded according to social station, and JPs and mayors of the cities and boroughs were ordered to investigate any offences against the Act of Apparel. In 1510 the idea of paying half of the fine to an informer was adopted. In 1515 the ushers of the king and queen's chambers were empowered to seize apparel worn illegally at courts, and outside the court anyone could seize unlawful garments. Any resistance to such seizure was to be met by doubling the appropriate fine. In 1533 the right of seizure was abolished and instead clothing was to be forfeited and a single fine of ¾*d* per day was to be paid. Apart from one short-lived experiment in 1562 there was never any special administrative or legal machinery instituted in England to cope with the provisions of the Acts of Apparel.[6]

In Switzerland, before the Reformation, the administration of sumptuary and moral laws was entrusted to an ecclesiastical court called the

furberia delle donne per eludere le severe pragmatiche e costrinsero i legislatori a moltiplicare inutilmente le legge, spesso a corregerle e riconoscere che i freni troppo stretti erano stati praticamente oltre che inutili, dannosi.'

[6] Harte, 'State Control of Dress', 143.

Chor-Gericht which also dealt with marriages. After the Reformation these functions were separated and, while marriages were still left to the ecclesiastical tribunal, a new court was set up to administer sumptuary laws. Members of this court were chosen by the city council from men of mature age and good reputation. This body, known in the late seventeenth century as the 'Reformation-Chamber', functioned until the French Revolution. In addition, in each town a commission was appointed to carry out sumptuary and minor police regulations.[7]

What is surprising in Italian legislation, by contrast, is not just how much information is provided for enforcement of the law, but how early such details appear. All the Italian sumptuary laws of the thirteenth century, no matter how brief, have provisions for enforcement, and the methods specified are almost as various as they are numerous, which suggests that some thought went into their formulation. For instance the Reggian funeral law of 1242 imposed a fine of 100 *soldi* on those contravening the law and urged the *podestà* to hold diligent inquiries on the matter.[8] The Sienese law of 1249 entrusted enforcement to nine citizens, three per *terziere*.[9] The law of Bassano of 1259 provides the earliest example of the use of informers who had to be of 'bone fame' and who could receive half of the fine of 100 *soldi*.[10] The Perugian law of 1266 specified that the custodians of the law should be appointed secretly by the *capitano del popolo* and the *podestà*. In order successfully to prosecute someone for breaking the law, these custodians had to have one witness of good faith and opinions. Whoever was found guilty of breaking the law was to be fined and excommunicated. Half of the fine was to be given to the commune and the other half to those who had made the accusation. Finally, the *podestà* and the *capitano* were ordered not to alter any part of the statute under threat of a deduction of 50 lire from their salaries.[11] The 1267 law from San Gimignano specified not only that women were to be fined 100 *soldi* for breaking the clothing restrictions, but that husbands were to be held responsible for payment of the fine.[12] The Bolognese wedding law of 1276 decreed that public notification of a wedding had to be given to the relevant parish three days before the wedding with a list of all those invited.[13] The Pisan law of 1286 declared that any citizen was allowed to denounce his fellow citizens and, if he did so, secrecy was to be guaranteed and a reward of half of the fine was

7 Vincent, *Costume and Conduct*, 3–8.
8 Cerlini (ed.), *Consuetudini reggiani*, 36.
9 Casanova, *Donna senese*, 47.
10 Fasoli (ed.), 'Statuti di Bassano', 134.
11 Fabretti, 'Statuti suntuari', 156–8.
12 Davidsohn, 'Jagd, Spiel, Luxus', 325.
13 Frati, *Vita privata*, 49–50.

to be given to him.[14] In Florence in 1290 in the *Consulte e Pratiche*, reference is made to a law requiring all women to register their garments with the commune and have them marked with a special seal, the earliest reference to the so-called *vesti bollate*.[15] By 1300 we have at least one example of each of the many methods that over the following two centuries governments were to refine and elaborate or abandon and replace as they sought the most effective means for enforcement of their laws.

Perhaps the most important factor in effective sumptuary control was to ensure that all the relevant members of the population were aware that sumptuary laws were in force and what precisely they proscribed. Hence most Italian sumptuary laws provide instructions for publication of the law. In Reggio, for example, in 1277, a funeral law required that the various provisions be publicly cried out through the city and district (*burgo*) once a month.[16] In Siena the sumptuary law compiled between 1277 and 1282 required that the law be announced publicly every four months.[17] The wedding and funeral restrictions contained in the Florentine statute of 1322–5 were to be announced publicly by a *bannitor* on the staff of the *capitano del popolo* every two months during his term in office.[18] In the Modenese sumptuary law of 1327–36, the *podestà* was to have the law cried out within twenty days of assuming office.[19] The Venetian sumptuary law of 1334 specified that it was to be proclaimed every six months by criers on the Rialto and in the Piazza di San Marco.[20] In Milan in 1396 the *podestà* was to proclaim the sumptuary provisions concerning excessive meals on feast days on the day before the feast of Saint John.[21]

A few laws enlisted the help of the clergy in their promulgation. The provisions on ornaments contained in the Florentine statute of 1322–5 were to be proclaimed at least once a month by the relevant magistrate and the *capitano del popolo* and, in addition, priests were to read them in their parish churches and notify the *capitano* of any violations discovered among their congregations.[22] The funeral law of Faenza of 1410 also called upon the help of the clergy. Not only were the *podestà* and the officials employed during his time in office to have the law proclaimed through the city and its environs, but the chaplains were to announce it in every customary place of

[14] Simoneschi, *Ordinamenti pisani*, p. xii and F. Bonaini (ed.), *Statuti inediti della città di Pisa dal XII al XIV secolo*, 2 vols. (Florence, 1854–70), i. 434.

[15] Rainey, 'Legislation in Florence', 45 citing the Florentine *Consulte e Pratiche*.

[16] Cerlini (ed.), *Consuetudini reggiani*, 45–6.

[17] Mazzi, 'Leggi senesi', 134.

[18] Rainey, 'Legislation in Florence', 65.

[19] Campori, 'Del governo in Modena', 480.

[20] Newett, 'Laws of Venice', 265.

[21] Verga, 'Leggi milanesi', 39.

[22] Rainey, 'Legislation in Florence', 65.

prayer, and the chapters of the ecclesiastical schools were to instruct and remind everyone of the contents of the statute.[23] This law also ensured that spice and drug dealers (*speciari* [*sic.*]) knew which items of weights of wax and candles were forbidden. So that they could not claim ignorance of the law, they were to place the sumptuary statute among their own guild statutes and have a member of their guild announce the law in the assembly at least every six months 'in a loud voice so that everyone can understand it well'.[24]

Knowledge of the laws, however, was not enough to encourage their observance. All of the Italian sumptuary laws imposed some kind of penalty. The most common was a monetary fine. Many sumptuary laws have one standard fine for contravention of any part of the law. Sometimes, however, the law would specify a particular monetary fine for each section of the law. The sumptuary law from Aquila of 1375, for instance, had a series of rubrics covering restrictions for marriages, funerals, gift-giving, and women's clothing, and each rubric had a different penalty as various as 1 gold florin; 1 ounce of gold; 1 or 2 gold *augustalii*; 1, 2 or 3 *tarenorii*; and 5, 10, or 20 *sollorii*.[25] Likewise the Milanese funeral law approved by Bergamo in 1343 had several chapters with separate monetary fines varying from 100 *soldi terziolorum*, 10 or 100 *lire terziolorum*, to 100 *soldi Imperialium*.[26]

The different fines imposed in another Bergamese law, this time from 1491, are instructive as to the way in which legislators regarded different offences. For example, the restrictions concerning women's clothing and ornaments each had a fine of 100 imperial lire. The one rubric concerned with men's clothing, however, imposed a fine of only 50 imperial lire. But when it came to the question of modesty in clothing, the situation was reversed. Women wearing garments deemed to be immodest were fined only 50 imperial lire while men in a similar situation were to be fined 6 gold ducats.[27]

The graded fines in the law from the Kingdom of Sicily of 1290 are also indicative of the preoccupations of the legislators. This royal law had different fines graded, not according to the type of restriction, but rather according to the social status of those breaking the law. Counts were to pay 50 lire, *banderese* were to pay 30 lire, barons and knights 15 lire, and valets, shield bearers, and others were to pay only 8 lire.[28] Concern to maintain class distinctions and to discourage ambitious aristocrats seems to have

[23] Rossini (ed.), *Statuta Faventiae*, 348–9.
[24] Ibid.
[25] Piacentino, 'Statuti in Abruzzo', 73.
[26] Pinetti, 'Limitazione del lusso', 55–7.
[27] Ibid. 58–63.
[28] Del Giudice, 'Legge del 1290', 8.

been greater here than that of distinguishing the severity of any particular offence against sobriety.

Very often, however, it was felt that a monetary fine was not sufficient by itself to discourage excessive attachment to luxury. One of the most frequent additional penalties was that of excommunication, a penalty already dealt with at some length.[29] In other cases, where the law was concerned with clothing and ornaments, in addition to a fine, the forbidden items were to be forfeited and given up to the enforcement officials.[30] Still other clothing laws, while targeted primarily at women, held the male members of the household responsible for payment of the fine and this was usually to be deducted from the dowry. San Gimignano (1267), Perugia (1318), Lucca (1337), and Bergamo (1491) provide just a few examples of a practice that was common.[31] In Venice not only were husbands and fathers held to be responsible for the conduct of their wives and daughters, but they were occasionally called upon to contribute to the treasury in the form of an extra loan, the luxury of their women being taken as proof of their ability to pay more than others.[32] Clearly it was hoped that the men of a household would help the government in the policing of the law by holding the women of the household in check.

Men were dealt with more severely in a Venetian law of 1443. If any patrician or member of his family was found breaking the law, then he was to be excluded from the *Maggior Consiglio* and all other offices for five years.[33] Likewise, a Perugian law of 1445 decreed that tailors making the forbidden items of women's clothing were to be fined 500 *lire di denarii* and they and the husbands of the women who had broken the law were forbidden for three years to take part in any public office and, if their names had already been *insaccati* or *imborsiati*, they were to be removed from the electoral bags within three days.[34] In Venice in 1459 and again in 1465, attempts were made to restrict the excessive feasts of the notorious *compagnie delle Calze*. Any man breaking these feasting restrictions was, if noble, to be fined 2 ducats for each offence and excluded from all councils and offices for two

[29] See Ch. 5 above.

[30] See e.g. Gubbio in 1371 (Mazzatinti, 'Leggi suntuarie eugubine', 289): 'in amissione rerum predictarum prohibitarum'; and Brescia in 1477 (Cassa, *Funerali*, 70–1).

[31] See e.g. San Gimignano 1267 (Davidsohn, 'Jagd, Spiel, Luxus', 325); Perugia 1318 (Fabretti, 'Statuti suntuari', 167); Lucca 1337 (Bongi (ed.), *Bandi lucchesi*, 47–8); Bergamo 1491 (Pinetti, 'Limitazione del lusso', 58 ff.); Newett, 'Laws of Venice', 257; ASV, Senato, Terra, Reg. I, p. 91; Fabretti, 'Statuti suntuari', 189.

[32] ASV, Senato, Terra, Reg. IV, fo. 133, 14 Jan. 1459, also Newett, 'Laws of Venice', 273.

[33] Rainey, 'Legislation in Florence', 167, item 26.

[34] Cassa, *Funerali*, 70–1.

years. If plebeian, he was to be refused access to the Piazza di San Marco and the Rialto for two years.[35] Similar punishments were imposed upon men in a Florentine law of 1356 and a Brescian law of 1477. In the former, any husband who refused to pay the fine for any sumptuary law violations committed by his wife was to be considered ineligible to hold communal office.[36] In the latter, not only were men to be fined 100 ducats and to forfeit any garment which broke the clothing restrictions on the use of gold and silver cloth, but their tax estimate was to be doubled and they were to be deprived of any Brescian political office or benefice for five years.[37] Again in Brescia, in 1499, anyone found to be in contravention of the law who was holding an office at the time had to leave his position immediately.[38]

Corporal punishment was rarely adopted and the only cases of it are directed at people without much status in society such as prostitutes, madams, and male and female servants. In Lucca in 1337 the law decreed that if a servant girl broke the clothing restrictions and did not pay her fine within ten days then she was to be whipped through the streets. The same penalty applied to any woman who lived by herself, had no husband, kept prostitutes, or was held to be one, excepting widows and other women deemed to be living honestly. In order to impose such a punishment upon a woman, her dishonest nature had to be proved to be public knowledge by four men of good status and reputation.[39] In Florence in 1356 female servants breaking the clothing restrictions were to be fined 50 lire. However, if such a servant failed to pay within fifteen days she was to be arrested, taken to the *Stinche*, stripped naked, and then led through the city streets being flogged along the way until she arrived at the market place where she was to be flogged again before being released.[40] In Savona in 1452 a law was passed forbidding male and female servants the use of ornaments of gold, silver, or pearls; clothes of silk or with trains; and shoes of soft leather. If a servant was found to have broken this law then, in the first instance, his or her master was responsible for payment of the fine, but if the master failed to pay up then the hapless servant was to be flogged twenty-five times.[41] In Genoa in 1488 any male servant breaking the sumptuary law was to be placed in the stocks with a paper mitre on his head.[42]

[35] Ibid. 90.
[36] Bongi (ed.), *Bandi lucchesi*, 53–4.
[37] Rainey, 'Legislation in Florence', 154.
[38] Cassa, *Funerali*, 90.
[39] Bongi (ed.), *Bandi lucchesi*, 53–4.
[40] Rainey, 'Legislation in Florence', 154.
[41] Pandiani, 'Vita privata genovese', 157.
[42] Belgrano, 'Vita privata dei genovesi' (1866), 221: 'debba esser messo [*sic.*] alla cattena con una mitra di pappero in testa'. This law also specified that female slaves breaking the law 'debbano avere patte 25 in mezzo di Banchi'.

That corporal punishment was applied only in such cases is not really surprising. By publicly flogging or humiliating such helpless and politically impotent members of society, a government could proclaim its commitment to sumptuary control and possibly instil a sense of fear in others, while not risking the disaffection of more powerful members of society. The only other instance in which corporal punishment was specified as a penalty for people other than servants and prostitutes was in a Florentine law of 1325. In this men and women were forbidden to wear the clothing of the opposite sex. If found doing so, such men and women were to be flogged through the city beginning at the law courts and finishing where the violation had occurred.[43] Perhaps such a penalty was justified in this instance on the grounds that such a citizen had demonstrated a moral perversity or a desire to deceive that deprived him or her of the right to more humane treatment, and that he or she was therefore to be considered on a par with servants and prostitutes.

Only one city, Venice, used the threat of imprisonment as a penalty for breaking the sumptuary laws and the singularity of this should be emphasized given the rarity of imprisonment as a punitive rather than custodial measure in early modern Europe as a whole. In June 1334, a Venetian sumptuary law decreed that any offender would be imprisoned until he paid the fine imposed.[44] In 1430 any shoemaker making a shoe with platforms higher than half of a *quarta* was to be fined 25 lire and imprisoned for three months.[45] In 1443, in a law bearing resemblance to the Florentine law of 1325 cited above, any man found wearing a woman's dress or other unsuitable garment ('habito desconveniente') was liable to lose the garment, pay a fine of 100 lire and go to prison for six months.[46]

A more lenient and possibly moralistic method of punishment, encountered in none of the other laws examined, was specified in the sumptuary law from Imola of 1334. Here we are told in the usual fashion that the fine for breaking the sumptuary law was to be paid by the man responsible for the woman from her dowry. If, however, she proved insolvent, then the woman was to be imprisoned in any place for religious women.[47]

Nearly all the sumptuary laws that contain a penalty of money specify

[43] Rainey, 'Legislation in Florence', 55.

[44] Newett, 'Laws of Venice', 265.

[45] ASV, Maggior Consiglio, Reg. Ursa, XXIX, 2 Mar. 1430; also Newett, 'Laws of Venice', 274.

[46] ASV, Senato, Terra, Reg. I, fo. 105, also Newett, 'Laws of Venice', 266.

[47] Gaddoni (ed.), *Statuti di Imola*, 225: 'si vero ipsam non habuerit unde solvat, tunc debeat mulierum talem facere carcerari apud aliquem locum religiosarum mulierum'.

how that money was to be distributed. Occasionally the entire fine was to be given over whole. For instance the 1375 law of Aquila specified that any fine was to be paid to the city's treasurer (*camerario*) with no further instruction as to what he was to do with it.[48] Likewise the Brescian funeral law of 1277 decreed that the *podestà* should be subject to a 50 lire fine if he failed to perform his duty with regard to enforcing the law and that this fine should be given over to the bailiff (*massaro*).[49]

Other laws used part of the fine as a means to encourage enforcement. Most common in this respect was the payment of a portion of the fine, usually half, to whoever had denounced those breaking the law. The Bolognese law of 1289 and the Lucchese law of 1308 both specify that, while half of the fine was to be given over to the Commune, whoever had accused the offender should be given the other half.[50] Similar specifications are to be found in the Florentine laws of 1299 and 1322–5,[51] and the Venetian laws of 1334 and 1336.[52] Perhaps most tempting of all was the offer in a Venetian law of 1465, directed at the *compagnie delle Calze*, which allowed that if an informer was a slave then he or she was to be set free.[53] The Perugian law of 1342 encouraged the *podestà* and the *capitano del popolo* to punish offenders by specifying that they should be given 12 *denarii* for every *lira* of any fine collected.[54] A Brescian funeral law of 1473 appointed five *sindaci* to make inquiries about offenders and denounce them to the *podestà*. Of the fines collected, three-quarters of each was to go to the community of Brescia and the other quarter to the *sindaci*. However, if anyone made an accusation against someone who was then successfully prosecuted, this accuser could have the quarter of the fine normally reserved for the *sindaci* if they had failed to make their own inquiries concerning the case, thereby encouraging vigilance by the population as well as by the *sindaci*.[55]

In the Faenzan funeral law of 1410, distribution of the fine was used to encourage officials to keep a check upon one another. Any fines received by the Commune were to be entered in an official book of the Commune stating how much had been received, from whom, and for what particular offence. Officials could collect 4 *soldi* from every lira received and 2 *soldi* were to be reserved for the *podestà*. But, if any official was found to have defrauded the Commune in any matter, he was to be punished with a fine of

48 Piacentino, 'Statuti in Abruzzo', 72.

49 Cassa, *Funerali*, 38.

50 Frati, *Vita privata*, 269 and G. Tommasi, 'Sommario della storia di Lucca dall'anno MIV all'anno MDCC', *Archivio storico italiano*, 10 (1847), 90.

51 Rainey, 'Legislation in Florence', 46 and 56.

52 ASV, Senato, Delib. Miste, Regs. 1333–4, fo. 69 and Regs. 1335–8, fo. 71.

53 ASV, Senato, Terra, Reg. V, fo. 149.

54 Fabretti, 'Statuti suntuari', 167.

55 Cassa, *Funerali*, 40.

25 lire and removed from office. Of this fine, half was to go to the Commune and the other half to whoever had revealed the fraudulent activities.[56]

The Florentine law of 1356 encouraged prompt payment of fines and discouraged prolonged court proceedings by reducing fines under certain circumstances. If those charged with violating the law confessed to the charges brought against them, the prescribed fine was to be cut in half. If those sentenced made their payment within ten days, the fine was also cut in half. But if the fine was not paid within ten days then an additional penalty of one quarter more had to be paid and the person who had posted bond *(fideiussor)*, or any relative mentioned in the ordinance as being responsible for a woman's fine, would be compelled to pay the fine.[57]

By use of other laws, attempts were made to put the fines to more constructive, long-term use. In Perugia in 1460 the law decreed that one quarter of the fine was to be used to repair the palace of the *Signoria* or that of the *podestà*, or to buy more vestments (*paramenti*) for the chapel of the Priors.[58] In Brescia in 1499, a severe law against feasts was passed with a hefty fine of 100 ducats imposed upon offenders. One third of this fine was to go towards the building of the city's *palazzo*.[59] The Florentine sumptuary statute of 1322–5 decreed that all the money collected from the fines was to be used for the construction of the new walls around the city.[60] One law, that of Gubbio in 1469, determined that the fine should be put to a charitable use. Although one quarter of the fine was to go to the official of the Commune, the remaining three-quarters were to be given to the *Monte de la Pietà*, which gave money to various charities.[61]

II

Who was to be responsible for enforcing these laws and how were they to set about their daunting and unpopular task? On this matter too the sumptuary laws give ample instruction, and what soon becomes apparent is that governments spent much time in establishing what they felt to be the best means for enforcement of their laws. Every Italian city that enacted sumptuary laws ensured that there was at least one government official responsible for enforcing them. Nor was it just a simple matter of delegation that enabled governments to feel that the matter had been dealt with. If sumptuary violations continued to occur, then discussions would ensue and a

[56] Rossini (ed.), *Statuta Faventiae*, 351.
[57] Rainey, 'Legislation in Florence', 167.
[58] Fabretti, 'Statuti suntuari', 192.
[59] Cassa, *Funerali*, 89–90.
[60] Rainey, 'Legislation in Florence', 64.
[61] Mazzatinti, 'Leggi suntuarie eugubine', 294.

new combination of officials would be appointed, or different qualifications established, or increased judiciary powers given to officials. Given the lengths to which some governments went in their efforts to hit upon just the right combination, it is impossible to maintain that governments did not really intend that their numerous laws be enforced.

The majority of Italian cities that concerned themselves with sumptuary matters employed a variety of different officials to enforce their laws but rarely attempted to institute a permanent magistracy. Very often the task was assigned to existing officials. In Lucca, for example, in the fifteenth century, the office known as the *fondaco* was given the additional task of sumptuary enforcement.[62] In Venice, in 1299, the *Avogadori di Comun* were to see to the penal procedure while the *Signori di notte* were to collect the fines.[63] The officer most frequently chosen by cities, however, was the *podestà*. One of the earliest instructions to a *podestà* is contained in Reggio's funeral law of 1277. In this the *podestà* for the time of his office was to send a member of his official household and one of his notaries to every funeral. If anything was seen to be in contravention of the law then the notary was to write down the name of every guilty person. Then the official was to demand the penalty specified in the law. If the *podestà* was at all negligent in making inquiries or punishing offenders then he himself was to be punished with a deduction of 25 lire from his salary.[64]

Similarly in Siena, in 1292, the *podestà* was to appoint one of his foreign notaries to deal with, among other duties, funeral and clothing regulations. In the case of a funeral, this notary was to go to the deceased's house and to the vigil to check that all was in order and to write down any contraventions. To ensure that women were not breaking the clothing laws, this notary was to go through the district of Siena and to churches on feast days. If he found any guilty woman he was to write down her name and that of her husband or father, and then give her three days within which to present her defence. If her defence was not considered legitimate, the *podestà* was to proceed with a condemnation against her. If the notary was at all lazy or negligent in carrying our these duties, the *Sindaco* was to fine him 10 lire. If the *podestà* failed to proceed with any condemnation, the treasurer and the four directors of the *Biccherna* were to withhold from his salary a sum of 25 *lire di denarii*.[65]

[62] Bongi (ed.), *Bandi lucchesi*, 312.

[63] Bistort, 'Magistrato alle pompe', 45.

[64] Cerlini (ed.), *Consuetudini reggiani*, 47.

[65] *R. Archivio di stato in Siena. Il costituto del comune di Siena volgarizzato nel MCCCIX–MCCCX*, 2 vols. (Siena, 1903), vol. i, distinzione 1, cap. CLIX, pp. 147–8.

A Bolognese law of 1289 specified the three means by which a *podestà* or his notary were to establish whether the law had been broken:

the *podestà* and his notary can inquire for themselves and through rumour [*per famam*], by seeing [*per aspectam*], through proof [*per probationes*], indictment, and presumption, and whichever other means are considered to be best, personally sending notaries both publicly and secretly to obsequies for the dead, to wedding festivities, to the ceremonies for nuns and priests and to festivities, to interdict the crowns and clothes of the women, and the notary is to bring back those contravening to be punished by the *podestà* under the aforesaid penalties.[66]

Similar additional duties laid down for the *podestà* are to be found, among many others, in Padua (1277),[67] Bologna (1289),[68] Bassano (1295),[69] Lucca (1308),[70] Parma (1316–25),[71] Perugia (1318),[72] Modena (1327–36),[73] Bergamo (1343),[74] and Milan (1396).[75] Nor were the Reggian and Sienese laws cited alone in making provision for a negligent *podestà*. Nearly always it was specified that an official not performing his duties satisfactorily was either to have a sum deducted from his salary or was to be fined an additional sum. Nor was any attempt at fraud to be tolerated as a law from Imola clearly states: the *podestà* must be 'diligent and efficacious, he must not feign or pretend to make inquiries'.[76]

In their efforts to achieve the most effective enforcement body, a few cities instituted a special magistracy to deal with luxury offences. As early as 1286 in Bologna there is reference to a magistracy to control sumptuary matters.[77] Again in Bologna, in 1294, there is a group known as the 'notaries of vice'.[78] In Cremona in 1300 a provision refers to 'the officials on ornaments'.[79] In Siena during the 1320s, a special official called the *donnaio* supervised enforcement and, in the following century, in 1472, the Sienese instituted a body known as the *Tre segreti sopra le vesti*.[80] But it was Venice and Florence which were to become most involved in the idea of establishing a permanent

66 Frati, *Vita privata*, 270.
67 Bonardi, 'Lusso di altri tempi', 9.
68 Frati, *Vita privata*, 267–74.
69 Fasoli, 'Statuti di Bassano', 328–9.
70 Tommasi, 'Della storia di Lucca', 90.
71 Ronchini (ed.), *Statuta communis parmae ab anno MCCCXVI ad MCCCXXV*, p. xvii.
72 Fabretti, 'Statuti suntuari', 165.
73 Campori, 'Del governo in Modena', 480.
74 Pinetti, 'Limitazione del lusso', 57.
75 Verga, 'Leggi milanesi', 24 and 39.
76 Gaddoni (ed.), *Statuti di Imola*, 225.
77 O. Mazzoni Toselli, *Racconti storici estratti dall'archivio criminale di Bologna*, 3 vols. (Bologna, 1866–70), 537 ff.
78 Frati, *Vita privata*, 249.
79 L. Astegiano (ed.), *Codice diplomatico cremonese, 715–1334*, 2 vols. (*Historiae patriae monumenta*, 2nd ser., 21–2; Augusta Taurinorum, 1895), ii. 140.
80 W. M. Bowsky, *A Medieval Italian Commune: Siena under the Nine, 1287–1355* (Los Angeles, 1981), 81–2.

sumptuary magistracy, although they were both to encounter considerable difficulties in doing so. A brief look at the efforts of both these cities is quite instructive as to the kinds of problems facing governments bent on sumptuary enforcement.

In the case of Venice, the first attempt at a sumptuary magistracy was in May 1334. In this year the *Maggior Consiglio* instituted a council of five *Savii* with seemingly unlimited power to deal with and administer cases 'expensarum inordinatarum'.[81] But these five wise men were a short-lived creation for just a month later, in June, a sumptuary law was approved which entrusted execution of its ordinances to the *Officiali del Levante*.[82] In 1360 a sumptuary law gave responsibility for execution to the *Avogadori di Comun* and then in 1389 the Senate included the *Officiali del Cataver*, the *Provveditori di Comun*, the *Signori di notte*, the *Capi-Sestiere* and all other officials concerned with contraband goods together with the *Avogadori* in this task.[83]

It was not until 1476 that the Venetians made another attempt at creating a stable magistracy. On 17 November of this year the *Maggior Consiglio* nominated three nobles on whom would rest the task of seeing scrupulously to the execution of the sumptuary provisions. They were to receive denunciations, arrange the trials, and apply fines. Any appeal against their sentences by the accused was to be made to the doge and his councillors. The appointment of these three nobles was to be renewed every two years.[84] Just seven years later, in 1483, it appears that this 'stable magistracy' had already fallen into disuse, for a decree of 27 January on the excesses of banquets entrusted execution of the law to the five *Savii di Rialto*.[85] But that the magistracy continued to exist in some limited form is indicated by the fact that, sixteen years later, on 29 November 1499, a decree issued by the Senate formally abolished the magistracy of the three *Savii* and once more gave the task of enforcement to the *Avogadori*.[86] From this date there is a rather confusing series of orders and commissions in which the fate of the three *Savii* is not at all clear.[87] However, on 8 February 1514, a truly stable magistracy was created called the *Magistrato alle pompe*. This consisted of three nobles with the title of *Provveditori* whose office was renewable every two years with an obligation not to abandon their position until a successor had been

81 Bistort, 'Magistrato alle pompe', 45 and ASV, Maggior Consiglio, Spiritus (copy), C. 162t.

82 Bistort, 'Magistrato alle pompe', 45–6.

83 Ibid. 46.

84 Ibid. 48–9.

85 Ibid. 49.

86 ASV, Senato, Terra, Reg. XIII, c. 103t.

87 Bistort, 'Magistrato alle pompe', 50–1.

elected. This body was purely executive as the legislative function resided exclusively with the Senate.[88]

Similar difficulties were encountered in Florence. In 1330 an official was appointed to search for violators and impose penalties who came to be known as the *ufficiale delle donne* (the Official on Women). In an effort to ensure impartiality it was specified that this official be a foreign notary who must not have come from any town within 60 miles of Florence nor from the same town as the *podestà*, *capitano del popolo*, or the Executor of the Ordinances of Justice. He was to be supplied with a notary and six assistants (also foreigners) as his official *familia*. He was appointed for a six-month term, paid a salary of 80 *lire di fiorini piccioli* per month, and had to pay his staff a salary from his remuneration.[89]

Nearly a century later, in 1420, the Official on Women was allowed to be a citizen of Florence or a foreigner,[90] but in 1427 the situation was changed once more with the establishment of a magistracy whose members were called the *Officiales super ornamentis mulierum*. Now it was specified that the officials in this body had to be not only Florentine citizens but also *popolani* and Guelfs. These officers were to be responsible for revising the laws as well as for enforcing them. They were to have a staff of a superintendent and as many messengers as they needed, although they were not to appoint their own notary, and they were to have a salary paid by the commune.[91]

In 1433 the Florentines added new clauses to the provision electing the *Officiales super ornamentis mulierum* in an effort to ensure impartiality. While they were still to be citizens, *popolani*, and Guelf, now it was also specified that they were to be at least 35 years old and that five of them were to be members of the seven major guilds and one a member of one of the fourteen minor guilds. The Priors, advisory college members, the captain of the Guelf party, the *Otto di Guardia*, and the six officials of the Merchant Court were all ineligible for this office as were any of their relatives or members of their *consorteria*. In addition, no more than one official was allowed from any one family or *consorteria*. Anyone elected to the position was forbidden to accept election to any other communal office whether in or outside Florence. The only exception to this rule was if an official was elected to one of the three major offices of the commune during his term of office. Then he was allowed to resign. Otherwise the only way for him to leave his position was to petition the *Signoria* for permission to do so, receive approval from at least

[88] Bistort, 'Magistrato alle pompe', 53–4.
[89] Rainey, 'Legislation in Florence', 295–6.
[90] Ibid. 455–6.
[91] Ibid. 456–7.

thirty-two members of the *Signoria* and its advisory colleges, and pay a fee of 10 gold florins.[92]

Despite these new guidelines, in 1439 the *Signori di notte* assumed responsibility for enforcement.[93] A decade later the *Conservatori delle Leggi* were given the task.[94] In March 1467 the Council of 100 elected five men as the *Officiales super ornamentis*. Just three weeks later, however, there was a need to elect four new officials as four of the others had resigned. While the provision announcing the newly elected officials does not explain why the others had resigned, there are indications that the major motive was a financial one. This provision notes that 'since there is need to have servants and secret informers and to make expenditures which arise from such matters, and lest on account of these things such responsibilities be postponed or neglected', expenses for these salaries, for books, parchment, and so on were now to be paid to the officials on top of their normal salary of 5 florins per month. This provision also allowed the officials to hold more than one communal office at the same time (but only if it was within Florence), and to accept the salaries of both offices.[95] Once more, however, these measures were insufficient to guarantee permanency, and in 1472 the *Conservatori delle Leggi* became responsible for enforcement and kept this task into the sixteenth century.[96]

Clearly, the position of sumptuary official was not a pleasant, popular, or indeed easy one. We already saw in Chapter 6 examples of legislators in Perugia (1366 and 1402) and in Verona (1441) dealing sternly with men and women who obstructed enforcement of clothing laws. These laws are not isolated examples. The Pisan law of 1350 declared that anyone who gave a false name when interrogated by enforcement officials was to be fined 55 *lire di denarii*.[97]

In Venice in 1512, waiters and cooks serving at banquets were compelled, under threat of a fine and imprisonment, to lead enforcement officers through the house so that they could perform their duty. If any person in the house

> should interfere with our officers, and forbid them to do their duty, or should molest them in any way by making use of injurious epithets, or throwing bread or oranges at their heads, as certain presumptuous persons have done, or should be guilty of any insolent act, it will be the duty of the waiters to leave the house immediately, and not to serve nor to be present at the banquet, under the aforesaid penalty, and nevertheless they shall have their salary as if they had served.[98]

[92] Ibid. 458–9.
[93] Ibid. 459.
[94] Ibid. 459–60.
[95] Ibid. 462–3.
[96] Ibid. 464.
[97] Simoneschi, *Ordinamenti pisani*, 31.
[98] ASV, Senato, Terra, Reg. XVIII, fo. 11.

A lengthy chapter in the Florentine law of 1384 makes it clear not only that those breaking the law would often resort to subterfuge to escape conviction, but also that they could rely on a network of friends and relatives to assist them. In this, penalties were prescribed for those refusing to give names to officials, or giving false ones. It gave officials the authority to impose fines on those who lied or concealed the truth when testifying about their sumptuary charges in the courts. Those presenting any impediment whatsoever to officials in discharging their duties were subject to a fine determined by the official according to the nature of the case. In addition, fines were to be imposed on those who allowed into their homes anyone who had been charged with a sumptuary violation or who had fled from enforcement officials. Anyone allowing such a fugitive into his home and refusing to reveal the fugitive's name was to be fined between 10 lire and 50 lire. If the enforcement official then discovered the offender's name, the latter was to be fined both for the violation itself and for withholding his name.[99] This law also imposed fines on any householder who refused to allow officials into his house to see whether wedding or funeral laws were being violated.[100]

Such unpopularity among the city's inhabitants must have made the job of sumptuary official isolating and demoralizing. Not only are the frequent fines for negligent officials referred to earlier an indication of the fear-induced lethargy that could be felt by officials, but another law from Genoa in 1483 suggests that officials were not immune to corruption for it imposed fines upon those who corrupted magistrates 'with money or by other means'.[101] Certainly, if enforcement of sumptuary laws was to succeed, officials had to rely on information gleaned from a network of secret informers, such as servants, cooks, waiters, and gravediggers, for their job represented an intrusion into an aspect of the private lives of Italian citizens which they prized above many others. In sumptuary, as in other offences, procedure by secret denunciation was most frequently relied upon. These secret informers could be officially delegated, as in thirteenth-century Padua,[102] or simply be any man off the street so long as he was of good repute, as in thirteenth-century Bassano[103] or fourteenth-century Lucca.[104] In Siena in 1343, a sumptuary law specified exactly how many of

99 Rainey, 'Legislation in Florence', 281 nn. 131–3 citing ASF, Statuti, 34, fo. 15^{r-v}.

100 Ibid. 282 n. 136 citing ASF, Statuti, 34, fo. 16^{v}.

101 Belgrano, 'Vita privata dei genovesi' (1866), 221.

102 Bonardi, 'Lusso di altri tempi', 9.

103 Fasoli (ed.), 'Statuti di Bassano', 328–9.

104 Tommasi, 'Storia di Lucca', 91, funeral law of 1308.

what type of informer were required before an official could press charges: 'and sufficient proof is considered to be two witnesses of truth or one witness of truth with two of rumour, or five of rumour or five of trust'.[105] More simple was the requirement of the Perugian law of 1266 that the custodians of the law were to have one witness of 'good faith and opinions' before they could accuse anyone.[106]

At least four cities hoped to encourage accusations by providing a special box in which secret accusations could be placed. In the sumptuary decree of Viterbo of 1449 provision was made for a chest to be placed in the church of S. Angelo. This chest, locked with three keys, was to be opened every fifteen days by the *Magnifici Signori Priori* and any denunciations placed within had to cite two witnesses to the contravention of the law, as well as the name of the offender and the place where the offence had occurred.[107] The Perugians also erected such a box in the cathedral in 1460 so that the denouncer could ensure that his identity remained secret. This box, also locked with three keys, was to be opened every fifteen days by the *Priori delle Arti.* [108] A similar practice was adopted in Venice, although we do not know how early it began. Certainly when the *Magistrato alle pompe* was moved to the ducal palace in 1562, two *bocche* or 'mouths' were sculpted into the stone on the outside wall of the office to receive denunciations. These *bocche* may still be seen today, complete with inscriptions, one of which declares: 'Secret denunciations concerning every sort of luxury against any person whatsoever with rewards of 42 ducats per 100 according to the laws';[109] while the other announces it is for 'Secret denunciations against ministers of luxury with impunity, secrecy and benefices according to the laws'.[110] In Florence, secret accusations known as tamburations could be deposited in one of several *tamburo* boxes. There was one of these boxes in each palace of every communal office and, as in Perugia, there was also a box located in one of the columns inside the cathedral.[111]

Those involved in the performance of, or witnessing of, a ceremony were

[105] Casanova, *Donna senese*, 60: 'ad qua probanda sufficiant duo testes de veritate vel unus testis de veritate cum duobus de fama, vel quinque de fama vel quinque de credulitate'.

[106] Fabretti, 'Statuti suntuari', 156–67.

[107] Lombardi, *Galiane in rivolta*, vol. i, p. cclxxviii.

[108] Ibid. 192.

[109] 'Denontie secrete in materia d'ogni sorte di pompe contro cadauna persona con benefici de ducati 42 per cento giusto alle leggi.'

[110] 'Denontie secrete contro ministri dele pompe con l'impunità secreteza e benefitii giusto alle legi.'

[111] Rainey, 'Legislation in Florence', 423 n. 229, cites Crusca's dictionary s.v. *tamburo* for this information about a box in the cathedral.

often called upon to assist in denunciations. In a Lucchese wedding law of 1362, the notary witnessing any stage of a marriage ceremony was to look out for infractions of the law under pain of a 100 *soldi* fine,[112] as were any notaries in a similar position in a Perugian law of 1366.[113] A slight variation of this practice was to be found in the Perugian law on weddings of 1445 in which any notary falsely witnessing the sum of a dowry was subject to a fine.[114] In the Faenzan funeral law of 1410, if the deceased was old enough to be given a proper burial, then the chaplain of his or her parish church was to notify the *podestà* or his official in writing before the burial giving the forename and surname of the deceased, his status, and where he was to be buried and at what hour. Moreover, if anyone from a particular ecclesiastical school died, then the chapter of the school was to go himself or send sufficient men to the house of the deceased and then go to the church at the time of the burial. If anyone was seen to contravene the law, then the chapter was obliged to inform the *podestà* within three days.[115] The Florentines relied upon more lowly workers for information in a law of 1356. In this, cooks had to notify communal officials in advance of any nuptial banquet giving a list of the types and quantities of food that were to be prepared, the name and address of the groom, and the day on which the *nozze* were to be celebrated.[116] In the case of funerals, gravediggers were to submit to officials in writing the name and address of any deceased before the public announcement of his death could be made.[117]

Cooperation was often called for from the people subject to the law as well, although this was only necessary for sumptuary occasions which had a private component. For instance, notification of weddings or funerals very often had to be given a few days before the planned event so that officials could go and see that all was in order. A Bolognese wedding law of 1294 is fairly typical in requiring not only that the cooks present themselves to the 'notaries of vice', but also that 'No person of any status is to hold a wedding without first presenting officials with a list of the names of the guests, the chapel, and the district where it is to take place.'[118] In a law against excessive feasting in Perugia in 1366, it was specified that anyone entertaining more than six people at a feast had, under penalty of 25 *lire di denarii*, to send for an official or notary to check that all was in order.[119]

[112] Tommasi, 'Storia di Lucca', 102.

[113] Fabretti, 'Statuti suntuari', 169–70.

[114] Ibid. 191.

[115] Rossini (ed.), *Statuta Faventiae*, 350–2.

[116] Rainey, 'Legislation in Florence', 160.

[117] Ibid. 165.

[118] Frati, *Vita privata*, 249. See also Bassano, 1295 (Fasoli (ed.), 'Statuti di Bassano', 329), in which those having a wedding are to go before the *podestà* or his judge and his officials three days beforehand so that they can then ensure that someone is at the wedding to see that all is in order.

[119] Fabretti, 'Statuti suntuari', 171.

Sumptuary officials also depended upon the help of craftsmen involved in the luxury trade itself. This was because, in order to press charges against those breaking the laws on clothing and ornaments, sumptuary officials required a detailed knowledge of cloth types and the weights and possible components of metals that was usually beyond the scope of their training. In particular, craftsmen were called upon to assist in the practice of registering clothes and ornaments, the so-called *vesti bullati* or *vesti timbrati*. Legislators recognized that, if their laws were to be adhered to, men and women would often be involved in extra expenditure as they would no longer be allowed to wear their old costly clothes and so would have to have new clothes made. Consequently, many cities instituted the practice of registering clothes and ornaments that had been made before the laws came into force and marking them with a special seal. This enabled men and women to continue wearing these clothes, thereby getting good use out of them, and enabled enforcement officials to see at a glance whether garments had been made after the laws came into force and, if so, whether they broke the laws. This policy was attempted in Florence in 1290 and again in 1356,[120] Lucca in 1337,[121] Pistoia in 1360,[122] Gubbio in 1371,[123] Bologna in 1398,[124] and Perugia in 1445 and 1460.[125] The Florentine law of 1356 instructed that garlands and circlets had to be appraised to see whether they were within the proper limits and stamped with the commune's seal. They then had to be registered with the communal notary who had to note down the woman's name and that of her husband, her parish, and the estimate of the garland's value. For performing this service the notary was entitled to charge a fee of 2 *soldi*. Further, before a jewellery box could be given as a wedding gift, its contents had to be appraised and marked with a leaden seal bearing the lily of the commune and then registered by a notary. The officials of the *Saggio* were allowed to charge 12 *denarii* for appraisal. The Gubbian law of 1371 specified that a goldsmith be elected to the position of *bullandum* and that he could receive a salary of 12 *denarii* for each *bulla* that

[120] Rainey, 'Legislation in Florence', 45 refers to the *Consulte e Pratiche* in which there is mention of a discussion concerning a law requiring all Florentine women to register their garments with the commune and have them marked with a special seal. See also ibid. 150–4.

[121] Bongi (ed.), *Bandi lucchesi*, 48–9 in which head ornaments, belts, and decorated fabrics 'debbia quelli marchiare fare' within a month.

[122] Zanelli, 'Predicatori a Brescia', 208. Forbidden clothes that were registered could be worn for up to two years.

[123] Mazzatinti, 'Leggi suntuarie eugubine', 291. Prohibited clothes made before this provision came into effect could be worn so long as they were registered within fifteen days.

[124] Frati, *Vita privata*, 277.

[125] Fabretti, 'Statuti suntuari', 191 and 194.

he registered. If, however, he charged a greater sum than this, he was to be fined 20 *soldi*. The Perugian law of 1460 instructed that clothes made before the law came into force were to be registered within thirty days and that members of the relevant guilds were to help estimate their values.

Craftsmen could themselves become targets of the law for if they manufactured any items prohibited by law then they were very often subject to a fine. This applied most frequently to tailors,[126] but also to goldsmiths,[127] to cooks,[128] and, on one occasion, to shoemakers.[129] A law of Ferrara of 1447, stated in more general terms that a fine of 35 ducats of gold was to be paid by any 'notaries, tailors, goldsmiths and others that were complicit in the disobedience',[130] while a Venetian law of 1299 insisted not that tailors be fined but that they take an oath to obey the law.[131]

III

The evidence provided above should make it clear that Italian legislators grounded their sumptuary laws upon a thorough base of guidelines for enforcement and that sumptuary officials could, in theory at least, turn for assistance to a complex network of informants and advisers. That established, it remains to be seen to what extent the laws were enforced, and here we confront difficulties of documentation. In trying to locate sumptuary violations, as in so many other areas of Renaissance crime, the situation is complicated by the fact that responsibility for enforcement was tossed from one government office to another. This means that records of searches conducted and charges pressed are dispersed throughout numerous different official registers. While more research is clearly called for, the picture is not, however, as bleak as some historians seem to believe. Prosecutions and court proceedings are extant in at least eight cities: Florence, Perugia, Siena,

[126] Parma 1258–1266 (Ronchini (ed.), *Statuta communis parmae digesta anno MCCLV*, 406); Gubbio 1371 (Mazzatinti, 'Leggi suntuarie eugubine', 292); Florence 1377 (Rainey, 'Legislation in Florence', 222: tailors fined 100 lire for each violation); Faenza 1410 (Rossini (ed.), *Statuta Faventiae*, 349: no tailor to make mourning clothes against the statutes under penalty of 40 Bolognese *soldi*); Bergamo 1491 (Pinetti, 'Limitazione del lusso', 63).

[127] Florence 1318 and 1330 (Rainey, 'Legislation in Florence', 49 and 73): goldsmiths and other artisans were forbidden to make or sell ornaments forbidden by law.

[128] See Brescia 1499 (Cassa, *Funerali*, 89–90); and Genoa 1484 (Belgrano, 'Vita privata dei genovesi' (1866), 171) in which a fine of between 5 and 10 ducats was imposed upon cooks, servants, and others preparing or serving prohibited items.

[129] Venice 1330 (ASV, Maggior Consiglio, Reg. Ursa, XXIX and Newett, 'Laws of Venice', 274): no shoemaker to make any shoe higher than half a *quarta* under penalty of 25 lire and three months' prison.

[130] Frizzi, *Memorie di Ferrara*, iii. 502.

[131] Newett, 'Laws of Venice', 262.

Venice, Ferrara, Bologna, Lucca, and Viterbo. Of these, the archives of Florence, Siena, and Bologna are especially rewarding. A brief examination of all these records, while obviously not completely representative, gives the distinct impression that sumptuary prosecution was almost as much a feature of Renaissance life as was sumptuary legislation.

There are records of sumptuary prosecution nearly as early as there are of laws. In 1249 in Siena, in the records of the *Biccherna*, there are two entries of multiple prosecutions. In the first, 6 lire were charged to each of three men 'of the city', three men 'of the valley', and three men 'of Camollia'. These men were charged with various offences, all listed with no indication as to who had committed which offence, and among such items as blasphemy and gambling is that of their women having worn lengthy trains and head ornaments against the statutes. For the lesser fine of 25 *soldi* a further eight men were charged with offences which included having allowed their women the freedom of walking through the city, their young girls to wear dresses with trains, and having allowed certain of their women to wail in a loud voice in a funeral cortège and to linger mournfully over the deceased.[132]

For the rest of the thirteenth century only three other prosecutions are known, all in Perugia in 1277. In this year three women were charged with having violated the funerary regulations in a sumptuary law that instructed women to attend funerals with their heads covered and not with their hair in disarray as an ostentatious sign of grief. One Domina Richa, wife of Gigalius Abadenghe, was seen in the church of San Lorenzo with no veil and her hair dishevelled 'contra formam statuti'. She was charged and fined. Clara, wife of a member of the Tobaldurius family, was seen in the same condition at a burial in the church of Saint Peter. Although a defence was presented on her behalf, it was not considered legitimate, and she too was fined. Another Clara, wife of Galuci Ufredini, was seen at her husband's funeral in the church of San Lorenzo with her head uncovered and her hair in disarray and she too was fined after an unsuccessful attempt to defend her.[133] Other prosecutions for funeral violations have been found in only two other cities. In Florence in 1360, a gravedigger working for the church of San Jacopo was prosecuted by the *ufficiale delle donne* for failing to notify the appropriate official that he had buried a corpse.[134] And in

[132] Casanova, *Donna senese*, 48 n. citing ASS, Biccherna, reg. 16a, c. 52, Dec. 1249.

[133] ASP, Archivio Giudiz. Podestà 1277, Package no. 1, fasc. no. 6. I am indebted to Alexander Murray for giving me copies of his transcripts of these documents.

[134] Rainey, 'Legislation in Florence', 422 n. 227 citing ASF, Giudice 120, fo. 127^v, 26 Mar. 1360.

Bologna in 1365, of seventy-nine people prosecuted for various sumptuary offences, one was charged with the offence of excessive funerary pomp.[135]

Prosecutions for breaking the laws regulating betrothal and wedding ceremonies are also extant. In Siena in 1409 a secret accuser informed the appropriate officials that Battista di Bernardo, Nanni di Feo, and Scotto degli Scotti had each presented a ring to monna Niccola, the bride of their friend, the silk merchant Antonio di Vangelista. This gesture on their part broke the law limiting the number of rings that a new bride was allowed to receive and, accordingly, Antonio had to forfeit the rings and pay a fine of 18 lire and 15 *soldi* for having allowed his wife to accept the gifts.[136] Again in Siena, in April 1414, Antonio di messer Piero dei Tolomei da San Cristoforo was fined because he failed to give official notice of the feast for his daughter's wedding and, further, had provided a sumptuous meal for this feast which included the forbidden sweetmeats *megliaccios*, delicacies which he had also sent to the house of his son-in-law.[137] Four contraventions of the betrothal and wedding regulations are recorded in Bologna in 1365,[138] and in Florence, in May 1360, Bernardo Velluti was charged with giving a chest valued at 3 gold florins to his wife for their wedding (the law stipulated 2 gold florins as the maximum value for these chests).[139]

Prosecutions against men breaking the clothing laws have not so far come to light. There are, however, four instances in Florence of children having been dressed against the law and their fathers being charged for having allowed this. In January 1360, the father of the infant Gualberto Morelli was charged with allowing him to wear a bicoloured (red and yellow) cloak with eighteen silver buttons, and with gold ribbons running down either side of the buttons.[140] In February 1360, Amfriono de' Spini was charged with allowing his infant son Cotto to wear a particoloured hat trimmed with gold ribbons and tiny gilded silver buttons. Amfriono, however, claimed that he could not be prosecuted because, as prior during May and June 1359, he was immune from prosecution not only for the period of his term in office, but for one year after leaving office. The judge acknowledged this legal obstacle and ruled that the case could not proceed.[141] In March of the

[135] Frati, *Vita privata*, 35. Frati's reference is no longer correct. I am indebted to Dottoressa Bambi at the Archivio di stato, Bologna, for locating the correct reference for this information which is now in ASB, Curia del podestà, *Ufficio corone e armi*, b, n, 38 (anni 1364–9).

[136] Casanova, *Donna senese*, 18 citing ASS, Archivio Giudiz. Podestà, ant. num. T. 16 ac. 8687, anno 1408–9.

[137] Ibid. 27.

[138] Ibid.

[139] Rainey, 'Legislation in Florence', 415 n. 183 citing ASF, Giudice 120, fo. 140^v and following folios.

[140] Ibid. 395 n. 111, citing ASF, Giudice 120, fo. 26^v.

[141] Ibid. 348–9.

same year another father was charged with allowing his daughter, who was under 5, to wear a brown tunic with gold ribbons on the collar, twenty-six enamelled silver buttons on the breast of the tunic, and sixteen silver gilded buttons on the sleeves which extended beyond her elbow.[142]

A more interesting case occurred in 1344. In this, Antonia, the 9-year-old daughter of Alemanno de' Medici, was charged with wearing a silver gilded crown on her head while in the house of the physician messer Tommaso del Garbo. What is unusual in this case is that the tamburation in which the accusation against her was made, was bound together with the record of inquisition and is the only known surviving Florentine sumptuary tamburation. More remarkable still is that it was Tommaso del Garbo himself who denounced the young girl. While we cannot know what prompted Tommaso to make such an accusation, Ronald Rainey has suggested several possibilities. As del Garbo was a physician, he and his wife were exempt from the sumptuary laws concerning dress. Rainey suggests that perhaps it was to protect such prerogatives 'based on professional status rather than wealth and on professional achievement rather than birth', that Tommaso felt constrained to submit a tamburation. Alternatively, perhaps he simply felt contempt for the arrogance of a Medici girl. Or perhaps he was prompted by a more moralistic sense of repulsion at the 'senseless and wasteful ostentation of an age in which nine year old girls wore silver gilded crowns'.[143]

Apart from these few examples, the majority of prosecutions that have been discovered deal with women who had violated the clothing laws. This is not really surprising if we consider that laws regulating women's clothing far outnumbered those in any other area. In Siena, apart from the early cases in 1249 mentioned above, there were several prosecutions in the late fifteenth century. In 1472 the following women were all charged with wearing clothes made of the heavy silk known as *ciambellotto* in green or white: monna Feliciana, daughter of Lodovico de'Ciglioni; monna Alda, daughter of Angelo Piccolomo de' Piccolomini; and monna Lucrezia, daughter of Ambrogio Spannocchi and wife of conte de' Vini.[144] On 25 January 1473, monna Minoccia di Rainerio di Francesco da Siena, wife of Antonio di Cristoforo di Antonio, a pork butcher, was seen in the church of San Francesco dressed in mourning clothes with a train of more than the permitted one and one half of a *braccio*. Three days later, her husband appeared on her behalf before the magistrate and tried to excuse her on the

142 Ibid. 394 n. 110, citing ASF, Giudice 120, fo. 108^{v}.

143 Ibid. 356 and 362.

144 Casanova, *Donna senese*, 49, citing AS., *Tre segreti sulle vesti*, n. 1, cc. 11, 12, and 13.

grounds that, as her train was carried in her hand and affixed to the side of her tunic, she had not broken the law. Despite this admittedly dubious defence, the *Tre segreti* charged monna Minoccia on 24 June 1473, with a fine of 18 lire.[145] In January 1474, there was a round-up of *signore* and *signorine* among whom were Battista, daughter of Pietro Palmieri and wife of Giovanni Gabrieli; Margherita, daughter of Guglielmo del Taia; Laura of ser Pietro Porcari; Angelica of Giovanni Lotti; and Battista, wife of Bartolomeo Ciani. The husbands, fathers, or betrothed of these women were to appear before the tribunal and either defend the actions of their women or pay the appropriate fine.[146]

Also preserved in the Sienese archives are several secret denunciations against women who had broken the law. On 3 August 1475, we hear that the wife of Gionta should be castigated for wearing black damask and a crimson *cotta*: 'Put Gionta to the oath and he will tell you the truth concerning her. Her name is monna Lisabetta.'[147] On 21 November of the same year the following accusation was received: 'You do well to observe the laws. On Friday, the day of the Madonna of September, the daughter of Christofano Turamini, wife of one of the de' Nini, wore a jewel against the statute. She was seen by many citizens from the "mouth" of the family, and among the others, these; that is, Giovanni di Simone, ser Galgano del Fonda, ser Galgano di Petroccio, Pietro di Nanni di Bindo, Lodovico di maestro Pietro.'[148] More self-righteous still was a denunciation received on 14 January 1475:

> Although our statutes last little time and lack observation, nonetheless some evident and manifest things have been seen and we deem it necessary to remedy them. And accordingly, we say that Compagno della Ghazaia has had newly made for his woman . . . a beautiful dress with large sleeves and of foreign cloth; the which two things are manifestly against our statutes and a harm to our city in many respects. And this very same [type of dress] we believe missere Lodovico Martinozi to have had made. If you do not make a demonstration and example of these two dresses, all will return to using them, and the greater portion of the money, as you can see, will go to Florence, that is from the dowries of our girls. . . . [T]his has been recorded with good charity, without any malice toward the aforementioned.[149]

The final case from Siena concerns messer Lorenzo di messer Antonio de' Lanti and his wife. On 10 April 1476, an inquisition was conducted

[145] Casanova, *Donna senese*, 40 citing ASS, *Tre segreti sulle vesti*, n. 1, c. 2. Casanova also notes that Antonio appealed against this sentence but she does not relate the outcome of the appeal.

[146] Ibid. 49, citing ASS, *Tre segreti sulle vesti*, n. 1, c. 20.

[147] Ibid.

[148] Ibid.

[149] Ibid. 48–9 citing ASS, *Tre segreti sulle vesti*, n. 1, c. 17.

against Lorenzo's wife for wearing on two occasions a dress of silk velvet valued at 3,000 lire or more. Lorenzo, appearing on her behalf as was customary, presented an eloquent and convincing defence:

To which [accusation], with every proper reverence, he explained how he, well informed of our laws, as a son of obedience, seeing that dresses of silk were permitted to wives of knights, not just to be obedient, so much as for civil honour and his convenience, bought a dress made of silk which cost him less than it appeared to cost to them. . . . And this because his father, messer Antonio, being the councillor of Duke Francesco and in that capacity appointed to the company of the most serene King Ascanio of Cyprus when he was in Milan to journey to France, the aforesaid king, in his benignity, made me and one of my brothers knights, as can be seen in a privilege with a seal hanging off it. I did not believe, nor do believe, that I displeased the citizens of Siena, nor your office; and this it seems to me is necessary to say and much more, when my rights have suffered, particularly as the aforesaid woman is the first cousin of the wife of Lord Robert, marquis of Castelnuovo and count of Caiaza. This privilege he offers to show your Worthy Reverences whenever it should please you. He prays you to absolve her from the said molestation so that he may use his military rights according to your laws, and in any case he recommends himself to you.[150]

Despite this defence, Lorenzo was still fined 37 lire and 10 *soldi*. He appealed against this sentence, however, and this time won his case.[151]

More ambiguous was the treatment of a Ferrarese woman, Elisabetta, wife of Ludovico Pirundoli. The treasurer of the Ferrarese commune had ordered that Ludovico pay a fine of 50 lire because Elisabetta had worn a dress of the crimson colour permitted exclusively to noblewomen. Ludovico protested, however, that his father, Niccolò, had been a nobleman of the city of Ferrara and that it was the opinion of the commune that he, Ludovico, and his brother Giovanni, were also considered nobles. Against this claim was put forward the fact that he was a merchant, but to this Ludovico replied that the merchant trade of the Venetian nobles in no way diminished their prerogatives of nobility. At this point the treasurer was confused and, uncertain how to proceed, turned the case over to the magistrate. The latter's judgement was that, leaving aside the claim of noble status, Elisabetta was to be absolved from this particular condemnation but, with an implicit judgement of what he considered to be her true status, he forbade her the use of this and similar garments fitting for nobles on any future occasion.[152]

150 Ibid., 50 citing ASS, *Tre segreti sulle vesti*, n. 1, cc. 15.

151 Ibid.

152 ACF, Deliberazioni dei Dodici Savi, Libro I, carte 11, an. VI, fasc. n. 39, dall'anno 1457 all'anno 1460. Also mentioned briefly in Frizzi, *Memorie di Ferrara*, iv. 28–9.

In Bologna in 1365, seventy-four women were fined for contravening the laws regulating feminine attire. Among these was the wife of Pietro di Nicolò Albergati who was fined 5 lire for wearing buckles of silver leaf, and the wife of Egano Lambertini who was fined the same amount for wearing a dress with pearl buttons and a hood (*cappuccio*) against the style prescribed by law. Other women were also fined 5 lire for wearing such items as dresses of red velvet and dresses with trimmings of gold and vair.[153] The only other known case from Bologna, the women in the bridal retinue of Ginevra Sforza on the occasion of her marriage to Sante Bentivoglio, has already been discussed in Chapter 6.

From Venice we know of two prosecutions concerning women's clothing. In 1400, the wife of the nobleman Giovanni Georgio (formerly Bertuccio),[154] was seen on a Sunday during the Carnival wearing a white silk dress with sleeves and a collar in violation of the sumptuary law of 1400. The dress was measured to prove that it did in fact contravene the specifications of the law, and Giovanni had to forfeit the dress and pay the appropriate fine as did the tailor who made the dress.[155] In the following year, 1401, the wife of Pietro Contarini di San Pantaleone, was seen in a black velvet dress also with sleeves and a collar against the statute. The dress was duly measured and Pietro too had to forfeit it and pay the fine as did his tailor, Anechino de Francia.[156]

It is fourteenth-century Florence, however, on which most work has been done, principally by Ronald Rainey,[157] and the documents discovered from this period are most illuminating as to the time and effort invested by sumptuary officials in the discharge of their duties. What is also noteworthy is that the notaries who were sent out by the Executor of the Ordinances of Justice to patrol the city were scrupulous in accounting for their time. They kept logbooks indicating when they went out, recording details of violations when they discovered them, and making a note even when they did not. For instance, Ser Donato, the notary appointed for a six-month term in 1349, noted that he found eighteen women violating the laws during this period and that twice men had impeded him from writing his report.[158] In the six months following Ser Donato's time in office, twenty-five violations were reported.[159] But Francesco Ochi, who served from July

[153] Frati, *Vita privata*, 35. ASB, Curia del podestà, *Ufficio corone e armi*, b, n 38 (anni 1364–9).

[154] P. Molmenti, *La storia di Venezia nella vita privata* (Bergamo, 1905), p. 272 has 'Zorzi' for 'Georgio'.

[155] ASV, Compilazioni leggi, c. 160^{v}.

[156] Ibid.

[157] See 'Legislation in Florence', 302 ff.

[158] Ibid. 310.

[159] Ibid. 310–11.

1350 to January 1351, diligently filled his notebook with daily entries alleging that he found no violations at all.[160] Perhaps Francesco fell victim to intimidatory tactics from the public but also felt afraid of repercussions from his superiors if he did not fill in his book.

Further information regarding the scrupulosity of officials can be gleaned from the Florentine communal account books. These record the receipt of fines imposed by the *ufficiali delle donne* and collected by the *Camarlinghi* of the communal camera. For the 1330s such fines were collected on an average of two per month. This number increased during the 1340s, decreased in the 1350s, with sporadic periods of increase in the late 1350s and early 1390s.[161] In a comparison of the books noting violations with those noting fines collected, no evidence of fraud was discovered.[162] It should be emphasized that in fourteenth-century Florence, at least, most of the women prosecuted for violating the sumptuary laws confessed to the charges and agreed to pay the fines imposed.[163]

Moreover, in all the cities examined, there does not seem to have been any bias towards prosecuting those of a particular professional or social status or, for that matter, refraining from pressing charges against those with influence in communal government. It was not just pork butchers, tailors, and gravediggers who could expect to be prosecuted. In Bologna even men as powerful as Sante Bentivoglio had no influence in lifting the charges imposed upon women in their care. In Siena, members of families as influential as the Piccolomini and Tolomei, and in Florence members of families such as the Strozzi and the Medici were charged and successfully fined.[164]

Further evidence that the laws were not regarded as mere dead letters is underlined by an interesting case from Pisa. In 1473 Lucrezia Tornabuoni, wife of Piero de' Medici received a letter from Elisabetta Gaetani, a nun in the convent of San Matteo in Pisa. Elisabetta asked advice from Lucrezia on behalf of a friend of hers from Genoa who found herself in an ambiguous legal position. Her Genoese friend was married to Iacopino Boetio who, though originally from Pisa, was now a Genoese citizen. The two of them had come for a visit to Pisa and Elisabetta's friend wore clothing that was customary in Genoa but, unfortunately, was against the Pisan sumptuary statute. Accusations were made against the woman after which she had not

160 Rainey, 'Legislation in Florence', 311.
161 Ibid.
162 Ibid. 317.
163 Ibid. 323.
164 See all the cases above as well as that of Dragoncina, wife of Benedetto di Ser Giovanni Strozzi, prosecuted on 15 Nov. 1349, cited in Rainey, 'Legislation in Florence', 315. For evidence of sumptuary prosecutions in Viterbo, as well as examples of extant tamburations, see Lombardi, *Galiane in rivolta*, vol. i, pp. lxix–lxxii.

left the house. The letter continues: 'And she would like, and I together with her, to know whether this statute applies to her, and to be free of all doubt she would like from Your Excellency licence to be able to go around according to her custom and wear her dresses and her jewels.'[165] That this Genoese woman's illicit brocades and pearls had marked her out on arrival in Pisa suggests that Pisan women were, by and large, attending to the laws. Moreover, that she went to the trouble of exploiting her connections to clarify the law and gain a personal licence indicates that wearing finery legally was an important matter for this woman, and no doubt for many others.

It is clearly not sufficient to attempt to explain the ultimate failure of sumptuary laws by claiming that there was a lack of will to enforce them. If this were the case the Italians could have simplified the lengthy legislative process by merely banning certain items without detailing the means to implement these bans. As we have seen, however, every Italian city or town that devised sumptuary laws spent much time and effort in tailoring enforcement procedures to individual circumstances and, moreover, did not fail to strengthen or revise these procedures when necessary. That said, the task of the enforcement officials must have been extremely difficult and demoralizing. Not only did their necessary intrusion into people's private affairs make them extremely unpopular, but the very private nature of their targets itself made the policing necessary for proper enforcement time-consuming and expensive. Despite these obstacles, the fact that so many prosecutions have so far been discovered is impressive. To understand why sumptuary legislation failed we must, then, look elsewhere.

IV

The first point to be made concerning the failure of sumptuary laws is one related to the job for which the legislation was designed. Legislators did not seek to proscribe luxury as such, but only luxury put to certain uses, or in certain areas of life or society, or, for example, at times of war. The objects of proscription had, therefore, to be identified in terms of specific items and practices. Hence, any who wished to continue in their luxurious ways whilst remaining within the letter of the law needed only to adopt a new set of items or practices. The letter of the law needed repeatedly to be rewritten precisely because often it was observed or enforced.

Nowhere was this problem more acute than in the area of clothing. As

[165] Lucrezia Tornabuoni, *Lettere*, ed. P. Salvadori (Florence, 1993), letter 76, pp. 125–6.

we saw in Chapter 2, whilst there were several sumptuary laws restraining excess at funerals and weddings, they were far outnumbered by those restricting clothing, and women's clothing in particular. Several reasons have already been suggested in Chapters 3 and 6 for this greater concern with women's dress, but one further point needs to be emphasized. Although there is quite a large margin for pomp and excess at funerals and weddings, such ceremonial occasions, couched in tradition, are slower to change and have certain fixed forms for luxurious expression. In these areas the law was dealing with relatively static phenomena and needed correspondingly less revision. Clothing, on the other hand, presented a never-ending problem. As argued previously, in order to proscribe luxurious clothing, legislators had to identify such clothing by employing specific fashion terminology. Sumptuary legislation against clothing, then, was required to take the form of fashion legislation. But legislative regulation of fashion proved impossible to them. Each time the hydra was decapitated, two new heads immediately grew in its place. A fashion might well have died and been replaced merely in the time it took to frame and pass a law proscribing it. So, rapid changes in fashion meant that the laws had constantly to be revised. And, as noted, passing a law could itself precipitate a change in fashion (at least amongst the law-abiding). It should be stressed, then, that the great increase in laws against women's clothing and indeed the increase in sumptuary laws of any sort, despite their manifest failure, derived to a large degree from the interaction between the law and what it sought to contain, and had little to do with a lack of regard for the law or a lack of desire to enforce it.

Sumptuary legislation, moreover, would have had more chance of success if it sought to outlaw all expressions of luxury per se in all sectors of society. The legislators in late medieval and Renaissance Italy never aimed at blanket proscription. As stressed earlier, luxury had a positive as well as a negative role to play in Italian life. Fine costumes and dazzling ceremonial displays could confer honour upon a city by demonstrating its wealth, good breeding, and technical expertise. For these reasons women were sometimes instructed to wear their finest clothes when foreign dignitaries visited a city and city councillors were ordered to dress in costly clothes fitting to their high office. Moreover, the luxury goods industries stimulated the local economy and allowed for the influx of foreign capital. Lawmakers of the period did not restrict the consumption of luxury goods per se because in principle they were not against such consumption. It was when luxury consumption was in excess or for the wrong purposes that lawmakers were prepared to condemn it. Throughout the period of this study, then, Italian legislators displayed an ambivalent attitude towards excess[166] that had unfortunate consequences for the efficacy of their numerous provisions. Furthermore, they did not have the manpower or the desire to institute the powerful and wide-ranging police force necessary to make a blanket sumptuary law enforceable, even had they wanted such a law.

Sumptuary law continued to be a feature of European life into the sixteenth and seventeenth centuries until it was finally abandoned in the eighteenth century (although provisions in times of war were still enacted even in the twentieth century). Throughout this later period, however, criticism of sumptuary policy, seen already in the petitions and letters of the mid-fifteenth century, continued to mount, until by the eighteenth century the very notion of sumptuary law was often treated with scorn.

One of the earliest and most significant criticisms of sumptuary law from this later period is an anonymous complaint of 1566 from Milan, written one year after a comprehensive sumptuary law had been approved by the Milanese authorities.[167] This document reverses all the traditional condemnations of luxury consumption. In reply to the old criticism of luxury, whereby God would have created us complete with ornaments if he had wished us to wear such items, this anonymous writer declares that God has in fact made us with the skill and the wherewithal to produce beautiful clothing and ornaments. To make and wear them, therefore, is to praise rather than to scorn God's bounty. Then, in response to the economic rationale usually proffered for the laws (that they keep capital within the city), the writer replies that such reasoning does not apply to Milan as the city produces so much that, not only will capital remain within the city, but foreign money will also enter it. Milan's greatness lies in her industry, this writer cautions: if industry should die, then one-third of the Milanese population would be deprived of their livelihoods and the city's great source of capital would disappear.

Against the argument that God will seek retribution against a city that revels in luxury, the anonymous author argues that, since God's mercy and his retribution are already active within the world, then if luxury were so bad, Milan should already have declined; but instead the city is flourishing, and flourishing more than other cities that have had regular sumptuary provisions for several centuries. Moreover, if such laws are passed in order to increase class distinctions, is it, he asks, worth such a major sacrifice? In

[166] There are, as we have seen, preambles that decry the evil effects of luxury, but this is consistent with its being a good in itself and capable of being put to good use. The distinction was important for the legislators.

[167] E. Verga, 'Le leggi suntuarie e la decadenza dell'industria in Milano, 1565–1750', *Archivio storico lombardo*, 27 (1900), 62–3.

words that could have come straight from a sermon condemnatory of luxurious clothing (and which are reminiscent of Guarino Veronese's arguments seen in Chapter 6), he writes that it is not clothing but virtue which distinguishes men, and therefore one's clothing is unimportant, luxurious or otherwise. His final conclusion is that 'il lusso è morale': it promotes industry and keeps men occupied, thereby distracting them from other serious vices.

The letter expresses the gradual transformation of the traditional medieval view of commercial activity as a necessary but potentially sinful activity, into a positive one blessed and approved by God.[168] Its argument also expresses and depends upon another gradual change in Italian society, that from precarious to more robust, resilient economies. Sumptuary laws were often framed with a view to the protection of fragile economies, since, as Montesquieu was to argue, 'the poorer a state, the more it is ruined by its relative luxury; and consequently the more occasion it has for relative sumptuary laws'. But, as Montesquieu continues (in line with the anonymous author of the letter), the 'richer a state, the more it thrives by its relative luxury; for which reason it must take care not to make any relative sumptuary laws'.[169]

By the eighteenth century, the cities and countries that had used sumptuary law as an integral part of governmental policy had changed in ways which would have made their use inappropriate. For the most part their economies were richer and more stable, and their attitudes to luxury consumption less ambivalent. The societies that had required sumptuary laws had outgrown their use.

The emerging commerce of the Renaissance brought luxury to people whose ethical culture was alien and often inimical to it, and which could not have anticipated its vitality. The impulse to legislate against luxury was to a great extent a product of that ethical culture. Fashion was the means by which luxury, and the burgeoning commerce of the Renaissance, repeatedly escaped regulation. And it was not for centuries that an accommodation was eventually achieved between the legislators and luxury, and that was only reached because the legislators finally separated themselves from that ethical world which had existed for centuries before the Renaissance.

[168] In A. O. Hirschman's terminology, a 'passion' was coming to be understood as an 'interest'. See Hirschman, *The Passions and the Interests: Political Arguments for Capitalism before its Triumph* (Princeton, 1977).

[169] Baron de Montesquieu, 'Consequences of the Different Principles of the Three Governments with Respect to Sumptuary Laws, Luxury, and the Condition of Women', in *The Spirit of the Laws*, trans. T. Nugent (New York, 1949), 99.

BIBLIOGRAPHY

MANUSCRIPT SOURCES

Archivio di Stato, Bologna

Curia del podestà, *Ufficio corone e armi*, b, n 38 (anni 1364–9).

Biblioteca Universitaria, Bologna

Cesare Nappi, *Zibaldone*, 'Palladium eruditum', 52, busta II, n. 1.

Archivio comunale, Ferrara

Deliberazioni dei Dodici Savi, libri C, D, G, I, M.
Archivio segreto del Comune, libro 4, n. 8.
Archivio segreto del Magistrato, libro 6, nn. 20 and 39; libro 8, n. 6; libro 9, n. 31.

Archivio di Stato, Venice

Compilazioni leggi, Busta 305, Pompe-Magistrato, Filza T.
Provveditori alle pompe, Busta, n. 1.
Senato Terra, Regs. I, III, IV, V, VI, XIII, XV, XVIII.
Senato, Delib. Miste, Regs. 1333–4, 1335–8, III, XXIV, XXIX, XLV, XLVI, LIII, LV, LIX, LX.
Avvogaria del Comune, Reg. A.
Maggior Consiglio, Regs. Fractus, XL. 94; Capricornus, XV. 32; Delib. Spiritus, XXIV; Novella; Ursa, XXIX; Regina, XXX; Diana, XXXIII.

Archivio di Stato, Milan

Carteggio Sforzesca, interno, cartella 1092 (Milano, città), 7 April 1490.

Archivio di Stato, Perugia

Archivio Giudiz. Podestà 1277, Package no. 1, fasc. no. 6.

PRINTED SOURCES

Sumptuary Statutes

ANDERLONI, E. (ed.), *Statuti dei laghi di Como e di Lugano del sec. XIV*, i: 'Statuti di Averrara e val Taleggio degli anni MCCCXIII e MCCCLXVIII'; 'Statuto di Dervio e Corenno dell'anno MCCCLXXXIX'; 'Statuti della Valsassina dell'anno MCCCLXXXVIII' (*Corpus statutorum italicorum*, 3; Rome, 1913).

ASTEGIANO, L. (ed.), *Codice diplomatico cremonese, 715–1334*, 2 vols. (*Historiae patriae monumenta*, 2nd ser. 21–2; Augusta Taurinorum, 1895).

BETTO, B. (ed.), Gli statuti del comune di Treviso, sec. XIII–XIV (*Fonti per la storia d'Italia*, 109; Rome, 1984).

BONAINI, F. (ed.), *Statuti inediti della città di Pisa dal XII al XIV secolo*, 2 vols. (Florence, 1854–70).

BONGI, S. (ed.), *Bandi lucchesi del secolo decimoquarto: Tratti dai registri del R. Archivio di Stato in Lucca* (Bologna, 1863).

BORELLI, C. B., 'Della prammatica o sia regolamento sopra il sontuoso vestire degli huomini e donne, e sopra le larghe spese dei convitti e funerali', in *Editti antichi e nuovi di sovrani principi della Real Casa di Savoia* (Turin, 1681).

BRUSASCA, M. (ed.), *Statuti di Gabiano* (Milan, 1955).

CAGGESE, R. (ed.), *Statuti della Repubblica fiorentina*, i. *Statuto del Capitano del Popolo degli anni 1322–1325* (Florence, 1910).

CALAMARI, G., *Lo statuto di Pescia del MCCCXXXIX* (Pescia, 1927).

CAMPORI, C., 'Del governo a comune in Modena secondo gli statuti ed altri documenti sincroni', in *Statuta civitatis mutine*, pp. ix–cclxxviii.

CARNESECCHI, C., *Cosimo I e la sua legge suntuaria del 1562* (Florence, 1902).

CECCHI, D. (ed.), *Statuta castri campirotundi* (Milan, 1966).

CERLINI, A. (ed.), *Consuetudini e statuti reggiani del secolo XIII* (*Corpus statutorum italicorum*, 16; Milan, 1933).

CIAMPI, S. (ed.), *Statuti suntuari ricordati da Giovanni Villani circa il vestiario delle donne, i regali e banchetti delle nozze e circa le pompe funebri, ordinati dal comune di Pistoia negli anni 1332 e 1333* (Pisa, 1815).

CISCATO, A., *Una legge suntuaria e altre leggi agrigentine del 1426* (Girgenti, 1905).

DALLARI, A., and GANDINI, L. A., *Lo statuto suntuario bolognese del 1401 e il registro delle vesti bollate* (*Atti e memorie della reale deputazione di storia patria per le Romagne*, ser. 3a, 7; Bologna, 1880).

DEL GIUDICE, G., 'Una legge suntuaria inedita del 1290: Commento storico-critico', *Atti dell'accademia pontaniana*, 16/2 (1886), 1–319.

DUPLÈS-AGIER, H., 'Ordonnance somptuaire inédite de Philippe le Hardi', *Bibliotheque de l'École des Chartres*, 3/5 (1854), 176–81.

FABRETTI, A., 'Statuti e ordinamenti suntuari intorno al vestire degli uomini e delle donne in Perugia dall'anno 1206 al 1536 (raccolti ed annotati)', *Memorie della reale accademia di scienze di Torino*, ser. 2b, 38 (1888), 137–232.

FASOLI, G. (ed.), 'Statuti del comune di Bassano dell'anno 1259 e dell'anno 1295', *Reale deputazione di storia patria per le Venezie: Monumenti storici*, NS 2 (1940), 41–403.

FEDERICI, V. (ed.), *Statuto di Tivoli del MCCCV con aggiunte del MCCCVII–MCCCVIII* (Rome, 1910).

FOUCARD, C., *Lo statuto inedito delle nozze venetiane nel 1299* (Venice, 1858).

GADDONI, S. (ed.), *Statuti di Imola del secolo XIV*, i. *Statuti della città (1334)* (Milan, 1931).

GHETTI, B., *Di alcune leggi suntuarie recanatesi* (Fano, 1905).

GIULIANI, M. (ed.), *La prammatica senese per le nozze, dell'anno MCCCCXII, febraio XXIV, pubblicata nel suo testo originale* (Siena, 1879).

GIULIOZZI, G., and RAFFAELLI, F., *Gli statuti suntuari del secolo XV al XVIII per la città di Macerata: Memorie storica seguita da tre statuti non mai pubblicati* (nozze Bonaccorsi-Labia) (Fano, 1879).

GLORIA, A., *Statuti del comune di Padova del sec. XII all'anno 1285* (Padua, 1875).

GREGORIO, R., 'Leges somptuariae', in *Bibliotheca scriptorum qui res in Sicilia gestas sub Aragonum imperio retulere*, 2 vols., ii (Palermo, 1792), 529–35.

LISINI, A., 'Le leggi prammatiche durante il governo dei Nove, 1287–1355', *Bollettino senese di storia patria*, 37 (1930), 41–70.

MAGNANO, A., 'Documenti per una storia delle leggi suntuarie veronesi', *Atti e memorie della accademia de agricoltura scienze e lettere di Verona*, 6th ser., 22 (1970–1), 247–401.

MANFREDINI, M., *Contro i superflui ornamenti delle donne: 1460* (Padua, 1896).

MANGANELLI, G. (ed.), *Statuti di Como del 1335 volumen magnum*, 2 vols., i (*Reale deputazione di storia patria per la lombardia sezione di Como*; 1936).

MARRI-CAMERANI, G. (ed.), *Statuto di Arezzo (1327)* (Florence, 1946).

MAZZATINTI, G., 'Di alcune leggi suntuarie eugubine dal XIV al XVI secolo', *Bollettino della Regia deputazione di storia patria per l'Umbria*, 3 (1897), 287–301.

MAZZI, C., 'Alcune leggi suntuarie senesi del secolo XIII', *Archivio storico italiano*, 4th ser., 5 (1880), 133–44.

MENCHETTI, A. (ed.), 'Gli statuti di Montalboddo dell'anno 1366 con le modificazioni e le aggiunte degli anni 1369, 1371, e 1375', appendix in *Storia d'un comune rurale della Marca Anconetana* (Iesi, 1913).

MONTORSI, W. (ed.), *Statuta Ferrariae anno MCCLXXXVII* (Ferrara, 1955).

MORELLI, G., *Deliberazione suntuaria del comune di Firenze, xiii aprile 1439* (nozze Stefanini–Morelli) (Florence, 1881).

MUNICCHI, A., *Una provvisione suntuaria della repubblica fiorentina* (Florence, 1909).

NICCOLAI, F., *Contributo allo studio dei più antichi brevi della campagna genovese* (Milan, 1939).

ORTALLI, G., PAROLIN, G., and POZZA, M. (eds.), *Statuti di Cittadella del secolo XIV* (Rome, 1984).

PAPA, P. (ed.), 'Miscellanea documenti degli archivi toscani; Capitoli del Comune di Firenze; Ordinamenti suntuari' (Florence, Palagio dei Priori), in *Alcune rubriche della prammatica sopra il vestire promulgata dalla Repubblica Fiorentina nel 1384* (nozze Cian Ciappa) (Bergamo, 1894).

PIACENTINO, M., 'Gli statuti in Abruzzo', *Bullettino della deputazione abruzzese di storia patria*, 5th ser., 9–11 (1947–9), 5–89.

PIERI, P. F., *Lo statuto di Vellano del 1367 e brevi notizie storiche anteriori* (Pisa, 1968).

POLIDORI, F. L., and BANCHI, L., *Statuti senesi scritti in volgare ne' secoli XIII e XIV* (Bologna, 1863–1877).

R. Archivio di stato in Siena: Il costituto del comune di Siena volgarizzato nel MCCCIX–MCCCX, 2 vols. (Siena, 1903).

Rinaldi, E. (ed.), *Statuti di Forlì dell'anno 1359* (*Corpus statutorum italicorum*, 5; Rome, 1913).

ROBOLOTTI, F., 'Pragmatica o vero ordini sopra il vestire et banchettare fatti per la città de Cremona: Con l'autorità del Senato di Milano', *Archivio storico lombardo*, 5 (1878), 725–35.

RONCHINI, A. (ed.), *Statuta communis parmae digesta anno MCCLV* (Parma, 1856).

—— *Statuta communis parmae ab anno MCCCXVI ad MCCCXXV* (Parma, 1859).

ROSSINI, G. (ed.), *Statuta Faventiae* (L. A. Muratori (gen. ed.), *Rerum italicarum scriptores*, 28/5; new edn. Bologna, 1929).

SACCUS, F. C., *Statuta civilia et criminalia civitatis Bononiae* (Bologna, 1735).

SANDRI, G. (ed.), *Gli statuti veronesi del 1276, colle correzioni e le aggiunte fino al 1323*, 2 vols. (*Reale deputazione di storia patria per le Venezie, monumenti storici*, NS 3/13; Venice, 1940).

SANESI, G., *Le ultime leggi suntuarie della Repubblica Fiorentina* (Pistoia, 1893).

SANTOLI, Q., SORBELLI, A., and JACOLI, F. (eds.), *Statuti dell Apennino Tosco-Modenese (Sambuca Pistoiese, Frignano) secoli XIII–XIV* (*Corpus statutorum italicorum*, 2; Rome, 1913).

SIMEONI, L. (ed.), 'Statuto suntuario a Verona nel XIV secolo.', *Studi storici veronesi*, 2 (1949–50), 235.

SIMONESCHI, L., *Ordinamenti suntuari pisani per gli anni 1350, 1386* (Pisa, 1889).

SORBELLI, A. (ed.), *Corpus chronicorum bononiensum*, 2 (L. A. Muratori (gen. ed.), *Rerum italicarum scriptores*, 18; new edn., Città di Castello, 1905).

Statuta civitatis mutine (*Monumenti di storia patria delle provincie modenesi, Serie degli statuti*, 1; Parma, 1864).

STEFANI, F., *Legge suntuaria circa il vestire degli uomini e delle donne ordinata intorno all'anno 1432 dalla città di Treviso: Tratta da un testo latino a penna del secolo XI* (Venice, 1880).

'A Thirteenth-Century Castilian Sumptuary Law', *Business History Review*, 37/1–2 (1963), 98–100.

TOUBERT, P., 'Les Statuts communaux et l'histoire des campagnes lombardes au XIVe siècle', *Mélanges d'archéologie et d'histoire*, 72 (1960), 397–508.

TREXLER, R. C., 'Synodal Law', *Studi e Testi*, 268 (1971), 227–87.

—— 'The Episcopal Constitutions of Antoninus of Florence', *Quellen und Forschungen aus Italianischen Archiven und Bibliotheken*, 59 (1979), 244–72.

VERGA, E., 'Le leggi suntuarie milanesi: Gli statuti del 1396 e del 1498', *Archivio storico lombardo*, 25 (1898), 5–79.

—— 'Le leggi suntuarie e la decadenza dell'industria in Milano, 1565–1750', *Archivio storico lombardo*, 27 (1900), 49–116.

ZANELLI, A., 'Di alcune leggi suntuarie pistoiesi dal XIV al XVI secolo', *Archivio storico italiano*, 5th ser., 16 (1895), 206–24.

ZDEKAUER, L., *Leggi suntuarie maceratesi del 1563* (Siena, 1901).

—— (ed.), *Statutum potestatis communis Pistorii anni MCCLXXXXVI* (Milan, 1888).
—— and SELLA, E. P. (eds.), *Statuti di Ascoli Piceno dell' anno MCCCLXXVII* (*Fonti per la storia d' Italia*, 47; Rome, 1910).
ZOLI, A., and BERNICOLI, S., *Statuto del secolo XIII del comune di Ravenna* (Ravenna, 1904).
ZONGHI, A., *Prammatiche fabrianesi nei secoli XIII, XV e XVI* (nozze Bigonzetti-Amici) (Fabriano, 1881).

Treatises and Sermons

AQUINAS, THOMAS, *Summa Theologica*, trans. fathers of the English Dominican Province, 3 vols. (New York, 1947).
AUGUSTINE, *De doctrina christiana*, ed. H. J. Vogels (*Florilegium patristicum*, 24; 1930), 1–103.
—— *Saint Augustine's Commentary on the Lord's Sermon on the Mount*, trans. D. J. Kavanagh, *Writings of Saint Augustine*, 3 (R. J. Deferrari (gen. ed.), *The Fathers of the Church*, 2; Washington, 1963).
—— *Saint Augustine Letters*, vol. v, trans. W. Parsons, *Writings of Saint Augustine*, 13 (R. J. Deferrari (gen. ed.), *The Fathers of the Church*, 32, New York, 1956).
BERNARDINO DA FELTRE, 'De vanitatibus mulierum'; 'De vanitatibus et pompus', in *Sermoni del beato Bernardino Tomitano da Feltre*, ed. P. C. Varischi da Milano (nella redazione de Bulgarino da Brescia), 3 vols. (Milan, 1964), sermon 38, i. 475–87; sermon 100, ii. 121–31.
BERNARDINO DA SIENA, 'Questa è la predica de la vanità del mondo e massimo ne le donne', in C. Cannarozzi (ed.), *Le prediche volgari*, 2 vols. (Florence, 1958), ii. 82–97.
—— 'Come ogni cosa di questo mondo è vanita', ed. L. Banchi, in *Le prediche volgari di San Bernardino da Siena: Dette nella piazza del campo l'anno MCCCCXXVII*, 3 vols. (Siena, 1888), iii. 185–213.
—— 'Contra mundanas vanitates et pompas'; 'De multitudine malorum quae ex vanitatibus subsequuntur'; 'Contra se fraudantes et capillos adulterinos portantes, atque contra feminas caudatas', in *Opera omnia*, ii (Florence, 1950), sermon 44, pp. 45–58; sermon 46, pp. 73–85; and sermon 47, pp. 86–99.
BOSSO, MATTEO, 'Matthaei Bossi Veronensis canonici regularis ne feminis varia ornamentorum luxuries indigne ac irreligiose restituatur ad d. B(essarionem) cardinalem Tusculanum Bononie legatum', in *Opera varia* (Bologna, 1627), 156–65.
CYPRIAN, 'The Dress of Virgins' (De habitu virginum) in *Saint Cyprian Treatises*, trans. R. J. Deferrari (gen. ed.), *The Fathers of the Church*, 36 (New York, 1958), 25–52.
DELLA MARCA, GIACOMO, 'De vanitate mulierum', in R. Lioli (ed.), *Sermones Dominicales*, 3 vols., i (Ancona, 1978), sermon 4, pp. 107–26.
SANUTI, NICOLOSA, 'Nicolosae Sanutae matroniae bononiensis ad

Reverendissimum in Christo patrem dominum d. Legatum bononiensum ut mulieribus ornamenta restituantur', in L. Frati, *La vita privata in Bologna dal secolo XIII al XVII* (2nd edn., Bologna, 1928), 251–62.

TERTULLIAN, 'The Apparel of Women' (*De cultu feminarum*), trans. E. A. Quain, in *Tertullian: Disciplinary, Moral and Ascetical Works* (R. J. Deferrari (gen. ed.), *The Fathers of the Church*, 40; New York, 1959), 111–49.

Other Sources

ADY, C. M., *The Bentivoglio of Bologna: A Study in Despotism* (Oxford, 1969).

ALTIERI, M. A., *Li nuptiali*, ed. E. Narducci (Rome, 1873).

ANDREWES, A., 'Eunomia', *Classical Quarterly*, 32 (1938), 89–102.

ANTAL, F., *Florentine Painting and its Social Background* (1948; Boston, 1965).

ARISTOTLE, *Politics*, *De generatione animalium*, *Physics*, in *The Complete Works of Aristotle: The Revised Oxford Translation*, ed. J. Barnes (Princeton, 1984).

—— *Nicomachean Ethics*, trans. M. Ostwald (Indianapolis and New York, 1962).

BALDWIN, F. E., *Sumptuary Legislation and Personal Regulation in England* (Baltimore, 1926).

BARBADORO, B., *Le finanze della repubblica fiorentina* (Florence, 1929).

BARONIUS, C., *Annales ecclesiastici denuo excusi et ad nostra usque tempora perducti ab Augustino Theiner*, 37 vols. (Paris, 1864–83), 22 (1870).

BAUDRILLART, H. J., *Histoire du luxe privé et public depuis l'antiquité jusqu'à nos jours*, 4 vols. (Paris, 1878–80).

BELGRANO, L. T., 'Della vita privata dei genovesi', *Atti della società ligure di storia patria*, 4 (1866), 79–273.

—— *Della vita privata dei genovesi* (2nd edn., Genoa, 1875).

—— 'Usanze nuziali in Genova nel secolo XV', *Giornale ligustico* (1887), 446–51.

BELL, Q., *On Human Finery* (London, 1947).

BENADUCCI, G., 'Contributo alla bibliografia di Francesco Filelfo', *Atti e memorie della R. deputazione di storia patria per le provincie delle Marche*, 5 (1901), 459–535.

BENSON, P., *The Invention of the Renaissance Woman: The Challenge of Female Independence in the Literature and Thought of Italy and England* (University Park, Pa., 1992).

BERGER, A., *Encyclopedic Dictionary of Roman Law* (*Transactions of the American Philological Society*, NS 43/2; Philadelphia, 1953).

BIAGI, G., *The Private Life of the Renaissance Florentines* (London, 1896).

—— *Fiorenza fiore che sempre rinnovella* (Florence, 1925).

BISTORT, G., *Il magistrato alle pompe nella repubblica di Venezia: Studio storico* (*Miscellanea di storia veneta*, 3rd ser., 5; Venice, 1912).

BOERIO, G., *Dizionario del dialetto veneziano* (Venice, 1867).

BONARDI, A., 'Il lusso di altri tempi in Padova: Studio storico con documenti inediti', *Miscellanea di storia veneta*, 3rd ser., 2 (1910), 1–292.

BONDS, W. N., 'Genoese Noblewomen and Gold Thread Manufacturing', *Medievalia et humanistica*, 17 (1966), 79–81.

BONELLI-GANDOLFO, C., 'La legislazione suntuaria senese negli ultimi 150 anni della Repubblica', *Studi senesi*, 35 (1920).

BONOLI, P., *Istorie della città di Forlí intrecciate di varii accidenti della Romagna e dell'Italia* (Forlí, 1661).

BOSELLI, G. V., *Delle storie piacentine*, 3 vols. (Piacenza, 1793–1805).

BOWSKY, W. M., *A Medieval Italian Commune: Siena under the Nine, 1287–1355* (Los Angeles, 1981).

BRENTARI, O., *Storia di Bassano e del suo territorio* (Bassano, 1884).

BRESC, H., *Un monde méditerranée: Économie et société en Sicile 1300–1450* (École français de Rome), 2 vols., ii (Palermo, 1986).

BREWARD, C., *The Culture of Fashion* (Manchester, 1995).

BRIDENTHAL, R., and KOONZ, C. (eds.), *Becoming Visible: Women in European History* (Boston, 1977).

BRIDGEMAN, J., ' "Pagare le pompe": Why Quattrocento Sumptuary Law Did Not Work', in L. Panizza (ed.), *Women in Italian Renaissance Culture and Society* (Oxford, 2000), 209–21.

BRUCKER, G. A. (ed.), *Two Memoirs of Renaissance Florence: The Diaries of Buonaccorso Pitti and Gregorio Dati*, trans. J. Martines (New York, 1967).

—— *Renaissance Florence* (1969; Los Angeles, 1983).

—— *The Society of Renaissance Florence: A Documentary Study* (New York, 1971).

BRUNDAGE, J. A., 'Sumptuary Laws and Prostitution in Late Medieval Italy', *Journal of Medieval History*, 13 (1987), 343–55.

BULLARD, M. M., 'Marriage Politics and the Family in Florence: The Strozzi-Medici Alliance of 1508', *American Historical Review*, 84 (1979), 668–87.

BURCKHARDT, J., *The Civilization of the Renaissance in Italy* (1860; Oxford, 1945).

CANTINI, L., *Saggi storici d'antichità toscane*, iii (Florence, 1906).

CARTLEDGE, P., and SPAWFORTH, A., *Hellenistic and Roman Sparta* (London and New York, 1989).

CASANOVA, E., *La donna senese del quattrocento nella vita privata* (Siena, 1901) (separately published extract from *Bollettino senese di storia patria*, 8).

CASINI, B., *Aspetti della vita economica e sociale di Pisa dal catasto del 1428–1429* (Pisa, 1965).

CASSA, A., *Funerali, pompe, conviti* (Brescia, 1887).

CECCHETTI, B., 'La vita dei Veneziani nel 1300: Le vesti', *Archivio veneto*, 31 (1886).

CHISHOLM, J., 'The Sumptuary Laws of Scotland', *Journal of Jurisprudence*, 414/35 (June 1891), 290–7.

CHOJNACKI, S., 'The Power of Love: Wives and Husbands in Late Medieval Venice', in M. Erler and M. Kowaleski (eds.), *Women and Power in the Middle Ages* (Athens, Ga., and London, 1988), 126–48.

CHORLEY, P., 'The Cloth Exports of Flanders and Northern France during the Thirteenth Century: A Luxury Trade?', *Economic History Review*, 2nd ser., 40/3 (1987), 349–79.

CICERO, *The Republic; and, The Laws/Cicero*, trans. N. Rudd (New York, 1998).

CIPOLLA, C. M., 'The Italian and Iberian Peninsulas', in M. M. Postan, and E. E. Rich, and E. Miller (eds.), *The Cambridge Economic History of Europe*, iii (Cambridge, 1963), 397–429.

—— *The Monetary Policy of Fourteenth-Century Florence* (Berkeley and Los Angeles, 1982).

COLLISON-MORLEY, L., *The Story of the Sforzas* (London, 1933).

COMELLI, G. B., 'Di Nicolò Sanuti primo conte della Porretta', *Atti e memorie della reale deputazione di storia patria per le provincie di romagna*, 3rd ser., 17 (1899), 101–61.

CROUCH, D., *The Image of the Aristocracy in Britain, 1000–1300* (London and New York, 1992).

CULHAM, P., 'The Lex Oppia', *Latomus*, 41 (1982), 786–93.

D'ARCO, C., *Della economia politica del municipio di Mantova a' tempi in cui si reggeva a repubblica* (Mantua, 1842).

DAREMBERG, C., and SAGLIO, F. (eds.), *Dictionnaire des antiquités grecques et romaines*, 5 vols. (Paris, 1873–1917).

DAUBE, D., *Roman Law: Linguistic, Social and Philosophical Aspects* (Edinburgh, 1969).

DAVIDSOHN, R., 'Jagd, Spiel, Luxus', in *Forschungen zur Alteren Geschichte von Florenz*, ii (Berlin, 1900), 324–5.

—— *Storia di Firenze*, 8 vols. (Florence, 1956–68).

DAVIS, C. T., 'Il buon tempo antico', in N. Rubinstein (ed.), *Florentine Studies: Politics and Society in Renaissance Florence* (London, 1968), 45–69.

DAVIS, F., *Fashion and the Construction of Identity* (Chicago, 1993).

DAVIS, N. Z., 'Women in Politics', in ead. (ed.), *Renaissance and Enlightenment Paradoxes: A History of Women in the West*, iii (Cambridge, Mass., and London, 1993), 167–83.

DEAN, T., 'Notes on the Ferrarese Court in the Later Middle Ages', *Renaissance Studies*, 3/4 (1989), 357–69.

DEGLI ARIENTI, SABADINO, *Le Porretane*, ed. G. Gambarin (Bari, 1914).

DELLA TOSA, SIMONE, 'Annali di Simone della Tosa', in D. M. Manni (ed.), *Cronichette antiche di varj scrittori del buon secolo della lingua toscana* (Florence, 1733), 125–71.

DE MATTEIS, M. C., 'La donna e la vita quotidiana nell'Italia tardo medievale', *Sitzungsberichte der akademie der Wissenschaften*, 473 (1986), 409–28.

DENHOLM-YOUNG, N., and KANTOROWICZ, H., 'De Ornatu Mulierum: A Consilium of Antonius de Rosellis with an Introduction on Fifteenth Century Sumptuary Legislation', *Bibliofilia*, 35 (1933), 315–35 and 440–56.

DILL, S., *Roman Society in the Last Century of the Western Empire* (London, 1905).

DONALDSON, J., *Woman: Her Position and Influence in Ancient Greece and Rome and among the Early Christians* (London, 1907).

EILERS, C., 'Roman Republican Sumptuary Legislation', MA thesis (McMaster Univ., Ontario, 1989).

EISENBART, L. C., *Kleiderordnungen der deutschen Städte zwischen 1350 und 1700: Ein Beitrag zur Kulturgeschichte des deutschen Burgertums* (Gottingen, 1962).

EVANS, J., *Dress in Medieval France* (Oxford, 1952).

FAVIER, J., *Philippe le Bel* (Paris, 1979).

FERRANTE, J. M., 'The Education of Women in the Middle Ages in Theory, Fact, and Fantasy', in Labalme (ed.), *Beyond their Sex*, 1980), 9–42.

FERRO, M., *Dizionario del diritto comune e veneto*, XIV (Venice, 1778–81), s.v. 'Lusso'.

FINKELSTEIN, J., *After a Fashion* (Melbourne, 1996).

FLETCHER, A., and STEVENSON, J. (eds.), *Order and Disorder in Early Modern England* (Cambridge, 1985).

FRATI, L., 'Lettere amorose di Galeazzo Marescotti e di Sante Bentivoglio', *Giornale storico della letteratura italiana*, 26 (1895), 305–44.

—— *La vita privata di Bologna dal secolo XIII al XVII* (2nd edn., Bologna, 1928).

FREUDENBERGER, H., 'Fashion, Sumptuary Laws, and Business', *Business History Review*, 37/1 (1963), 37–48.

FRIZZI, A., *Memorie per la storia di Ferrara*, 5 vols. (Ferrara, 1847–50).

GABOTTO, F,. 'Per la storia del costume nel medio evo subalpino', *Bollettino storico bibliografico subalpino*, 13 (1909), 1–28.

GAGARIN., M., *Early Greek Law* (Los Angeles, 1986).

GARNER, R., *Law and Society in Classical Athens* (London, 1987).

GEHRKE, H. J., 'Politik und Philosophie bei Demetrios von Phaleron', *Chiron*, 8 (1978), 149–93.

GENICOT, L., 'Crisis: From the Middle Ages to Modern Times', in M. M. Postan and H. J. Habakkuk (eds.), *The Cambridge Economic History of Europe*, i (2nd edn., Cambridge, 1966), 660–742.

GILCHRIST, J., *The Church and Economic Activity in the Middle Ages* (London, 1969).

GIOMO, G., 'Il lusso: Leggi moderatrici—pietre e perle false', *Nuovo archivio veneto*, NS 31, 16/1 (1908), 103–14.

GOLDTHWAITE, R., 'The Economy of Renaissance Italy: The Preconditions for Luxury Consumption', *I Tatti Studies: Essays in the Renaissance*, 2 (1987), 15–39.

—— 'The Empire of Things: Consumer Demand in Renaissance Italy', in F. W. Kent and P. Simons (eds.), *Patronage, Art, and Society in Renaissance Italy* (Oxford, 1987), 153–75.

GREEN, L., *Chronicle into History: An Essay on the Interpretation of History in Florentine Fourteenth-Century Chronicles* (Cambridge, 1972).

GREENFIELD KENT, R., 'Sumptuary Law in Nürnberg: A Study in Paternal Government', *Johns Hopkins University Studies in Historical and Political Science*, 36th ser., 2 (1918).

GREGOROVIUS, F., *History of the City of Rome in the Middle Ages*, trans. G. W. Hamilton, 8 vols. (London, 1900–2).

GRUBB, J. S., *Firstborn of Venice: Vicenza in the Early Renaissance State* (Baltimore, 1988).

GUNDERSHEIMER, W. L., 'Women, Learning and Power: Eleanora of Aragon and the Court of Ferrara', in Labalme (ed.), *Beyond their Sex*, 3–65.

HALE, J. R., 'Violence in the Late Middle Ages', in L. Martines (ed.), *Violence and Civil Disorder in Italian Cities 1200–1500* (Berkeley and Los Angeles, 1972).

—— *Florence and the Medici: The Pattern of Control* (London, 1977).

HAMMOND, W. A., 'Sumptuary Laws and their Social Influence', *Popular Science Monthly*, 37 (1890), 33–40.

HAMPEL-KALLBRUNNER, G., *Beiträge zur Geschichte der Kleidordnungen, mit besonderer Berücksichtigung Österreichs* (Vienna, 1962).

HARTE, N. B., 'State Control of Dress and Social Change in Pre-Industrial England', in D. C. Coleman and A. H. John (eds.), *Trade, Government and Economy in Pre-Industrial England: Essays presented to F. J. Fisher* (London, 1976), 132–65.

HASTINGS, J. (ed.), *Encyclopaedia of Religion and Ethics* (Edinburgh, 1915).

HEERS, J., 'La Mode et les marchés des draps de laine: Gênes et la montagne a la fin du moyen âge', *Annales*, 26 (1971), 1093–1117.

HEFELE, K. J., *Histoire des conciles d'après les documents originaux*, trans. H. Leclerq, 11 vols. (Paris, 1907–52).

HERALD, J., *Renaissance Dress in Italy, 1400–1500* (London, 1981).

HERLIHY, D., *Medieval and Renaissance Pistoia: The Social History of an Italian Town, 1200–1430* (New Haven, 1967).

—— 'The Medieval Marriage Market', *Medieval and Renaissance Studies*, 6 (1976), 3–27.

—— and KLAPISCH-ZUBER, C., *Les Toscans et leurs familles* (Paris, 1978).

HIRSCHMAN, A. O., *The Passions and the Interests: Political Arguments for Capitalism before its Triumph* (Princeton, 1977).

HOLLIDAY, A. J., 'Spartan Austerity', *Classical Quarterly*, 17 (1977), 111–26.

HOOPER, W., 'The Tudor Sumptuary Laws', *English Historical Review*, 30 (1915), 433–9.

HUNT, A., *Governance of the Consuming Passions: A History of Sumptuary Law* (Houndmills, Basingstoke, 1996).

INFESSURA, STEFANO, *Diario della città di Roma di Stefano Infessura scribasenato*, ed. Oreste Tommasini (*Istituto storico italiano fonti per la storia d'Italia*; Rome, 1890).

JARDINE, L., *Worldly Goods: A New History of the Renaissance* (London, 1996).

JONES, A. R., and Stallybrass, P., *Renaissance Clothing and the Materials of Memory* (Cambridge, 2000).

JONES, P. J., 'La storia economica: Dalla caduta dell'impero romano al secolo XIV', in *Storia d'Italia*, 2* (Turin, 1974), 1469–1810.

—— 'Economia e società nell'Italia medievale: La leggenda della borghesia', in *Storia d'Italia, Annali*, i (Turin, 1978), 185–372.

JUVENAL, *The Sixteen Satires*, trans. P. Green (London, 1967).

KELLY-GADOL, J., 'Did Women Have a Renaissance?', in Bridenthal and Koonz (eds.), *Becoming Visible*, 137–64.

KELSO, R., *Doctrine for the Lady of the Renaissance* (Urbana, Ill., 1956).

KENT, F. W., 'A Proposal by Savonarola for the Self-Reform of Florentine Women (March 1496)', *Memorie domenicane*, 14 (1983), 335–41.

—— and SIMONS, P., 'Renaissance Patronage: An Introductory Essay', in eid. (eds.), *Patronage, Art, and Society in Renaissance Italy* (Oxford, 1987), 1–21.

KING, M. L., 'Book-Lined Cells: Women and Humanism in the Early Italian Renaissance', in Labalme (ed.), *Beyond their Sex*, 66–90.

—— *Women of the Renaissance* (Chicago and London, 1991).

KIRSCHNER, J., *Pursuing Honor while Avoiding Sin: The Monte delle Doti of Florence* (Milan, 1978).

KLAPISCH-ZUBER, C., *Women, Family and Ritual in Renaissance Italy* (Chicago, 1985).

KÖHLER, C., *A History of Costume*, ed. E. Von Sichart, trans. A. K. Dallas (London, 1928).

KÖNIG, R., *The Restless Image: A Sociology of Fashion*, trans. F. Bradley (London, 1973).

KOVESI KILLERBY, C., 'Practical Problems in the Enforcement of Italian Sumptuary Law, 1200–1500', in T. Dean and K. J. P. Lowe (eds.), *Crime, Society and the Law in Renaissance Italy* (Cambridge, 1994), 99–120.

—— ' "Heralds of a Well-Instructed Mind": Nicolosa Sanuti's Defence of Women and their Clothes', *Renaissance Studies*, 13/3 (1999), 255–82.

KRAEMER, P., *Le Luxe et les lois somptuaires au moyen âge* (Paris, 1920).

KRISTELLER, P. O., 'Learned Women of Early Modern Italy: Humanists and University Scholars', in Labalme (ed.), *Beyond their Sex*, 91–116.

KÜBLER, B., 'Sumptus', in A. Pauly, G. Wissowa, W. Kroll, and K. Witte, *Real-Encyclopädie der klassischen Altertumswissenschaft*, 4a (Stuttgart and Munich, 1894–), 901–8.

KURTZ, D. C., and BOARDMAN, J., *Greek Burial Customs* (London, 1971).

LABALME, P. H. (ed.), *Beyond their Sex: Learned Women of the European Past* (New York, 1980).

—— 'Women's Roles in Early Modern Venice: An Exceptional Case', in Labalme (ed.), *Beyond their Sex*, 129–52.

LACEY, W. K., *The Family in Classical Greece* (London, 1968).

LANE, F. C., *Venice: A Maritime Republic* (Baltimore, 1973).

LANGLOIS, C. V., 'Project for Taxation presented to Edward I', *English Historical Review*, 4 (1894), 517–29.

LARNER, J., *The Lords of Romagna: Romagnol Society and the Origins of the Signorie* (London, 1965).

LARNER, J., *Italy in the Age of Dante and Petrarch 1216–1380* (New York, 1980).

LAVER, J., *A Concise History of Costume* (London, 1969).

LAZZI, G., 'Abbigliamento e costume nella Firenze dei primi granducati: Fonti e documenti', in *La Famiglia e la vita quotidiana in Europa dal '400 al '600: Fonti e problemi. Atti del convegno internazione Milano 1–4 dicembre 1983* (Rome, 1986), 295–319.

LÉRIGET, M., *Des lois et impôts somptuaires* (Montpellier, 1919).

LEVI PISETZKY, R., 'Nuove mode della Milano Viscontea nello scorcio del '300', in *Storia di Milano*, 16 vols., v (Milan, 1955), 875–908.

—— *Storia del costume in Italia*, 5 vols. (Milan, 1964–9).

—— 'Mode e costume', in *Storia d'Italia*, i (Turin, 1973), 932–79.

LEWIS, P., *Later Medieval France: The Polity* (London, 1968).

LIGHTBOWN, R. W., 'Portrait or Idealization: The Ravello Bust', *Apollo* (Feb. 1988), 108–12.

LIVY, *Rome and the Mediterranean: Books XXXI–XLV of The History of Rome from its Foundation*, trans. H. Bettenson (Harmondsworth, 1976)

LIZIER, A., 'Contributo alla bibliografia della legislazione suntuaria in Italia', *Miscellanea storica novarese* (1906), 107–14.

LOMBARDI, G., *Galiane in rivolta: Una polemica umanistica sugli ornamenti femminili nella Viterbo del Quattrocento*, 2 vols. (Rome, 1998).

LOMBARDO, M. L., 'Abbigliamento e moda a Roma nel secolo xv: Fonti documentarie', in *La famiglia e la vita quotidiana in Europa dal '400 al '600: Fonti e problemi etc.* . . . (Rome, 1986), 321–41.

LURIE, A., *The Language of Clothes* (London, 1992).

LUZIO, A., and RENIER, R., 'Il lusso di Isabella d'Este marchesa di Mantova', *Nuova antologia*, ser. 4a, 63 (1896), 441–69.

MACDOWELL, D. M., *The Law in Classical Athens* (London, 1978).

MACHIAVELLI, NICCOLÒ, *Istorie fiorentine*, in *Opere di Niccolò Machiavelli*, ed. E. Raimondi (Milan, 1966).

MACINGHI STROZZI, ALESSANDRA, *Selected Letters of Alessandra Strozzi*, trans. and ed. H. Gregory (Berkeley, 1997).

MCKENDRICK, N., BREWER, J., and PLUMB, J. H., *The Birth of a Consumer Society: The Commercialization of Eighteenth-Century England* (London, 1982).

MACK SMITH, D., *A History of Sicily: Medieval Sicily 800–1715* (London, 1968).

MACLEAN, I., *The Renaissance Notion of Woman: A Study in the Fortunes of Scholasticism and Medical Science in European Intellectual Life* (Cambridge, 1980).

MCNAMARA, J., and WEMPLE, S. F., 'Sanctity and Power: The Dual Pursuit of Medieval Women', in Bridenthal and Koonz (eds.), *Becoming Visible*.

MALESPINI, RICORDANO, *Istoria fiorentina di Ricordano Malespini coll'aggiunta di Giachetto Malespini e la cronica di Giovanni Morelli* (Florence, 1718).

MALLETT, M., *The Borgias: The Rise and Fall of a Renaissance Dynasty* (London, 1971).

MANSI, G. D. (ed.), *Sacrorum conciliorum nova et amplissima collectio* (continued and supplemented under the editorship of L. Petit and J. B. Martin), 53 vols. (Florence, 1759–1962).

MANZI, G., *Discorso di Guglielmo Manzi sopra gli spettacoli, le feste, ed il lusso degl'italiani nel secolo XIV* (Rome, 1818).

MARTIGNONE, F., 'L'importanza del danaro nella mentalità dei Genovesi alla fine del Medio Evo', *Studi genuensi*, 9 (1972), 73–86.

MARTINES, L., *Power and Imagination: City-States in Renaissance Italy* (Harmondsworth, 1979).

MASSÉRA, A., 'Dante e Riccobaldo', *Bollettino della società dantesca italiana*, NS 22 (1915), 168–200.

MAZZONI TOSELLI, O., *Racconti storici estratti dall'archivio criminale di Bologna*, 3 vols. (Bologna, 1866–70).

MEISS, M., *Painting in Florence and Siena after the Black Death* (Princeton, 1951).

MILES, D. P., 'Forbidden Pleasures: Sumptuary Laws and the Ideology of Moral Decline in Ancient Rome', Ph.D. thesis (London, 1987).

MILLER, E., Introduction to Cipolla, 'The Italian and Iberian Peninsulas', pp. 281–90.

MINUTOLI, C. (ed.), 'Sommario della storia di Lucca dall'anno MIV all'anno MDCC', *Archivio storico italiano*, 1st ser., 10 (1847), 89–103.

MOLMENTI, P., *La storia di Venezia nella vita privata*, ii (Bergamo, 1905).

MONTAIGNE, 'Of Sumptuary Laws', in *Essays of Montaigne*, ed. W. C. Hazlitt, trans. C. Cotton, 5 vols., ii (London, 1923),149–52.

MONTESQUIEU, BARON DE, 'Consequences of the Different Principles of the Three Governments with Respect to Sumptuary Laws, Luxury, and the Condition of Women', in *The Spirit of the Laws*, trans. T. Nugent (New York, 1949), 94–108.

MURATORI, L. A., *Dissertazioni sopra le antichità italiane*, ed. G. F. Soli, 3 vols. (Milan, 1751).

MURRAY, A. O., 'Archbishops and Mendicants in Thirteenth-Century Pisa', *Stellung und Wirksamkeit der Bettelorden in der städtischen Gesellschaft*, Band 3, Ordensstudien 2 (1981), 19–75.

MUZZARELLI, M. G., ' "Contro mundans vanitates et pompas": Aspetti della lotta contro i lussi nell' Italia del XV secolo', *Rivista di storia della Chiesa in Italia*, 40/2 (1986), 371–90.

MYERS, G., 'Blue Laws', in *Encyclopaedia of the Social Sciences*, ii (New York, 1930–4).

NASALLI ROCCA DI CORNELIANO, E., 'Il cardinale Bessarione legato pontificio in Bologna (1450–1455): Saggio sulla costituzione dello stato pontificio e sulla legislazione e la vita giuridica del '400', *Atti e memorie della reale deputazione di storia patria per le provincie di Romagna*, 4th ser., 20 (1930), 17–80.

NEWETT, M. M., 'The Sumptuary 'Laws of Venice' in the Fourteenth and Fifteenth Centuries', in T. F. Tout and J. Tait (eds.), *Historical Essays by Members of the Owens College, Manchester* (London, 1907), 245–77.

O'CALLAGHAN, J. F., 'Paths to Ruin: The Economic and Financial Policies of Alfonso the Learned', in R. I. Burns (ed.), *The Worlds of Alfonso the Learned and James the Conqueror: Intellect and Force in the Middle Ages* (Princeton, 1985), 41–67.

ODORICI, F., *Storie bresciane*, 11 vols. (Brescia, 1853–65).

ORIGO, I., *The Merchant of Prato* (1957; London, 1984).

OVID, *The Art of Love, and Other Poems*, trans. J. H. Mozley, ed. G. P. Gould (Cambridge, Mass., 1979).

OWEN HUGHES, D., 'Sumptuary Law and Social Relations in Renaissance Italy', in J. Bossy (ed.), *Disputes and Settlements: Law and Human Relations in the West* (Cambridge, 1983), 69–99.

—— 'Distinguishing Signs: Ear-Rings, Jews and Franciscan Rhetoric in the Italian Renaissance City', *Past and Present*, 112 (Aug. 1986), 3–59.

—— 'Invisible Madonnas? The Italian Historiographical Tradition and the Women of Medieval Italy', in S. Mosher Stuard (ed.), *Women in Medieval History and Historiography* (Philadelphia, 1987), 25–58.

—— 'Regulating Women's Fashion', in C. Klapisch-Zuber (ed.), *Silences of the Middle Ages: A History of Women in the West*, ii (Cambridge, Mass., and London, 1992), 136–58.

PANDIANI, E., 'Vita privata genovese nel rinascimento', *Atti della società ligure di storia patria*, 47 (1915), 119–201.

PANOFSKY, E., *Early Netherlandish Painting: Its Origins and Character*, 2 vols., i (New York, 1971).

PASOLINI, P. D., 'Delle antiche relazioni fra Venezia e Ravenna', *Archivio storico italiano*, 3rd ser., 16 (1872), 307–23.

PATON, B., *Preaching Friars and the Civic Ethos: Siena, 1380–1480* (London, 1992).

PERTILE, A., *Storia del diritto italiano dalla caduta dell'impero romano alla codificazione*, v (2nd edn., Turin, 1892).

PEZZANA, A., *Storia della città di Parma*, 5 vols., ii (Parma, 1842).

PIERRO, M., 'Le leggi suntuarie e il problema demografico nel medioevo', *Politica sociale*, 2 (1930), 13–23.

PINETTI, A., 'La limitazione del lusso e dei consumi nelle leggi suntuarie bergamesche (sec. XIV–XVI)', *Atti dell'Ateneo di scienze lettere ed arti in Bergamo*, 24 (1915–17), 3–94.

PIPONNIER, F., 'Le Costume nobiliaire dans la France du bas moyen âge', *Sitzungsberichte der Akademie der Wissenschaften*, 400 (1982), 343–63.

PLUTARCH, *Lives, Agis*, in *Plutarch on Sparta*, trans. R. J. A. Talbert (Harmondsworth, 1988), 53–70.

—— *Solon*, in *Greek Lives: A Selection of Nine Greek Lives/Plutarch*, trans. R. Waterfield (Oxford and New York, 1998), 46–77.

POLIDORI CALAMANDREI, E., *Le vesti delle donne fiorentine nel quattrocento* (Florence, 1924).

POMEROY, S., *Goddesses, Whores, Wives and Slaves: Women in Classical Antiquity* (New York, 1975).

RABIL, A., *Laura Cereta: Quattrocento Humanist* (Binghamton, NY, 1981).

RAINEY, E. R., 'Sumptuary Legislation in Renaissance Florence', Ph.D. thesis (Columbia Univ., 1985).

—— 'Dressing Down the Dressed-Up: Reproving Feminine Attire in Renaissance Florence', in J. Monfasani and R. G. Musto (eds.), *Renaissance Society and Culture: Essays in Honor of Eugene F. Rice* (New York, 1991).

RIBEIRO, A., *Dress and Morality* (London, 1986).

ROBINSON, D. E., 'The Importance of Fashions in Taste to Business History: An Introductory Essay', *Business History Review*, 37 (1963), 5–36.

RODOCANACHI, E., *Histoire de Rome de 1354 à 1471* (Rome, 1922).

RODOCANACHI, S., *La Femme italienne à l'époque de la Renaissance* (Paris, 1907).

ROMANIN, S., *Storia documentata di Venezia*, 10 vols., iii (Venice, 1853–61).

RUIZ, T. F., 'The Transformation of the Castilian Municipalities: The Case of Burgos 1248–1350', *Past and Present*, 77 (Nov. 1977), 3–32.

RYDER, A., *The Kingdom of Naples under Alfonso the Magnanimous: The Making of a Modern State* (Oxford, 1976).

SACCHETTI, FRANCO, *Il trecentonovelle*, ed. A. Lanza (Florence, 1984).

—— 'Canzone distesa di Franco Sacchetti contro a le nuove foggie'; 'Canzone distesa di Franco Sacchetti contra a la portatura de le donne fiorentine', in *Franco Sacchetti Opere*, ed. A. Borlenghi (Milan, 1957), 978–81 and 1011–16.

SALIMBENE DE ADAM, *Cronica*, ed. G. Scalia, 2 vols. (Bari, 1966).

SCHMEIDLER, B. (ed.), *Die Annalen des Tholomeus von Lucca in Doppelter Fassung: Nebst Teilen der Gesta Florentinorum und Gesta Lucanorum* (*Monumenta Germaniae Historica Scriptores*, NS 8; Berlin, 1930).

SCHOLES, P. A., *The Oxford Companion to Music* (9th edn., London, 1955).

SCHROEDER, H. J., *Disciplinary Decrees of the General Councils* (St Louis, Mo., 1937).

SENECA, *De Tranquillitate Animi*, in *Four Dialogues: De Vita Beata, De Tranquillitate Animi, De Constantia Sapientis, Ad Helviam matrem de Consolatione*, ed. C. D. N. Costa (Warminster, Wilts., 1994).

SHAW, F. J., 'Sumptuary Legislation in Scotland', *Juridical Review*, NS (1979), 81–115.

SOMBART, W., *The Quintessence of Capitalism: A Study of the History and Psychology of the Modern Business Man*, trans. and ed. M. Epstein (London, 1915).

SPUFFORD, P., 'Coinage and Currency', in M. M. Postan and E. Miller (eds.), *The Cambridge Economic History of Europe*, ii (2nd edn., Cambridge, 1987), 788–873.

STAFFORD, P., 'More than a Man or Less than a Woman? Woman Rulers in Early Modern Europe', *Gender and History*, 7 (1995), 486–90.

STAGLIENO, M., 'Le donne nell'antica società genovese', *Giornale ligustico di archeologia, storia e belle arti* (1878), 275–329.

STROCCHIA, S. T., *Death and Ritual in Renaissance Florence* (Baltimore, 1992).

SUETONIUS, *The Twelve Caesars*, trans. R. Graves (Harmondsworth, 1989).

TACITUS, *The Annals of Imperial Rome*, trans. M. Grant (Harmondsworth, 1989).

THIRSK, J., *Economic Policy and Projects: The Development of a Consumer Society in Early Modern England* (Oxford, 1978).

THORNTON, P., *The Italian Renaissance Interior 1400–1600* (London, 1991).

TOMAS, N., 'Alfonsina Orsini de' Medici and the "Problem" of a Female Ruler in Early Sixteenth-Century Florence', *Renaissance Studies*, 14/1 (2000), 70–90.

TOMMASI, G., 'Sommario della storia di Lucca dall'anno MIV all'anno MDCC' (with documents ed. C. Minutoli), *Archivio storico italiano*, 10 (1847), 89–103.

TORNABUONI, LUCREZIA, *Lettere*, ed. P. Salvadori (Florence, 1993).

TREXLER, R. C., *Public Life in Renaissance Florence* (New York, 1980).

URBINI, G., 'Per la storia del costume in Italia', *Nuova rivista storica* (Sept.–Oct. 1921), 481–95.

VAINI, M., *Dal comune alla signoria: Mantova dal 1200 al 1328* (Milan, 1986).

VASINA, A., *Romagna medievale* (Ravenna, 1970).

VEBLEN, T., 'The Economic Theory of Women's Dress', *Popular Science Monthly*, 46 (1894–5), 198–205.

—— *The Theory of the Leisure Class: An Economic Study of Institutions* (1899; London, 1924).

VERONESE, GUARINO, *Epistolario di Guarino Veronese*, ed. R. Sabbadini (Miscellanea di storia veneta, 3rd ser. 11 and 14; Venice, 1916 and 1919).

VILLANI, GIOVANNI, *Croniche storiche di Giovanni, Matteo e Filippo Villani*, ed. F. Gherardi, 7 vols. i (Milan, 1848).

VINCENT, J. M., 'European Blue Laws', *American Historical Association Annual Report (1897)* (1898), 355–72.

—— 'Sumptuary Legislation', in *Encyclopaedia of the Social Sciences*, xiv (New York, 1930–4).

—— *Costume and Conduct in the Laws of Basel, Bern, and Zurich, 1370–1800* (Baltimore, 1935).

WATSON, P. F., 'Virtu and Voluptas in Cassone Painting', Ph.D. thesis (New Haven, 1970).

WIESNER, M. E., *Women and Gender in Early Modern Europe* (Cambridge, 1993).

WIRSZUBSKI, C., *Libertas as a Political Idea at Rome during the Late Republic and Early Principate* (Cambridge, 1968).

ZANELLI, A., 'Predicatori a Brescia nel Quattrocento', *Archivio storico lombardo*, 3rd ser., 15 (1901), 83–138.

INDEX

Abadenghe, Gigalius and Richa 153
Acciaiuoli, Bishop 100–1
Agis, king of Sparta 10
Agrigento 28
Albergati, Pietro di Nicolò and wife 158
Albornoz, Cardinal 98
Alexander of Hales 96–7
Alfonso, king of Naples 44
Alfonso X, king of Castile 24, 25
'Allelujah movement' 26
Ammannato, Giacomo 110
Ancient Rome:
  ambitus 16
  clothing 12, 13–15
  Digest 2, 114, 129
  dining habits 2, 12, 16
  dowries 13
  funerals 2, 12–13, 16
  furniture 12–13
  gifts 12, 16
  gladiatorial displays 12, 16
  gravitas 15, 16
  inheritance by women 13, 14, 15
  jewellery for men 14
  jewellery for women 14
  music 13
  Twelve Tables 12, 16
  women 12, 13–15
Ancona 28
Annales Ecclesiastici 96
Anonymous 94, 95
Antonio, di Cristoforo di Antonio 155–6
Aquila 28
  funerals 72, 73, 75, 106, 137
  gift-giving 78, 137
  penalties 137, 141
  shortness of doublets 62
  weddings 67, 70–1, 77, 137
  women's clothing 137
Aquinas, Thomas ('Of Modesty in the Outward Apparel') 97–8, 104
Aragon 24, 32
Arezzo 28
Arienti, Sabadino degli (*Le Porettane*) 125
aristocracy, *see* Italy
Aristotle 10, 11, 114
Aspra Sabina 28
Athens, women 10, 11–12
Augustine 19, 22, 92, 96
Augustus (Caesar) 14
Averrara 30

baptisms 26, 38, 77–9
  gift-giving 78–9
  in Padua 26, 69, 77
  in Pisa 77
Baronius (*Annales Ecclesiastici*) 96
Bassano 28
  enforcement 135; enforcers 144; informants 148
  gift-giving 79
  weddings and funerals 26
Battista di Bernardo 154
Bellano, weddings and funerals 30
Bentivoglio family 43–4, 83
Bentivoglio regime 83, 125
Bentivoglio, Sante 129–30, 159
Bergamo 28, 32, 37
  breasts to be covered 62
  enforcers 144
  funerals 32, 76, 106
  gift-giving 79
  jewellery 39
  John of Bohemia's regime 83
  Milanese domination 83, 106, 137
  penalties 137, 138
  preamble to laws 37, 41–2
  women's clothing 59, 137
Bernadino of Siena 109
Bessarion, Cardinal 88, 99, 110, 124–30 *passim*
Biliotti, Bishop 100
Bini, Maria di Piero 55
Black Death 53; *see also* plagues
Boccardo 5
Boetio, Iacopino and wife 159–60
Bologna 26, 28, 29, 33, 34, 37, 99
  Bentivoglio regime 83, 125
  class distinctions 86, 88, 124
  enforcement 101, 129, 150, 159; enforcers 144; informants 141
  funerals 72, 73, 74, 153
  gift-giving 74, 78, 79
  laws favouring women 113
  ornaments on clothing 59
  papal authority 44, 83

Bologna (*cont.*):
  penalties 35, 46
  petition by Sanuti 124–32
  preambles to laws 103
  prosecutions 153, 158
  public debt 43–4
  registration of clothing and ornaments 151
  Religious 78
  Sedici 43–4
  silk industry 48
  Visconti regime 83
  weddings 69–70, 135, 154
Bonardi, Antonio 3–4, 33
'bonfire of the vanities' 109
Borso d'Este dowries 58
Bosso, Matteo 130, 131
Brescia 26, 28, 34
  Anziani (council) 63
  'bonfire of the vanities' 109
  enforcement and informants 141
  family devices 80
  funerals 39, 40, 43, 73, 76, 106, 107–8
  incentives to marriage 59
  modesty 65
  penalties 139, 141; not to hold office 139; use of fines 142
  preamble to laws 52
  prohibition on disguise 64
  prohibition on veils and masks 64
  Religious 78, 109
  signorial regimes 83
  social status 81

Cacciaguida (Dante's ancestor) 1
Camporotondo:
  domination by Lords Varano of Camerino 83
  weddings, funerals, and gifts 30
Cancellari, Orfeo de 96
Carrara, Francesco Novello da 71, 84
Castel Fiorentino 28, 83
Castello 103
Castracani, Castruccio 121
Catholic Church:
  appropriate dress for women 17, 63, 65, 92
  Aquinas' theology 97–8, 104
  clergy, *see* Religious
  conventual and observant friars 108–9
  Council of Constance (1414–18) 93
  Council of Constantinople (869–70) 20
  Council of Lyons (1274) 93
  Council of Montpellier (1195) 20
  Council of Montpellier (1216) 93
  Council of Nicaea (787) 20
  Council of Paris (1323) 93
  Council of Toulouse (1191) 20
  Council of Vienne (1311–13) 93
  excommunications 100, 101–2, 103, 105, 129, 138
  Gregory X 92–6; Lenten edict 93–6, 110
  Innocent VIII 99
  Julius II 107–8
  laity 19, 21, 92, 93, 96, 98, 108
  Lateran Council (1139) 20
  Lateran Council (1215) 20
  luxury 17–22, 77, 162; of clergy 4, 19–22, 23, 25, 37, 93, 97, 102; justification by Milanese writer 162–3
  Martin V 99
  Nicholas III 98
  Paul II 99, 105
  petition by friars of San Domenico 107–8
  Religious, *see* Religious
  Sixtus IV 99
  and state 98–110
  sumptuary laws 92–110
  women's clothing 93–5, 97
  see also Aquinas, Thomas; Augustine; Cyprian; Jerome; Tertullian
Cereta, Laura ('Curse against the ornamentation of women') 131–2
Charlemagne 21
Charles, duke of Calabria 121, 123
Charles I of Anjou 25, 120
Charles II of Anjou 86
children:
  baptisms 26, 38, 77–9
  clothing 38, 154–5
  decorations at birth 39–40
  gift-giving 78–9
Ciani, Bartolomeo 156
Ciani, Battista di Bartolomeo 156
Cicero 12, 15
Ciglioni, Feliciana di Lodovico de' 155
Ciglioni, Lodovico de' 155
Cittadella 30
city states, *see* Italy
class distinctions 80–1, 82, 84–90, 97, 124, 127, 137–9, 157, 159
  defined by luxury 7–8, 15, 24, 91
  see also enforcement; exemptions
clothing 6, 37, 160–3
  in Ancient Rome 2, 13–15

in Aragon 24
in Athens 10
changes in fashion 112, 161, 163
crowns 25, 46–7, 155
funerals 73, 161
furs 24, 86, 120, 122–3
gold ribbons 154, 155
as indicator of wealth etc. 112
main target of sumptuary laws 111–13
masks, veils, and cloaks 63–5
minors' 38
in northern Italy 4
pearl buttons 158
peasants' 38
prohibition on cross-dressing 64, 140
purple 14, 15, 86
registration 151
servants' 38, 88
silver buttons 112, 154, 155
weddings 161
woollen 86
see also class distinctions; funerals; men; weddings; women
Como, gift-giving 78
Contarini, Pietro and wife 158
Corenno 30
Corner, Cristina 104, 124, 125
Correggio, Giberto di 84
Cremona 27, 28
enforcers 144
Cyprian 19, 22, 92, 96

Dati, Gregorio and Isibetta 55
Datini, Francesco 55
Datini, Ginevra di Francesco 55
de Valois, Marie 121
debts, *see* dowries; economy
Delphi funerals 11
Demetrius of Phalerum 11
Dervio 30
despots (signorial regimes), *see* Italy
dining habits:
in Aragon 24
in Athens 10
extravagant Roman 2
in Sicily 86
see also feasts
Donato, Ser (notary) 158
dowries 54–60, 120
enrich other cities 156
fines from 59, 138, 140
taxes 55
Drakon laws 10n.
economy:
banking failures 44
credit 46
expansion 42, 44, 61
importance of circulation of money 45–6
interest rates 43
new opportunities for trade 81
opening of trade routes 7
poverty 43, 44
prohibitions on trade 48–9, 50
public debt of Bologna 43–4
public debt of Florence 44
public debt of Naples 44
scarcity of capital 43–4
and women's clothing 113, 161
Elagabalus 15
enforcement 1–2, 46, 100–2, 105, 121–2, 123, 129, 133–62
changes in fashion 112, 161, 163
enforcers 142–3, 160
excommunications 100, 101–2, 103, 105, 129, 138
failure 5–7, 17, 133–4, 160–3
informants 135–6, 141
prosecutions 152–3, 155–8
see also penalties
English sumptuary laws 23, 134
Este, Obizzo and Niccolò d' 84
exemptions 34, 47, 62, 64, 84, 85, 87, 90, 103–4, 115, 120, 121, 122
bought 47, 123
for doge and family 84, 90–1, 115
gabelle 46–7
for knights 89–90, 124
for Religious 85
in republics 82, 89
for social categories 84–6, 89–90, 124

Fabriano 27, 28
Faenza 28
class distinctions 86, 87–8
communal regime 83
enforcement 102; informants 141, 150
funerals 76, 87–8, 106, 136–7
penalties 141–2
proclamation of sumptuary laws 136–7
feasts 37, 38, 58, 66–7, 154
banning 75
in Perugia 150
Feo, Nanni di 154
Ferrara 28
class distinctions 89, 157
dowries 58

Ferrara (*cont.*):
- Este regime 83
- exemptions 84, 120
- penalties 152
- preamble to laws 52
- prohibition on cross-dressing 64
- prohibition on masks 64
- prosecutions 153, 157
- weddings 58

Ferrara, Riccobaldo da 1

Florence 1, 28, 31, 33, 34
- artisans 50
- Bishop Acciaiuoli 100–1
- Bishop Biliotti 100
- 'bonfire of the vanities' 109
- class distinctions 89–90
- constitutions 100–1
- decline in marriage 54
- decline in population 53, 54
- enforcement 102, 121–2, 136, 148, 159; enforcers 144–5, 146, 158–9; informants 141, 148, 149, 150
- as example 32
- exemptions 90; bought 47
- feasts 67
- funerals 4, 27, 47, 72, 73, 75–6, 153
- gift-giving 79
- Guelfs 146
- guilds 146
- importation of clothes 123
- Merchant Court 146
- modesty 62–3, 65
- most laws against women 112–13
- number of rubrics 37
- Official on Women 146
- officials, *see* politics
- *Otto di Guardia* 146
- penalties 46, 139, 148; corporal punishment 140; fines and use of fines 142, 148, 154, 159; for servants 139
- petitioned by Pisa 31, 51
- petitions 121
- politics 81, 146–7; women excluded 115
- preamble to laws 52
- Priors 146
- proclamation of sumptuary laws 136
- prohibition on cross-dressing 64, 140
- prohibition on disguise 64–5
- prosecutions 152, 153
- protectionism 48–9
- public debt 44
- publication of sumptuary laws 136
- registration of clothing and ornaments 151
- taxes and *gabelle* 47, 62
- weddings 68, 71, 154
- women blamed for ills 118–19
- wool industry 48

Forli 28
- funerals 73

France:
- dining habits 25
- men's clothing 24
- royal decrees 24
- women and crowns 25

Francia, Anechino de 158

Frederick, Emperor 122

Fregoso, Cardinal Paolo 99

Frignano 30

Fronto, Octavius 15

funerals 37, 38, 39, 40, 71–6, 153–4
- in Ancient Rome 2, 12–13, 16
- in Aquila 72, 73, 75, 106, 137
- in Athens 10–11
- in Bassano 26
- in Bellano 30
- in Bergamo 32, 76, 106
- in Bologna 72, 73, 74, 153
- in Brescia 26, 39, 40, 43, 73, 76, 106, 107–8
- in Camporotondo 30
- clothing 64, 71, 73, 161
- in Delphi 11
- extreme unction 74
- in Faenza 76, 87–8, 106, 136–7
- family devices 79–80
- in Florence 4, 27, 47, 62–3, 72, 73, 75–6, 153
- in Forli 73
- gift-giving 78
- hair 153
- head coverings 153
- in Isola d'Orta 30, 73
- in Keos 11
- limits on noise 72–3
- in Lucca 31, 73, 75
- in Milan 72, 74–5, 76, 79–80, 137
- in Modena 72, 73, 75
- in Orzinuovi 30
- in Padua 71, 76, 106
- in Parma 106–7
- participation of Religious 71, 74, 76, 77, 106–7
- in Pavia 74
- in Pisa 72, 76–7, 106

and politics 71, 74, 76
in Reggio 26, 34, 35, 72
in Riperia d'Orta 30, 70
segregation of sexes 74
in Siena 43, 72–4 *passim*, 75
in Venice 91
in Verona 43
weeping and wailing 72, 153
furnishings 30, 39–40
Fusacchi, Giuliano di Michele 56

gabelle 46–8, 62
Gabiano 30
Gabrieli, Battista 156
Gabrieli, Giovanni 156
Gaetani, Elisabetta 159
Gallicciolli *re* petitions 103–4
Gallus, Gaius Asinius 15
Garbo, Antonio del 155
Genoa 24, 26, 27, 28, 34, 99
domination of Savona 84
dowries 57
exemptions 34, 90
furs 34
gabelle 47
gift-giving 79
modesty 63
Pisan clothing not acceptable 159–60
preamble to laws 52
protectionism 49
silk industry 48
stocks as penalty 139
sugar industry 49
trade 45
weddings 67
Gente, Giberto da 84
Georgio, Giovanni and wife 158
Gesta Florentinorum 95, 96
gift-giving 37, 38, 74, 77–80
Ancient Rome 12, 16
baptisms 78–9
Camporotondo 30
funerals 78
to Religious 77–8, 107
weddings 78–9
Gionta's wife (Lisabetta) 156
Giustiniani, Bernardo 103
Giustiniani, Lorenzo 103, 104
gold and silver 45–6, 90, 121, 122; *see also* jewellery and ornaments
Gritti, Andrea 104–5, 124
Gubbio 28, 98
clothing of laity 64
dowries 57–8
Guidubaldo I regime 83
prohibition on cross-dressing 64
prohibition on masks 64
registration of clothing and ornaments 151–2
Religious 109–10
use of fines 142
Guelfs 146
Guidubaldo I of Gubbio 83, 110

Haterius, Quintus 15
Honorius 16

Imola 28
exemptions 90
penalties 140
preamble to laws 36, 42–3
industries:
cotton 49–50
new 81
silk 48
skilled artisans 43, 49–50
sugar 49
wool 48
inheritance:
by women in Ancient Rome 13, 14, 15
by women in Sparta 10
Isola d'Orta, weddings and funerals 30, 73
Italy:
aristocracy 81, 82
compared with England and Switzerland 23, 134
despots (signorial regimes) 82, 83–4, 86
monarchies 44, 81, 82, 86
papal states 43–4, 83, 86, 98–9, 124
positive aspects of luxury 7–8, 15, 24, 91, 124, 161–2
republics 81–2, 89, 121, 122
south compared with north 25–6, 33, 81
Iulis on Keos 11

James, king of Aragon 24
Jeanne of Navarre, Queen of France 25
Jerome 19, 22, 92, 96
jewellery and ornaments 6, 9, 11, 14, 39, 45, 59, 109, 115, 121, 123, 125–6, 128
in Ancient Rome 14
in Aragon 24
crowns 25, 46–7
gold and silver 47, 88
pearls 45, 46–7, 48
registration 151

jewellery and ornaments (*cont.*):
  in Sparta 9
  see also women, jewellery and ornaments
John of Bohemia 83
Julius Caesar 14n.
Juvenal 15

Keos funerals 11

Lambertini, Egano and wife 158
land laws:
  in Ancient Rome 13, 14
  in Sparta 10
Lando, Archbishop Girolamo 105
Lanti, Antonio de' and wife 156–7
Latino, Cardinal 63, 98, 123, 124
le Débonnaire, Louis 21–2
Leonello, Marquis 58
Leonora of Portugal 122
licenziati (teachers of medicine, grammar, philosophy) 84, 85
Livy 17, 114
Lombardy 30
Lorenzo's wife 156–7
Lotti, Giovanni and Angelica 156
Louis VIII, king of France 24, 33
Lucca 28, 31, 34
  Anziani (council) 31–2
  artisans 50
  class distinctions 88–9
  communal regime 83
  decline in marriages 51
  dining habits, funerals, weddings, and ornaments 31
  enforcement: enforcers 143, 144; informants 141, 148, 150
  funerals 73, 75
  gift-giving at baptisms 79
  hoods 63–4
  penalties 138
  prohibition on nudity 62
  prosecutions 153
  registration of clothing and ornaments 151
  servants 139
  silk industry 48
  violence at weddings 67–8
  weddings 68–9
Lupi, Angelo, bishop of Tubertino 65, 110
Lycurgus on Sparta 9

Maffei, Timoteo 110, 124, 130, 131
magnate families and politics 84, 87, 89
Malespini, Ricordano 92–5 *passim*
Manfredi, Giovanni Galeazzo 83, 87
Mantova, Fra Battista da 109
Mantua 27, 28, 29
  artisans 50
  Gonzaga regime 83
  weddings 70
Marca, Jacopo della 109
Mariani (friar) 108
marriages:
  incentives 58–60
  political 69, 117
  see also dowries; weddings
Medici, Alemanno de' 155
Medici, Antonia de' 155
Medici, Cosimo de' 61
Medici family 159
Medici, Piero de' 159
men:
  clothing 14, 15–16, 18–19, 24, 38, 112, 113; in Ancient Rome 14, 15–16; in Castile 24; Christian 18–19; comments by Aquinas 97–8; covering of genitalia 62; in France 24; furs 86, 90; gold and silver 139; modesty 62, 86, 118; not to wear silk 15, 86; penalties 137–8; and public roles 95, 114–15; shortness of doublets 62
  dowries 54–8
  encourage vanity in women 119
  and *gravitas* 15, 16
  jewellery and ornaments 86; in Ancient Rome 14; gold and silver 139
  liable for women's fines 135, 138, 139, 140, 153, 154–8 *passim*
  misogyny 111, 119
  in Piedmont 86
  prohibition on cross-dressing 64, 140
Messina 32, 120
  petition re clothing 120
  preamble to law on dowries 56–7
Messina trade 45
Milan 27, 28, 29, 33
  artisans 50
  class distinctions 86, 87
  domination of Bergamo 83
  enforcers 144
  exemptions 87
  funerals 72, 74–5, 76, 79–80, 137
  furnishings 39–40
  justification for luxury 162–3
  penalties 137
  preamble to laws 52

protectionism 49
publication of sumptuary laws 136
silk industry 48
Visconti and Sforza regimes 83
wealth 162
weddings 67, 69
Minerbetti, Andrea 55
Minerbetti, Andrea di messer Tommaso 55
Minerbetti family 55
Minoccia di Rainerio 155–6
Modena 28, 30
class distinctions 88
enforcers 144
funerals 72, 73, 75
petitions 120
publication of sumptuary laws 136
regime 84
Religious 77
weddings 70
monarchies, *see* Italy
money, *see* economy; penalties
Montalboddo 28
Montefalco, Battista da 110
Montefeltro, Federico da 83
Morelli, Gualberto 154
music:
at weddings 68–9
as luxury 13

Naples 27, 33, 44
Nappi, Cesare 131
Nero 15
Nini, de' (family) 156
noise, limitations on 68–9, 72
nudity, forbidden in Lucca 62

Ochi, Francesco 158–9
Oppian law 14, 17
Orvieto 29
Orzinuovi, weddings and funerals 30
Ovid 13

Padua 29, 30–1
artisans 50
Carrara regime 84
enforcement: enforcers 144; informants 148
funerals 71, 76, 106
preamble to laws 52
Religious 109
weddings and baptisms 26, 69, 77
women blamed for city's ills 52, 118–19
Pallavicino 84
Palmieri, Pietro 156
papal states, *see* Italy
Parenti, Marco 55–6
Parma 29
artisans 49–50
cloth trade 44
Correggio regime 84
cotton industry 49–50
da Gente regime 84
enforcers 144
funerals 106–7
preambles to laws 102–3
trade with Venice 44
Visconti regime 84
women's clothing 26
Pavia, funerals 74
penalties 46, 139, 148
for artisans 151, 152
being led naked through streets 139
class distinctions 139–40
corporal punishment 139–40
excommunication 100, 101–2, 103, 105, 129, 138
fines 59, 137–42, 148, 151, 152, 154, 159; paid by male relative 135, 138, 139, 140, 153, 154–5, 154–8 *passim*; use of 142, 148, 154, 159
imprisonment 140
not to hold office 139
for servants 139
stocks 139
for tailors 105, 138, 152, 158
for women 139, 159
see also enforcement
Perugia 29, 34, 98–9
'bonfire of the vanities' 109
enforcement 101–2, 105, 123, 135, 141, 147; enforcers 144; informants 149, 150
exemptions 64
feasts 26, 66–7, 150
gift-giving 78, 79
modesty in clothing 63, 65
penalties 138; use of fines 142
preamble to laws 36, 42
prosecutions 152, 153
registration of clothing and ornaments 151, 152
Religious 77–8, 110
tailors 105, 138
weddings 26, 66–7, 69
women: blamed for ills 118–19; head coverings 64

Pescia 29
petitions against sumptuary laws 103–5, 119–20, 121, 124–32, 133, 134, 162
  by friars 107–8
  by Sanuti 124–32
  by Venetian noblewomen 103–5, 124, 125
  Gallicciolli on 103–4
Petrucci, Battista 122, 126
Philippe le Bel, king of France 25
Philippe le Hardi, king of France 25
Piccolomini, Aeneas Silvius 54
Piccolomini, Alda di Angelo Piccolomo de' 155
Piccolomini, Angelo Piccolomo de' 155
Piccolomini family 159
Piedmont 33, 86
  class distinctions 86–7
  ducal family of Savoy 86
Pirundoli, Elisabetta di Ludovico 157
Pirundoli, Giovanni 157
Pirundoli, Ludovico 157
Pirundoli, Niccolò 157
Pisa 29
  baptisms 77
  Cardinal Federico Visconti 99–100
  class distinctions 88
  constitution of Visconti 99–100
  decline in marriages 51, 54
  decline in population 51, 53
  enforcement 101, 147, 159
  exemptions 90
  extreme unction 74
  funerals 72, 76–7, 106
  Genoese clothes not acceptable 159–60
  gift-giving 79
  number of rubrics 37
  petitions Florence 31, 51
  prohibition on veils 64
  protectionism 48
  Religious 78
  weddings 68
  wool industry 48
Pistoia 29, 32, 47
  artisans 50
  registration of clothing and ornaments 151
plagues 44, 53, 54, 117
Plutarch 10
politics 80–1, 146–7
  and funerals 71, 74, 76
  and magnate families 89
  and weddings 66
  women excluded 115
population:
  decline in 50–3, 61
  move from countryside 61, 81
  see also social mobility
Porcari, Laura di Pietro 156
Porcari, Pietro 156
Porcellini, Giovanni 117
Prato 29
  artisans 50
  decline in population 53
prosecutions, *see* enforcement
prostitutes:
  in Athens 10
  clothing 64
  corporal punishment 139
  northern Italy 4
protectionism 48–50
Puglia 33
  class distinctions 86
  preambles to laws 35–6

Rainerio, Minoccia di 155–6
Ravenna 29
Reggio 29
  enforcement 135; enforcers 143, 144
  funerals 26, 34, 35, 72
  penalties 34
  publication of sumptuary laws 136
Religious 78, 109
  church and state 98–110
  entering orders 107
  excommunication 129
  exemptions 85
  opinions on clothing 97–8, 104, 108–10
  opposition to laws 107
  participation in funerals 71, 74, 76, 77, 106–7
  power of 77–8, 99–102
  proclamation of sumptuary laws 136–7
republics, *see* Italy
Riperia d'Orta, weddings and funerals 30, 70
Robert, count of Arras 121
Robert, king of Naples 84
Romagna 123
Roman Catholic Church, *see* Catholic Church
Rome 29
  'bonfire of the vanities' 109
  papacy's return from Avignon 99
  see also Ancient Rome

Sacchetti, Franco 1, 122
Saccomurro 29

Salimbeni 119
Sambuca 30
San Gimignano 29
  enforcement 135
  penalties 138
  women's clothing 26
Sanuti, Nicolò, count of the Poretta 124–5
Sanuti, Nicolosa:
  treatise on women 124–32
  women's gifts to men 127–9
Sarzana 29
Sassetti, Letta 117
Sassetti, Paolo 117
Savona 29
  dominated by Genoa and Visconti family 84
  penalties, for servants 139
Scaligeri, *see* Lucca; Scala, Alberto and Mastino della
Scala, Alberto and Mastino della 31, 83, 84
Scannabecchi, Guglielmo 31
Scotti, Scotto degli 154
Sedici of Bologna 43
servants:
  clothing 139
  corporal punishment 139
  stocks 139
Sforza, Galeazzo Maria 116
Sforza, Ginevra 129
Sforza, Tristano 116
Sicily 29, 32
  class distinctions 86, 137–8
  penalties 137–8
  preamble to laws 35–6
Siena 29, 32, 34
  'bonfire of the vanities' 109
  dowries 58
  enforcement 159; enforcers 143, 144; informants 148–9, 154
  exemptions 90, 121, 122
  funerals 43, 72–4 *passim*, 75
  laws favouring women 113
  limitations on noise 68
  number of rubrics 37
  petitions 121
  preamble to laws 36, 41, 52
  prosecutions 152, 153, 155–7
  publication of sumptuary laws 136
  weddings 58, 69n., 71
  women:
    blamed for ills 118–19
    clothing 26, 155–6
silver, *see* gold and silver; jewellery and ornaments
social control 61, 66–81
  feasts 66
  and morality 62
  see also politics
social mobility 43, 61, 80, 81; *see also* population
Solon 10, 12
Spain, royal decrees 24
Spannocchi, Ambrogio 155
Spannocchi, Lucrezia di Ambrogio 155
Sparta:
  cosmetics 9
  dyed clothing 9
  perfume 9
  sumptuary laws 9
  women 9–10
Spini, Amfriono de' 154
Spini, Cotto de' 154
Strozzi, Alessandra 115–16
Strozzi family 159
Sulla 13
sumptuary laws:
  defined 2
  on dowries 56–7
  enforcement, *see* enforcement
  exemptions, *see* exemptions
  number 2, 133
  penalties, *see* enforcement; penalties
  petitions against, *see* petitions against sumptuary laws
  pre-medieval 23, 41; *see also* Ancient Rome; Athens; Sparta
  preambles 35–6, 37, 41–3, 47, 52, 102–3, 119, 133
  publication 135–6
  Renaissance 3, 161, 163
  social, economic, and political aspects 4–16, 33–4, 41–60, 81, 161
  usually urban 30
  see also economy; politics; social control
Switzerland, sumptuary laws 23, 134–5

Tacitus 17
Taia, Guglielmo del 156
Taia, Margherita del 156
Talenti, Francesca 55
taxes, *see gabelle*
Tertullian 18–19, 22, 92, 96
Tiberius 15, 16, 17
Tivoli 29
Tobaldurius, Clara 153

Tolomei da San Cristoforo, Antonio dei 154
Tolomei family 159
Tornabuoni, Lucrezia 115–16, 159
Tosa, Simone della (*Annals*) 93–5 *passim*
Treviso 29
  gift-giving 78–9
trousseaus, *see* dowries
Turamini, Christofano and daughter 156

Ufredini, Clara 153

Val Taleggio 30
Valsassina 30
Vangelista, Antonio di 154
Vangelista, Niccola di Antonio di 154
Vanucci, Bishop Giacomo 105
Varano, lords of Camerino 83
Vellano 29
Velluti, Bernardo 154
Venice 27, 29, 31, 33, 34
  decline in population 53
  dowries 57
  enforcement 102, 147; enforcers 143, 144–6; informants 141, 149
  exemptions: bought 123; for doge and family 84, 90–1, 115
  feasts 66, 67, 138
  funerals 91
  furnishings 39
  laws favouring women 113
  no lugubrious clothing for councillors 91, 115
  penalties 138–40; fines 140; imprisonment 140; on luxury 123; not to hold office 138
  petitions by noblewomen 103–5, 124, 125
  platform shoes 51–2, 117, 140
  preambles to laws 42, 52, 103
  prohibition on cross-dressing 64
  prosecutions 153, 158
  protectionism 49
  publication of sumptuary laws 136
  shoemakers 140
  silk industry 48
  social control 66
  sugar industry 49
  trade 45
  weddings 35, 58, 69
  women's dress and men's status 116–17
Verona 27, 29, 34
  artisans 50
  Della Scala regime 84
  enforcement 123, 147
  exemptions bought 123
  funerals 43
  preamble to laws 36
Verona, Guarino da 130–1, 132
Vicenza (commune), wool workers 50
Vicenza, Fra Giovanni da 26, 109
Villani, Giovanni 32, 94–6 *passim*, 121, 123
Vini, Lucrezia di conte de' 155
Visconti family 32, 76, 83, 84
Visconti, Cardinal Federico 99–100
Visconti, Filippo-Maria 106–7
Visconti, Gian Galeazzo 87
Vitelleschi, Bartolommeo 65
Viterbo 29, 46
  and Castel Fiorentino 83
  enforcement, informants 149
  prosecutions 153

wars, foreign mercenaries 90
wealth: vanity versus proper pride 127; *see also* dowries; economy; funerals; weddings
weddings 37, 38, 39
  in Ancient Rome 2
  in Aquila 67, 70–1, 77, 137
  in Bassano 26
  in Bellano 30
  in Bologna 69–70, 135, 154
  in Camporotondo 30
  clothing 161
  decline of 51, 52, 54
  in Ferrara 58
  in Florence 68, 71, 154
  in Genoa 67
  gift-giving 78–9
  in Isola d'Orta 30, 73
  limits on celebrations 58, 66–71, 154
  in Lucca 31, 68–9
  in Mantua 70
  in Milan 67, 69
  in Modena 70
  music at 68–9
  in Orzinuovi 30
  in Padua 26, 69, 77
  in Perugia 26, 66–7, 69
  in Pisa 68
  and politics 66
  ring ceremonies 67–8
  in Riperia d'Orta 30, 70
  in Siena 58, 69n., 71
  in Venice 35, 58, 69

violence at 67–8
see also dowries; feasts
women:
age at first marriage 54, 55
Ancient Rome 10, 13–15
Athens 10, 11–12
blamed for Padua's ills 52, 118
chastity 117–18
clothing 9–10, 11–12, 14, 17, 26, 38, 39, 155; breasts to be covered 62, 63; buttons and hooks 88, 112, 122; for Christian women 17; class distinctions 81, 88, 97, 120; comments by Aquinas 97; and decline in birth rates 113; and decline in marriages 113; designs 93; *Dress of Virgins* (Cyprian) 19; dyed 9, 11; and economy 113; justification 143, 161–2; length of train 26, 63, 86, 93, 98, 104, 110, 120, 123, 153, 155; life stages 116; main target of sumptuary laws 111–13; modesty 62–5, 110, 117–18, 137; penalties 137; provocative 96, 97, 118, 123, 124; purple 14, 86, 125; silk 88, 120, 125, 155–8 *passim*; sleeves 117, 120; and status 116–19, 127, *see also* class distinctions; veils and head coverings 63–4, 88, 98, 102, 109, 122, 123, 158
concubines 88–9
cosmetics 9, 18, 96, 97
dowries and trousseaus, *see* dowries
excesses 47
excluded from public life 113, 114, 115, 127
exemptions 103–4, 115, 121
false hair 18, 88, 96, 104, 121
fertility 54
footwear 88; platform shoes 51–2, 104, 117, 140
French 25
gabelle 47–8
guardians of virtue 10, 117, 127
headdresses 26, 86, 87, 88, 102, 109
and honour of city 127–8
and honour of family 117
influence 113–14, 116
jewellery and ornaments 9, 11, 14, 59, 109, 115, 121, 123, 125–6, 128, 153, 156; crowns 25, 46–7, 121; gold and silver 47, 88, 93, 120, 123, 128, 139; pearl buttons 158; pearls 45, 46–7, 48, 93, 121, 139; silver and gold 121; *see also* jewellery and ornaments
legal, political, and social position 113–14
married compared with unmarried 59–60, 97, 124
in monarchies and under despots 113–14, 120
Official on Women 146
penalties for prostitutes 139
penalties for single 139
perfume 9
petitions 103, 119–20, 124
private space 114
prohibition on cross-dressing 64, 140
prosecutions 152–3
in public 39
regulated 11
in republics 113–14, 121
sexual predators 118–19
and souls 11
of Sparta 9–10
suspected of being prostitutes 139
virgins 19, 59–60, 96, 97, 117
see also clothing

CPSIA information can be obtained
at www.ICGtesting.com
Printed in the USA
BVHW031444130323
660323BV00001B/79

9 780199 247936